The Spheres of Music

LEONARD B. MEYER

The Spheres of Music
A Gathering of Essays

THE UNIVERSITY OF CHICAGO PRESS
Chicago & London

Leonard B. Meyer is professor emeritus of music at the University of Pennsylvania, where he taught from 1975 to 1988 as the Benjamin Franklin Professor of Music.

The University of Chicago Press, Chicago 60637
The University of Chicago Press, Ltd., London

© 2000 by The University of Chicago
All rights reserved. Published 2000
Printed in the United States of America

09 08 07 06 05 04 03 02 01 00   1 2 3 4 5

ISBN: 0-226-52153-2 (cloth)
ISBN: 0-226-52154-0 (paper)

Library of Congress Cataloging-in-Publication Data

Meyer, Leonard B.
    The spheres of music : a gathering of essays / by Leonard B. Meyer.
        p.   cm.
    Essays previously published.
    Includes bibliographical references and index.
    ISBN 0-226-52153-2 (cloth : alk. paper). — ISBN 0-226-52154-0
(paper : alk. paper)
    1. Music—History and criticism.   I. Title.
ML60.M616S74   2000
780—dc21   99-34400
                                                                CIP

*To my students and my colleagues,
from whom I have learned so much*

Contents

Preface

Why collect one's essays? Well, in my case, one reason is what might be thought of as late-life reflection on problems that have concerned me over a span of almost fifty years. Another reason is the sociopsychological desire to disseminate one's conceptual genes. This helps explain the character of the collection. All the essays have been published previously—although not, for the most part, in musicological journals. And I want not only to make them more readily available but also to bring them together so that they can "converse" with and illuminate one another.

To collect and comment on completed studies is to choose rather "to bear those ill[usion]s we have than fly to others that we know not of." Over the years, however, I have changed my mind about a number of matters considered in these essays. And publishing them again gives me a chance not only to revise and recant but also to add to as well as comment on ideas presented in the original essays. For these reasons, a number of sentences and paragraphs of the original texts have been omitted and new ones inserted. Where it seemed appropriate, a few of these added texts have been enclosed in brackets. However, new notes, commenting on the main text, have not been marked.

Many of the ideas, comments, and observations in these essays will be familiar to those who have read my other work.[1] What is different is the emphasis, via both the gathering and the changes I have made, on their *inter*-relations. At this stage of my life, I want to "put it all together" in a more or less comprehensive vision that joins theory to history, history to culture, culture to aesthetics, aesthetics to methodology, and methodology back to theory. The result is a pastiche: bits of the old combined with bytes of the new

---

1. Those who know other work of mine will recognize that I have occasionally cribbed and, without acknowledgment, quoted from my own work. But, rather than sue myself for such infringement, I sue for the reader's understanding on the ground that redundancy in the service of dissemination is no sin. On the other hand, because the essays were published in journals dealing with different disciplines, not only is there more duplication than I would wish but also far too many references to my own work. For these defects, I apologize.

yield insights into the kinds of relations that are at the heart of the creation, comprehension, and history of music.

Something also needs to be said about the admittedly limited stylistic/ cultural scope of the essays—especially in the light of the emphasis on universals in the postlude. Frankly, I doubt that the addition of a small scattering of selected examples from other periods and cultures—for instance, pointing to the frequency of gap-fill melodies in Gregorian Chant—would significantly strengthen the plausibility of the many hypotheses present in these essays. All of them, whether explicit or implicit, need to be tested on the musics of a variety of styles and cultures. This is especially appropriate not only because of the essentially empirical stance of the essays but also because of their concern with the interaction of universal constants with cultural variables.

These essays owe so much to so many—my teachers (beginning with my family), my colleagues and students at the Universities of Chicago and Pennsylvania, and friends in and out of the academy—that thanking even a select list would be a thankless task. There must, of course, be a "however."

I cannot, however, fail to acknowledge the help of those who have been explicitly involved in getting this collation ready for distribution and dissemination. First and foremost comes my wife, Janet Levy, to whom I have continually turned for astute advice, cogent criticism, and expert editing. I am also indebted to Wye Allanbrook, one of the readers for the University of Chicago Press, who raised relevant questions and pointed to pertinent problems; to Kathleen Hansell of the University of Chicago Press, for helpful suggestions; to Joseph H. Brown for his thoughtful and meticulous editing; and to Christine Schwab for her patience and dedication.

I

Prelude

1

Concerning the Sciences, the Arts—
AND the Humanities

For the past few decades the relationships among the sciences, the arts, and the humanities have been a subject of continuing concern and often of acrimonious, sometimes confusing, debate. The failure of the intelligent lay public to understand science has been the cause for concern; doubtful analogies have created the confusion. Recently, Gunther S. Stent, a molecular biologist, considered some of these matters.[1] Since his discussion is representative of a viewpoint not infrequently espoused by scientists and occasionally by artists and laymen as well, I shall take his article as a point of departure and will, from time to time, use it as a foil for counterargument.

Like a number of other writers, Stent contends that in essential ways science and art are comparable. As he puts it: "Both the arts and the sciences are activities that endeavor to discover and communicate truths about the world."[2] Although one cannot but sympathize with the desire to bring the so-called Two Cultures together, a viable and enduring union will not be achieved by ignoring or glossing over important differences. Using the behavior of scientists, artists, and laymen as empirical evidence, the first part of this essay will argue that Stent's union is a shotgun marriage, not one made in heaven, and that his attempt to wed different disciplinary species results not in fecund insight but in barren misconception. In the second part, I will suggest that this misunderstanding arises because, like many scientists (as well as a goodly number of artists and laymen), Stent fails even to recognize the existence of the humanist—that is, the theorist and critic of the arts. Yet the humanities must

Reprinted from *Critical Inquiry* 1, no. 1 (1974): 163–217.

My brother Daniel W. Meyer suggested several changes that have improved this essay. His help is gratefully acknowledged. Especially I am indebted to Professor Janet M. Levy, not only for incisive criticism, but for calling attention to and helping formulate the discussion of a number of problems, particularly in the area of invention.

1. See Gunther S. Stent, "Prematurity and Uniqueness in Scientific Discovery," *Scientific American* 227, no. 6 (December 1972): 84–93. My concern will be with the second part of Stent's essay, in which he considers the relationship between the sciences and the arts.

2. Ibid., 89.

be included, and areas of inquiry within them differentiated, if diverse disciplines are to be related to one another in a coherent and consistent way.

1

Let us begin by considering the key terms in Stent's definition of the
arts and sciences. These are the notions of *discovery, truth,* and that unassuming little word *about*.

Scientists discover facts, and, when verified, these have the status of truths.
But science does not consist of a collection of facts, however true they may
be. (That the earth is round is a true statement, but it is not a scientific one.)
The sciences consist of theories and hypotheses devised to exhibit and explain
the relationships among verified facts. In addition, theories also encourage the search for, and discovery of, other facts. But the truth of a theory or
hypothesis is never more than provisional. It is provisional because it is impossible, in principle, to be certain that at some future time facts will not be
found that will prove the theory to be partly or wholly mistaken. Depending
on the completeness and "fit" of the data as well as on their relationships
to other theoretical formulations, hypotheses are confirmed with various degrees of probability. But it does not follow from this that theories are equally
probable. Current hypotheses in particle physics, for instance, are quite provisional, while theories of ordinary matter are evidently both rigorous and reliable. "Although it may involve a lack of vision on my part," writes Gerald
Feinberg, "I cannot see any . . . unknown regions on our present map of nature. Accordingly it seems to me that we now have a model of the structure
of bulk matter that is fairly complete and unlikely to change in its essential
aspects." [3]

It is important to notice that, although they can be confirmed only provisionally, theories and hypotheses can be *dis*confirmed unequivocally. And, as
mistaken theories are discarded, the validity of those that survive becomes
more probable. Thus, through a kind of cultural-historical trial and error, science moves toward truth—in some realms arriving at virtual certainty, in others achieving only tentative or partial answers to problems. Given these
qualifications, it seems reasonable to assert that the sciences not only endeavor but are able to formulate truths about the world.

The relationships that scientific theories explain *exist* in nature. The structure of the DNA molecule was what it was before Watson and Crick formu-

---

3. Gerald Feinberg, "Ordinary Matter," *Scientific American* 216, no. 5 (May 1967): 132.
The nature of scientific "truth" is also discussed below.

lated a theory of its structure. They did not create its structure; they *discovered* it. Or, lest this seem to deny creativity to scientists, they *created* a theory to explain the structure of DNA. Furthermore, although the theory of molecular structure—our explanation of it—was changed by their discovery, the nature of the relationships within the molecule was not changed by what Watson and Crick did. That is, we assume, evidently on good grounds, that, while our theories explaining nature may change, the principles governing relationships in the natural world are constant with respect to both time and place—for instance, that the double helix was the same ten thousand years ago and that it is invariant wherever it exists.

This is not, however, the case with works of art. *Hamlet, Guernica,* and the C♯-Minor Quartet quite simply *did not exist* prior to Shakespeare's writing, Picasso's painting, and Beethoven's composing. Our usual way of speaking is significant behavioral evidence of this difference between science and art. For, although aspects of the grammar and syntax employed in, say, the C♯-Minor Quartet existed prior to its composition—as part of early nineteenth-century musical style that Beethoven himself had helped shape—we do not say that Beethoven "discovered" the C♯-Minor Quartet but that he *created* or *composed* it. Conversely, one would not say that Watson and Crick "created" the double helix but, rather, that they *discovered* the structure of DNA or that they formulated a theory of its structure.

I referred to *Hamlet* at the beginning of the previous paragraph because, as he so often did, Shakespeare borrowed his plot from an existing source. Now if "we are not really interested in the exact word sequence" but are "concerned with the content,"[4] then it should not be important whether we read Shakespeare's play, the earlier one from which his plot was borrowed, or the tale that was the basis for the earlier play. Clearly, however, this is not the case. And Stent is certainly aware that there is a problem. But his discussion and "solution" of it seem to me fundamentally mistaken and misleading. Consequently, disputing individual points seriatim would be fruitless. Instead, I shall cut through his Gordian argument with a sharp, but simple, distinction: namely, there is a profound and basic difference between scientific theories, which are *propositional*, and works of art, which are *presentational*.

Scientific theories consist of propositional statements or hypotheses expressing and explaining recurring and orderly relationships found in the world of natural events, social behavior, and human action. They are general in that they refer to classes or types; they are abstract in that they account for only

4. Stent, "Prematurity," 89.

some attributes of the natural world. The law of gravity, for instance, expresses the relationship between the mass of, and the distance between, objects. But it asserts nothing about their shape, color, and texture or their size and material—except as these may affect their mass.

Works of art, on the other hand, are presentational patterns that, like phenomena in the worlds of nature and of human behavior, may be the occasion for experiences that are found to be enjoyable, intriguing, and moving. Even when art is representational, what is re-presented is not an abstract concept *about* relationships but a concrete exemplification *of* relationships—an exemplification whose specificity is crucially and critically consequential. Our experience of Michelangelo's *Moses,* for instance, is shaped not by abstracted variables such as mass, texture, color, form, and subject, taken individually, but by the unique relationships that result from the confluence of all these attributes. More important still, the statue is not understood as a general proposition about the chemical composition of marble, the proportions of the human body, the history of the Jewish people, the style of Renaissance sculpture, or even the nature of aesthetic experience. It is an object not for theoretical generalization but for aesthetic appreciation and response.[5]

Yet the matter is more complex. For understanding and responding to works of art do involve making classlike judgments. When we look at a statue, read a poem (internally performing it), or listen to a string quartet, appreciation depends upon our having internalized hypotheses (developed unconscious probability judgments) about how the work will proceed, develop, and achieve closure. Such internalized hypotheses depend in part upon our generalized experience of the world and specially upon our experience of other similar works of art—their style and form, genre, and subject matter. However, though our understanding of works of art, like our understanding of sunsets and football games, depends upon what might be called *propositional habits,* such habits are not explicitly formulated concepts, as scientific theories are. Nor are the works of art they enable us to enjoy themselves propositions. Michelangelo's *Moses,* the C♯-Minor String Quartet, and Keats's sonnet "When I have fears that I may cease to be" are presentational patterns whose specific nonrecurring relationships are the basis for, and shape, particular aesthetic experiences.

---

5. The difference between proposition and presentation is epitomized in the epigram that closes Archibald MacLeish's poem "Ars Poetica":

    A poem should not mean
    But be.

Even if it be granted that scientists do not create in the sense that artists do but discover and formulate, what about inventors? Surely they do more than construct theories explaining already existing relationships. They bring novelty into existence: the wheel and the airplane, the printing press and television, irrigation and indoor plumbing. Without belittling the creative aspects of invention, it is important to notice that inventions, too, are general and generic. They are comparable, not to the creation of particular works of art, but to the invention of repeatable artistic principles—that is, to poetic forms such as the sonnet, musical procedures such as imitative counterpoint, and visual structurings such as linear perspective. Because what is discovered is a generic principle, inventions are analogous to propositional theories rather than individual works of art. Consequently, as we shall see, simultaneous invention, like the simultaneous discovery of scientific theories and artistic techniques, is not uncommon.

What is invented, then, is a general technological principle. One does not invent a single, unique artifact. One automobile is almost as useless as one telephone. To put the matter differently: the making of a unique object would be not an invention but a work of art. Falling between true invention and a work of art is a single and signal creation in the useful arts—for instance, the George Washington Bridge or Frank Lloyd Wright's Robie House. And, even in these cases, what is "artistic" is not the generic principle (the technique of suspension or cantilever construction)—that is, the invention—but the individuality of the particular design.

The distinction between the propositional theories of science and the presentational presence of works of art is important because it helps account for interesting differences between the behavior of scientists, on the one hand, and artists and their audiences, on the other. In addition, such behavioral differences indicate that, while the psychology of scientific discovery, generic invention, and artistic creation may in many ways be similar, the results of these activities can be equated only by misconstruing the nature of each.

In this connection it needs to be emphasized that it is not enough merely to assert that later works of art "replace" earlier ones as scientific theories do. What is needed is empirical evidence of some sort. And, in the absence of experimentally validated psychological knowledge, the best evidence we have is the actual behavior of scientists, artists, audiences, and so on. Consider, then, the following contrasts in behavior.

1. Very rarely—and then for "kicks" rather than professional reasons—does a working scientist read an original work by an earlier scientist: for

instance, Newton's *Principia,* Darwin's *Origin of Species,* or even Einstein's papers on relativity. They read "textbook" summaries in which the results of past scientific discoveries are digested. As C. P. Snow writes: "No scientist, or student of science, need ever read an original work of the past. As a general rule, he does not think of doing so. Rutherford was one of the greatest of experimental physicists, but no nuclear scientist today would study his researches of fifty years ago. Their substance has all been infused into the common agreement, the textbooks, the contemporary papers, the living present."[6] Such cumulative summarizing is possible because scientific theories are propositional—are concerned with general, classlike statements describing and explaining relationships existing in nature.

In the arts, however, the opposite situation prevails. Artists, critics, and audiences frequently disagree. But they would all vehemently insist that works of art cannot be digested or summarized. Writers and readers do not study précis of plays, poems, or novels but the originals; artists and audiences insist upon seeing the original work of art—even good reproductions are scorned; and musicians emphasize the importance of hearing a composition as the composer wrote it, not some set of propositional statements about it. A scientist who has not read Newton, Darwin, or Einstein is not unusual. But a humanist who has not read *Hamlet,* seen paintings by Picasso, or heard a Beethoven string quartet is an anomaly.

A further difference is also evident: instruction in the arts does not consist in the study of a textbook presenting recent discoveries in the humanities. When textbooks are used, they are made up of excerpts and reproductions that illustrate historical or critical hypotheses. It is presumed that students have read, seen, or heard the originals referred to or excerpted. This is the case because works of art, even the most representational ones, are not general propositions about the world or about feelings but presentations of particular patterns that constitute a basis for aesthetic experience.

2. That the propositional character of science differs from the presentational nature of works of art is indicated by another significant contrast. As C. P. Snow and others have pointed out, scientific theories supersede one another, while works of art do not. Kepler's discovery that planetary orbits are

6. C. P. Snow, *Public Affairs* (New York, 1971), 94–95. Stent ("Prematurity," 91) makes brief reference to this fact. So does Thomas Kuhn, *The Structure of Scientific Revolutions* (Chicago, 1962). This educational technique is made possible not, as Kuhn suggests, primarily because scientists have "confidence in their paradigms" but because scientific education consists, in its beginning stages, of the acquisition of propositional knowledge.

elliptical confuted and replaced the theory of epicycles. Or, to quote a recent account, John T. Edsall, reviewing a history of biochemistry, writes: "The crucial period of transition here came in the mid-1930's when Rudolf Schoenheimer and David Rittenberg . . . demonstrated the incessant interchanges that occur between the materials supplied by the diet and the constituents of the tissues, and between one tissue and another. *This rapidly swept away the previous concepts* of 'exogenous' and 'endogenous' metabolism, which had dominated the thinking of biochemists for a generation after Otto Folin had formulated them in 1905" (emphasis added).[7]

Because scientific theories consist, as noted earlier, of general, abstract propositions referring to recurring relationships among selected variables, their validity can, at least in principle, be tested empirically and their "fit" with other knowledge assessed. Once this has been done, alternative hypotheses advanced to account for identical relationships are, as a rule, mutually exclusive: only one true proposition can occupy a given conceptual-explanatory "space." As a result, theories and hypotheses supersede one another.

This is not, however, the case with the particular phenomena that the theory explains. They are not general, abstract, or recurring. Thus, although only one true hypothesis accounts for the way that the refraction of light on water droplets produces the colors of a sunset, there are innumerable specific sunsets, each one of which can be enjoyed for its own special effect. And it would seem strange indeed to argue that one sunset confuted or superseded another.

Works of art, too, are particular, presentational phenomena—though ones created by man, rather than ones found in nature. Like natural objects and events, works of art may, as we shall see, be the subject of theoretical-critical inquiries. But, per se, they are not abstract, general propositions. They are— they present and re-present—concrete, particular relational objects or events. Works of art may follow one another in time, but, because they are not propositional, they are neither testable nor mutually exclusive. Ordinary experience offers unequivocal evidence that this is so: the scientific theories of Aristotle, Ptolemy, and Folin are now of only historical interest, but the music of Mozart, the sculpture of Michelangelo, the plays of Sophocles and Shakespeare, are continuing sources of aesthetic insight and enjoyment.

Even when the subject represented is the same and the quality of insight is comparable, later works do not supersede earlier ones. A Crucifixion by Rembrandt does not negate, replace, or supersede ones by Titian or Crivelli. Nor

7. John T. Edsall, "The Evolution of Biochemistry," *Science* 180 (11 May 1973): 607.

does *King Lear* supplant *Timon of Athens* in the same sense that Darwin's theory supersedes the hypothesis of special creation.[8] *Lear* is performed more often than *Timon,* not because it is propositionally or semantically "truer" (see below), but because it is presentationally and syntactically richer. Far from confuting, invalidating, or superseding one another, works of art—especially those that are similar in style and genre, subject matter and form—complement and illuminate one another.

3. Another difference between the behavior of scientists and artists indicates that the distinction between the discovery of propositional theories and the creation of presentational patterns is real and consequential—namely, scientists and artists make their major contributions at different periods of their lives.

It is, I believe, generally agreed that most major scientific discoveries— really new theoretical formulations—are made when scientists are quite young, even though publication may be delayed, as in Newton's case. But the greatest works of artists, writers, and composers have for the most part been created late in life—even though that life be short, as in the cases of Mozart and Keats.[9] One thinks of Beethoven's last string quartets; or of Verdi's *Otello,* written when he was seventy-four; of Rembrandt's greatest portraits, painted in his last years; or Michelangelo's *Last Judgment,* done when he was over sixty; of Goethe's *Faust* and Milton's *Paradise Lost,* written when their authors were almost sixty.

A further behavioral difference complements this. For the most part, the scientists who are considered "great" are those who formulated radically new theories about the natural world. They were innovators who, in Kuhn's terms,[10] overthrew an existing paradigm. The names of Kepler, Newton, Dar-

---

8. On this point Snow is more perceptive than Stent ("Prematurity," 91–92). He writes: "There is no built-in progress in the humanist culture. There are changes, but not progress, not increase of agreement" (*Public Affairs,* 95). But Snow is only half right. His statement applies to works of art. These, however, are only part of "humanist culture." Humanist theorists, as distinguished from artists, do formulate theories; and these *may* be cumulative, superseding one another. The difficulties of theory construction in the humanities, which have made cumulative development the exception, are considered in the second part of this essay.

9. Mozart's masterpieces and Keats's greatest poems were created during the last five years of their lives. And, had they lived longer, later works would in all probability have surpassed, but not superseded, those we have. As is often the case, some counterexamples come to mind. Wordsworth's greatest (and most innovative) poetry was written before he was thirty, and later works show an undeniable decline in quality.

10. Particularly when major paradigm changes are taking place, the relationship of data to theory is subtle and complex (see Kuhn, *Scientific Revolutions,* chaps. 8, 12).

win, and Einstein come readily to mind. But, despite the persistent myths inherited from the nineteenth century, this has not been the rule in the arts. Bach, Mozart, and even Beethoven; Raphael, Titian, and Rembrandt; Shakespeare, Cervantes, and Goethe were not radical innovators. They did not overturn an existing syntax, style, or genre. Rather they built on and elaborated an existing one. As R. S. Crane observed: "It is a great advantage to an original artist also . . . if the 'form' in which he proposes to write has already been extensively cultivated by his contemporaries and immediate predecessors, since in that case much of his work of material or technical invention has already been done."[11]

Thus, in music, the invention and initial cultivation of the sonata-form principle—an innovation that with important qualifications might be likened to a technological invention—by composers writing toward the beginning of the eighteenth century were a great advantage to Haydn, who built on their formal and technical innovations. And Haydn's cultivation of sonata form was similarly helpful to Mozart and Beethoven. The new paradigm, the sonata-form "idea," which can be thought of as propositional, was the work of the early Classical composers—Wagenseil, Sammartini, C. P. E. Bach, and others—whose music is seldom played and whose names are almost forgotten save by historians of music. In art, then, it is the elaborators of an existing stylistic paradigm who create the greatest works. In science, it is the other way around: the discoverers of new theories, which prove to be correct, are remembered, while the elaborators tend to be forgotten.

Why these contrasts in behavior? Partly, at least, they can be understood as consequences of the difference between the capacities and conditions favoring the discovery of novel propositions and those fostering the creation of original presentational patterns.

The scientist begins with a problem—usually one that arises because existing theory cannot adequately account for newly discovered empirical data. His goal is to formulate and, if possible, to test a hypothesis that fits the facts better than the prevalent one. To do this, he must be able to see "old facts" in a new way. But, the more the prevalent theory has become ingrained as the way of perceiving and conceptualizing relationships in the world, the more difficult it is to formulate alternative propositions—the harder it is to see the world without the biased glasses of tradition. Believing has a strong tendency to become seeing.

11. R. S. Crane, *Principles of Literary History* (Chicago, 1967), 70–71.

A simple and unscientific example will serve to illustrate this point. The data in this case are a series of words; the problem is to punctuate the series so that it makes grammatical-syntactic sense:

TIME FLIES YOU CAN'T THEY FLY TOO FAST

Many people have trouble making the series into intelligible English. They do so because their traditional mode of interpretation—their initial linguistic hypothesis—leads them to construe *time (tempus)* as a noun and *flies (fugit)* as a verb. Only by overthrowing this hypothesis, and recognizing that *time* can be a verb and *flies* a noun, can the series make sense. Construed in the light of this new formulation, the sentence can be explained and punctuated:

Time flies? You can't! They fly too fast.

In short, had linguistic habits been less firmly established, the problem might have been more readily "solved."

Similar considerations seem to play a role in the formulation of scientific hypotheses. The ability to discover new relationships in the world depends to a considerable extent on being naive enough to see data in a nontraditional way. Before he arrived at a new theory of planetary orbits, Kepler had to struggle against and escape from a traditional view that posited the perfection, and hence necessary ubiquity, of circular motions. Jeremy Bernstein makes the same point when he describes the difficulty that Lorentz had in accepting Einstein's theory: "Perhaps his resistance to Einstein's theory was a matter of age. Both Lorentz and Poincaré were in their late forties when they were responding to the crisis that they felt had been produced in physics by the Michelson-Morley experiment. In a sense, *they knew too much:* they had too much of a vested interest in classical physics to throw it away. Einstein was only twenty-six when he published the special theory (not only his discovery but nearly all the really great discoveries in theoretical physics have been made by men under thirty)" (emphasis added).[12] Because the young have, generally

---

12. Jeremy Bernstein, "Profiles—Albert Einstein—1," *New Yorker,* 10 March 1973, 101. See also Kuhn, *Scientific Revolutions,* 149; and Freeman J. Dyson, "Innovation in Physics," *Scientific American* 199, no. 3 (September 1958): 78.

As Kuhn points out (*Scientific Revolutions,* 165), one may also be naive because one is an outsider—someone new to a field. Similar considerations may also play a part in innovation in the arts. For instance, two of Milton's most innovative poems—"On the Morning of Christ's Nativity" and "Lycidas"—were written before he was thirty. The Camerata, whose experiments were to establish the foundations of opera, was made up of outsiders—literary men and dilettantes (such as the leader of the group, Count Bardi)—as well as a number of trained professionals. Innovators in the arts may, of course, go on to create masterpieces. However, those who promul-

speaking, been less thoroughly ingrained with prevalent ways of conceptualizing the world, novel theories are most often hit upon early in scientific careers. And, because science is chiefly concerned with discovering and accounting for the lawlike relationships among events, it is those who formulate new and consequential theories—theories that not only alter our concepts and cognitions but guide the search for new data—who are most honored and best remembered.

The artist, on the other hand, is concerned not with the discovery of general principles but with their use. He employs the rules and regularities of a prevalent paradigm—the grammar, syntax, and formal procedures of an existing style—in order to create an original pattern of particulars: a work of art. But, as I shall argue later, the artist need not have conceptualized the rules he uses—let alone be able to explain them. His "knowledge," based on practice and experience, may be tacit. He understands the rules in the sense of being able to employ them efficiently and effectively, not in the sense of being able to formulate them as propositional statements. Men can use, and have used, language with brilliant effect without being able to formulate or explain the rules of grammar and syntax, prosody or rhetoric—not to mention notions such as those of generative grammar. Similarly, men were able to build Chartres Cathedral without knowing the propositional principles of engineering—the laws of stress, force, pressure, and the like. And so it has been in the other arts as well. Composers, for instance, employed tonal syntax long before a viable theory of tonal harmony was formulated.

Styles are complex probability "systems" within which the artist chooses among alternative possibilities—that is, in terms of which he invents and combines patterns, develops and resolves tensions, devises and elaborates formal relationships. Without a probabilistic paradigm, creative choice would be impossible. For, if the rules specified precisely what was to be done, all choices would be preordained, and originality would be impossible. Academic art approaches this condition. On the other hand, were there no rules at all—were anything possible and all possibilities equally probable—the artist would be caught in trembling indecision. For an indefinitely large number of such alternatives virtually precludes intelligent choice.

Style is the artist's point of departure. It guides, but does not determine, the choices he makes. The syntactic norms, prosodic procedures, and dramatic conventions of Elizabethan England, for instance, limited many of

---

gate radically new stylistic changes seldom create works of the highest quality. Their importance is historical rather than artistic.

Shakespeare's choices. But they did not determine the specific words, gestures, and actions given to Hamlet, Gertrude, or Claudius. These depended not only upon Shakespeare's ability to invent interesting alternatives and to envisage their consequences but upon his capacity, as the first audience for his own inventions, sensitively to judge their effects and to choose accordingly.

The ability to invent and envisage creatively depends in part upon innate qualities of mind and feeling. Partly it is the result of the artist's experience —of his having learned, through patient and painstaking practice, to devise promising possibilities and to imagine their implications. Similarly, the capacity to choose with sensitivity and discernment depends in part upon experience—experience not only of the world but of other works of art. In other words, the artist's ability to choose *efficiently* depends upon the existence of viable stylistic rules; his capacity to employ such rules *effectively* depends upon his ingenuity and his judgment, both of which are to a considerable degree the result of experience.

It is because invention, discernment, and judgment increase with practice and experience that artists tend to create their greatest works late in life. For this reason, too, such works are produced not by those who promulgate a new stylistic paradigm but by those who are fortunate enough to build upon one that already exists—by artists who have had the opportunity to internalize the probabilities and procedures of a style, to explore their potentialities, and to become expert in selecting alternatives that are compelling and entertaining.

4. While my primary concern is to consider differences between the sciences and the arts, I do not wish to suggest that there are no similarities. Despite its manifold mysteries, the psychology of the creative process appears to be an area of clear commonality.[13] Both scientists and artists must possess qualities such as a high level of disciplined energy, the intelligence to comprehend complex relationships, the imagination to envisage the implications of concepts and patterns, and the ability to tolerate the tensions of uncertainty and ambiguity. More specifically, artists, like scientists, seem to use a kind of trial-and-error method. Beethoven, for instance, wrote: "I can remember for years a theme that has once occurred to me. I alter a lot, *reject and experiment until I am satisfied;* and then begins in my head the development *(Verarbei-*

13. In *The Creative Act* (New York, 1967), Arthur Koestler emphasizes that originality is a component of aesthetic value. But, if *originality* (the discovery of novel forms, syntax, etc.) is distinguished from *inventiveness* (the imaginative use of existing means), then originality has not been a criterion of value in all cultures—especially not in most non-Western cultures. For further discussion of this point, see below.

tung) in breadth, concentration, height and depth" (emphasis added).[14] But psychological similarities between the creative processes of scientists and artists do not warrant the conclusion that the results produced—theories and works of art—are comparable, any more than the fact that energy generates both sound and light warrants the conclusion that those phenomena are experientially and conceptually equivalent.

Even the idea of originality, often thought of as being characteristic of both science and art, seems to denote quite different sorts of behavior in the two realms—as a simple example will show. A South Indian musician, improvising on the sitar, employs tonal materials, syntactic procedures, and formal relationships that have been used time and time again. What are new are not the stylistic rules and the archetypal schema that guide his performance but their actualization as a specific work of art. The composer-performer is judged to be original, not because he overturns a traditional paradigm, but because, employing existing rules in an inventive and imaginative way, he creates a new presentational pattern for our aesthetic enjoyment. But a scientist whose work consisted of devising subtle variations within an existing theory—essentially performing the same experiment over and over—would not be considered especially original or creative, even though the need for his contribution would be readily acknowledged.

The distinction between the presentational character of works of art and the propositional nature of scientific theories is of more than philosophical interest. For, when these disparate ways of "knowing" are confounded, the practical consequences may be bizarre, if not deplorable.

Particularly in music and the visual arts, scientific discovery has in the recent past often been taken as the model for creativity. Originality has been equated with stylistic innovation. As Harold Rosenberg has pointed out, the search has been for propositional novelty. For instance, categorical rules stipulated: use only one color, paint only straight lines, wrap everything in canvas, choose musical relationships from a predetermined set of pitches and durations, or merely throw the dice.[15]

This search for novelty can be explained historically. The beginning of the twentieth century was characterized by stylistic diversity. Different national and personal idioms existed side by side. At the same time, there was a growing awareness that other cultures and earlier epochs had employed different

14. Quoted in Martin Cooper, *Beethoven: The Last Decade, 1817–1827* (London, 1970), 129–30.

15. Harold Rosenberg, *The Tradition of the New* (New York, 1959), 67.

styles. A pervasive sense of pluralism, coupled with a presumed weakening of the prevalent style, made it appear that art was indeed artificial, if not arbitrary. Nothing seemed impossible. As a result, choosing became traumatic. From this point of view, the propositional programs invented by contemporary artists can be understood as ways of limiting—or, in the case of chance art, of avoiding—choice.[16]

At the same time, Western thought and ideology came to be more and more dominated by science. Seeking to emulate its achievements and perhaps unconsciously to attain comparable prestige, many artists turned their attention and energies not to creating art but to proposing new theories of art. The supposed equivalence of art with science was made explicit when works were labeled *experimental.*

That these events are understandable historically is, however, no guarantee that the analogy is tenable. In addition to the more fundamental contrasts being considered, the fact that our criteria for originality are different in the arts and sciences indicates that the analogy is mistaken. Whether its consequences are aesthetically fruitful, history will decide.[17]

What is interesting, and also amusing, is that a concatenation of errors evidently underlies the premium currently placed upon novelty in art and science. In the arts, the value placed on novelty is largely confined to Western culture, where it is a relatively recent phenomenon. Until around the beginning of the eighteenth century, artists were by no means expected to fly in the face of what was established. Accomplishment and originality were equated with the inventive use of traditional means, not with the invention of revolutionary idioms. More surprisingly, Thomas Kuhn writes that "novelty for its own sake is not a desideratum in the sciences as it is in so many other creative fields."[18]

Paradox and irony are here compounded. Thinking it to be a goal of science, which they sought to emulate, many contemporary artists have searched for novelty. Not only was the analogy mistaken, but so was the presumed goal! And the ultimate irony is that, were works of art indeed comparable to scientific theories, then, like such theories, they might prove to be wrong and

16. Choice was not, of course, actually avoided, only displaced: after all, these artists *chose* not to choose.

17. In this connection, it is important to recognize that, in the arts as well as the sciences, fruitful consequences may follow from mistaken theories.

18. Kuhn, *Scientific Revolutions,* 168. With regard to the valuing of innovation, see also J. Bronowski, "The Creative Process," *Scientific American,* vol. 199, no. 3 (1958), quoted in essay 5 (pp. 189f.).

would be discarded. All that would remain of such experimental efforts would be historical curiosities comparable to ether or to phlogiston.

5. Another behavioral difference between science and art—one related to our conception of originality—is the occurrence of simultaneous discovery. The facts are as striking as they are indisputable. Independently of one another, and at roughly the same time, Newton and Leibnitz discovered calculus, Darwin and Wallace formulated similar theories of evolution—and these are only the most famous instances. But simultaneous creation of the same work by two artists working independently of one another has never occurred. It is difficult even to imagine two Elizabethan dramatists writing the play we call *Hamlet,* two composers of the early nineteenth century creating the C#-Minor String Quartet that Beethoven wrote, or two artists of the early twentieth century both painting *Les demoiselles d'Avignon.* Accusations of illicit Hegelianism or doubtful historicism cannot obscure the fact that, when conditions are propitious, the probability of making a particular scientific discovery becomes very high. Watson's account in *The Double Helix* makes it abundantly clear that, had he and Crick not hurried, someone else would have solved the problem before they did. Nor need one be a historical determinist to believe that, given the state of scientific knowledge in the 1950s, if Yang and Lee had not refuted the law of parity, some other scientist would soon have done so.[19] But, if Stravinsky had not composed the *Symphony of Psalms,* it would never have been written at all.

The contrast can, once again, be traced to the difference between propositional statements and presentational patterns. Because the number of true general statements that can be made about some class of natural phenomena would seem to be finite, it is not improbable that, given favorable cultural-historical conditions, more than one scientist will discover a particular relationship and formulate a theory to explain it. But, just as the principle of the refraction of light is the basis for the colors of countless specific sunsets, so the rules of a style, however constant and restricted they may be, can give rise to innumerable individual works of art. Consequently, the probability of simultaneous artistic creation is virtually nil.

19. This point is explicitly asserted by Harry D. Huskey: "It is this reviewer's opinion that no one is indispensable to a development when the time is right. . . . I feel certain that several of us on the Moore School team could have written a sample stored program if we had felt it necessary. This in no way detracts from von Neuman's ability to recognize the importance of an idea, and to develop such concepts at rates that the rest of us could only admire as spectators at a race" ("On the History of Computing," *Science* 180 [11 May 1973]: 589).

Earlier, I suggested that the invention of new artistic techniques and technological innovation are analogous. Because what is discovered is a repeatable, general principle—for example, sonnet form or invertible counterpoint, irrigation or the steam engine—simultaneous discovery should occur in both cases. That it does so in technology is well known. Indeed, John R. Pierce believes that, for various reasons, "the chance of simultaneous discovery is perhaps greater in technology than in science."[20] In the arts, unfortunately, the evidence is somewhat equivocal. Style changes and new techniques are seldom effected by a single work but through a host of often forgotten ones. And they evolve gradually over the years. Cubism, for instance, developed out of the work of Cézanne and his contemporaries. During the first decade of the twentieth century it was in the air. It could be "in the air" because it was a general concept. It would certainly be peculiar and improper, however, to assert that a specific pattern such as *Les demoiselles d'Avignon* was in the air. In music, the following decade saw the advent of serialism. And its beginning provides a clear instance of simultaneous discovery in the arts. Both Hauer and Schönberg evidently hit upon the idea—the general principle—of composing with twelve tones at roughly the same time and independently of one another.

6. Both the arts and the sciences are collective activities. But they are so in significantly different ways. Works of art illuminate one another. Our understanding and appreciation of *Hamlet* or the C♯-Minor Quartet depend upon our experience of other plays and compositions. To some extent such understanding is atemporal. Manet's paintings affect our appreciation of Goya's (and vice versa), just as Manet's paintings change our understanding of those by his contemporaries and followers. Granted this cultural interdependence, however, the specific relationships that constitute a work of art form a complete and coherent pattern that is "logically"—though not historically or psychologically—independent of other works of art.

Science is collective in a different and even more significant sense. Unlike works of art, scientific hypotheses do not possess internal integrity and completeness. Their interdependence is more than historical and psychological. They complement and entail one another in a logical and systematic way. It is not the individual hypothesis that creates coherence and integrity in science but the larger, more comprehensive set of interrelated discoveries. Joel H. Hil-

---

20. John R. Pierce, "Innovation in Technology," *Scientific American* 199, no. 3 (September 1958): 117.

debrand makes the point crystal clear: "We are building fragments of information into structures of great beauty, comparable as achievements of the human mind and spirit with the greatest works of art and literature."[21] Notice that what are compared are science as a collective activity and individual works of art. The collective character of science is also implicit in C. P. Snow's report that Dirac felt that "there was one supreme reward for his scientific work, the sense of having a share in the building of an *edifice.*"[22]

Because they are not propositional, works of art do not constitute a logical or systematic order. A late work of Manet cannot be inferred from an earlier one, let alone from ones by Courbet or Delacroix. Even taken as a whole, Manet's oeuvre does not entail other works of art in the way that the theory of evolution entails hypotheses about the transmission of hereditary traits. Perhaps it is because works of art are related to one another in more informal ways that artists rarely think of their activity as collective or communal.[23] Picasso certainly did not regard *Les demoiselles d'Avignon* primarily as a contribution to the "edifice" of contemporary painting—although it was unquestionably profoundly influential.

7. Turning now from a concern with the nature and genesis of scientific theories and works of art, let us consider the way that our apprehension of them changes over time.

When a great scientific theory is first formulated, it often seems strange, anomalous, and perplexing. For it asks us to "see" the world in a radically new way. If the theory is accepted and confirmed, it gradually becomes part of the culture's customary way of comprehending and explaining the world. As this occurs, what at first appeared to be anomalous and perplexing comes to seem ordinary and is taken for granted. Here is Freeman Dyson's account of the acceptance of Maxwell's theory: "The basic difficulty of the Maxwell theory in those days was that no one could conceive an electric field except in terms of a mechanical model. . . . Only very slowly did it become possible to forget the mechanical models and to picture an electric field as something basic and

21. Joel H. Hildebrand, "Order from Chaos," *Science* 150 (22 October 1965): 41.
22. Snow, *Public Affairs,* 97.
23. Again, there are counterexamples. As Professor Barbara H. Smith (to whom I am indebted for both cogent criticisms and specific suggestions) reminds me, "F. G. Lorca saw *Blood Wedding* as primarily a contribution to the renewal of the vitality of Spanish theater" (private communication). And Wagner evidently regarded his work as a contribution to the edifice of German culture. But such cases, attributable to relatively recent changes in cultural ideology (e.g., the rise of nationalism), are exceptional.

indivisible. . . . Once the change was made, the simplicity and beauty of the Maxwell equations were no longer hidden, and *it was hard to understand what all the fuss was about*" (emphasis added).[24]

Great works of art, too, often seem strange and perplexing at first. However, although they are based upon and form part of a stylistic paradigm, they never become fully absorbed into it. The "idea" of the sonnet, of the leitmotif, or of pointillism will, like a scientific principle, lose its original strangeness as it becomes part of common practice. But Keats's sonnet "When I have fears that I may cease to be," Wagner's *Tristan und Isolde,* and Seurat's *Grande jatte* do not do so. For, in each case, the general principles employed are actualized as a specific and unique pattern that retains much of its original strangeness.

To put the contrast concisely, a successful scientific theory tends to become so much a part of our ordinary way of perceiving relationships in the world that it loses its aura of strangeness and novelty. The success of a work of art, on the other hand, lies in its ability, despite repeated encounters, to remain fresh, remarkable, and mysterious. It is because general propositions can become absorbed into everyday thinking that a bright college student can comprehend concepts that Newton, for instance, had to struggle to formulate; while great works of art—*Hamlet, Les demoiselles d'Avignon,* and the C♯-Minor String Quartet—continue to excite our wonder and to perplex us.

*

Scientific theories, as we have seen, are constructs that formulate those relationships among phenomena that are found to be regular and invariant. The phenomena—planetary motions, molecular structures, economic behavior, and the like—are not themselves derived from, and consequently cannot refer to or be *about,* anything else. They neither disclose nor propose. They exist. Theories are, directly or indirectly, derived from and refer to such existent actualities. Because they are related to one another in these ways, it is both customary and reasonable to assert that theories are "about" phenomena: for instance, that the theory proposed by Watson and Crick is *about* the structure of the DNA molecule; that the law of supply and demand is *about* the behavior of prices given certain economic conditions; and that, in the humanities, a theoretical or a critical essay may be *about* sonata form or the *Moonlight* Sonata.

24. Freeman Dyson, "Innovation in Physics," *Scientific American* 199, no. 3 (September 1958): 76.

But what is the *Moonlight* Sonata about? According to legend, when asked what the sonata meant—what it was *about*—Beethoven went to the piano and played it a second time. His answer seems not only appropriate but compelling. Suppose, on the other hand, that a physicist, asked what the law of gravity was about, answered by letting some object fall to the ground. Surely, the inference would be that he was being disingenuously witty—that he had not responded properly. Beethoven's answer is reasonable, while the physicist's is not, because the *Moonlight* Sonata is not about the world in the sense that the law of gravity is. It does not refer to anything—not even to the tonal and temporal relationships of which it is constituted. It *is* something: a work of art.

Now it might be argued that music is a special case because it is not as a rule explicitly representational—as literature and the plastic arts generally are. But this contention, common though it is, is mistaken. Because the relationship between a work of art and what it refers to is both subtle and complex, it can be only summarily described here. But few serious critics would, I think, disagree with the basic position being espoused.

Many works of art make use of facts and events found in the world—words and gestures, lines and colors, forms and actions. But these are so transformed, when they are re-presented by the artist, that the resulting pattern acquires an integrity and autonomy characteristic of natural phenomena. Even when the subject is a historical event or character, as in *Julius Caesar* or *War and Peace,* the integrity of the aesthetic pattern is evident. For, while our ability to comprehend a play or a novel depends upon our experience of the world (including, especially, other fictional accounts) and upon our sense of what is probable and plausible, we do not judge *Julius Caesar,* say, in terms of the accuracy and veracity with which speeches, events, and actions are reported—as we would if the work were a history. Rather, it is judged in terms of its own internal coherence and plausibility. As Barbara H. Smith observes: "The work of art, then, provides the stimulus to and occasion for a highly distilled and rewarding cognitive experience, but also a highly artificial one; for in experiencing a work of art, we may have all the satisfaction that attends the pursuit and acquisition of knowledge without *necessarily* having acquired any knowledge at all. Or, rather, what we acquire knowledge *of* in a work of art is primarily the work itself, a fabricated microcosm designed to be knowable in just that way."[25]

Above all, works of art are not *about* the world in the sense of being general

25. Barbara H. Smith, "Literature as Performance, Fiction, and Art," *Journal of Philosophy* 67, no. 16 (20 August 1970): 562.

propositions. Although it is a fictional exemplification of the behavior of a prince caught in a particular set of domestic and political circumstances—circumstances that are understandable partly because they are recurrent kinds known through our experience of the world—*Hamlet* is not a theory about human behavior or political action. Were it about the world in the sense that science is, the play would have to be counted as one of the greatest failures ever. For theories about the world, and histories of it, are judged according to their precision, clarity, and empirical validity. But, as shelf after shelf of criticism testifies, *Hamlet*'s propositional "content" is anything but explicit and precise. Like phenomena in the world, the play may be the subject of theoretical inquiry, and audiences as well as critics may make inferences about its propositional "meaning." But, as a work of art, it is not a propositional explanation but a presentational exemplification.

Nor are works of art "about" the emotions, although their skillful representation or exemplification may strike us as poignant and illuminating. More importantly, works of art may evoke and shape affective experience, just as other phenomena—sunsets, football games, or political conventions—do. Psychology, not art, however, formulates theories about the emotions. The humanist-critic—using psychological theories or, because those are as yet inchoate and rudimentary, employing common sense—may attempt to explain our response to a particular work of art. But the work of art is not *about* such experiences, any more than a magnificent sunset, an exciting football game, or a rousing political convention is. Scientists have frequently noted the presence of a marked affective component in scientific discovery. But few, one suspects, would want to assert that the act of discovery was "about" their emotional experience.

The third term in Stent's troublesome triad—namely, *truth*—is more problematic. Not only is the validation of theories provisional, but it depends upon considerations such as the explanatory strength and simplicity of a hypothesis relative to possible alternatives and upon how it fits both with other theories and with the data. Even counterevidence is not always a decisive factor. Theoretical formulations may well go beyond the available facts, and known discrepancies are often disregarded for the sake of explanatory power and elegance. These complexities, together with the historical vicissitudes of once well-established beliefs, have made scholars reluctant to assert that theories are true.[26] It seems to me, however, that some theories are so securely

26. This seems the case with Thomas Kuhn. However, to achieve "an increasingly detailed and refined understanding of nature" is to do more than merely move "from primitive begin-

supported by the weight of evidence and by the larger pattern of hypotheses that their truth cannot be denied. Even to qualify them as provisional would be to cavil—like arguing that the statement "All men are mortal" is only probable because the evidence is not yet complete.

The validity of scientific theories can, after all, be tested empirically. As John C. Eccles has pointed out, although the insight provided by a new hypothesis may have "immediate esthetic appeal in its simplicity and scope, it must nevertheless be subjected to rigorous criticism and experimental testing. The illumination often has had the suddenness of a flash, as with Kekulé and the benzene ring, Darwin and the theory of evolution, Hamilton and his equations. But suddenness of illumination is no guarantee of the validity of a hypothesis. I have had only one such sudden illumination—the so-called Golgi-cell hypothesis of cerebral inhibition—and some years later it was proved false!" [27]

Scientific theories can be proved false because they are general propositions about the relationships among existing phenomena. A theory that relates the colors of a sunset to the refraction of light by water vapor, or one that relates the prices of goods in a free market to supply and demand, can, at least in principle, be tested empirically. But to assert that a particular sunset is true (or false) simply makes no sense. (It is possible, of course, to remark upon the quality of a sunset, noting that it was especially vivid and colorful. And a theory might be proposed that related our aesthetic or affective responses to such qualities.) Because sunsets and price changes are particular phenomena *in* the world, not propositions *about* the world, the terms *true* and *false* are irrelevant and unintelligible.

And so it is with works of art. We do not, save in a metaphoric sense, assert that they are "true." What could it possibly mean to confirm or disconfirm *Hamlet, Les demoiselles d'Avignon,* or the C♯-Minor String Quartet? What kind of data or experiment can be imagined that would test their validity? The

---

nings" (Kuhn, *Scientific Revolutions,* 169). It is to move toward and, at times, to arrive at truths. It is not necessary to adopt a teleological view of scientific progress—one that reifies *truth* as a kind of goal that is objectively "there" to be discovered—in order to believe that science moves toward truth. Kuhn's analogy between the history of science and biological evolution, which seems to play a part in his position, is misleading. Not only do scientists, like other human beings, have goals, while natural processes do not, but the relationships that science explains exist as phenomena in the world and provide data for the evaluation of theories, while the phenomena themselves (the facts of evolution) have no reference in terms of which either goals or truths could possibly be evaluated.

27. John C. Eccles, "The Physiology of Imagination," *Scientific American* 199, no. 3 (September 1958): 144.

answer is *none* because what can be tested are general theories about the world, not phenomenal patterns in it or even particular exemplifications of it. Simpleminded "tests," such as accuracy of representation, yield obviously ludicrous results: Is a "realistic" novel like Steinbeck's *Grapes of Wrath* truer than *Gulliver's Travels* or Goethe's *Faust*? Is an illustrative painting by Rockwell Kent true, while ones by Bosch or Picasso are false? (It is, however, entirely proper to argue that one work of art is more interesting and elegant, entertaining and moving than another, just as we do with other presentational phenomena—sunsets, football games, or political conventions.)

History, too, indicates that the notions of true and false are not applicable to works of art. For, were works of art propositional truths about the world, then their history would, like that of scientific theories, have been one of supersession. That is, later works of art would have been more convincing than earlier ones and would have replaced them. But this has not, of course, occurred. It would be preposterous to suggest that there has been a progression toward greater truth as we have moved from Sophocles to Shakespeare to Pinter, from Josquin to Mozart to Bartók, or from Phideas to Donatello to Rodin.

Great works of art command our assent. Like validated theories, they seem self-evident and incontrovertible, meaningful and necessary, infallible and illuminating. There is, without doubt, an aura of "truth" about them. However, they persuade and convince, not because they are validated general propositions about the phenomenal world, but because the patterns and relationships they present possess internal integrity and autonomous coherence. This is not to deny that representational art, and especially literature, must be credible in the sense of conforming (within broad and undefined limits) with our experience of the probabilities of the world and of human behavior.[28] Yet,

28. There are nonfictive kinds of representation—e.g., biographies—that seem to make explicitly empirical truth claims. The problem of classification raised by biography is beyond my competence. But a few observations seem pertinent.

Biographies represent specific events and personal characteristics. They must conform with some degree of accuracy to documented data. But they do not consist of propositional truths such as are found in science. Rather, they seem to be interpretive realizations of the patterns and relationships potential in the given data. For this reason there can be alternative biographies of the same person, just as there can be alternative interpretations of a musical score or a poetic text. And, just as the performance of a symphony may be pedestrian and boring, so a biography may be accurate but routine and lifeless. This suggests that there is a distinction between truth and accuracy. Though there may be innumerable inaccurate, and hence "untrue," biographies of an individual, no biography is ever the single "true" one, any more than there is a single "true" performance of a particular symphony.

Biographies are, as far as I can see, kinds of history. They may be more or less artful, as histories may be, but they are not works of literature in the sense that novels, even historical ones,

even in this seeming similarity, science and art stand in contrast to one another. For scientific theories are general propositions whose truth is tested with respect to specific phenomena, while works of art are specific phenomena whose credibility is corroborated by general experience.

If we keep in mind that works of art are comparable not to scientific theories *about* phenomena but to the phenomena themselves, then other relationships between art and truth become evident. Like natural phenomena, works of art may be the occasion for the development of general theories. Such theories, like those in the sciences, may be explicitly formulated: for instance, in philosophy and psychology, sociology and music theory. And the validity of such theories can at least in principle be tested. Often, too, members of the audience make inferences of an informal sort that result in what seem to be general truths. What must be emphasized is that the artist presents relationships from which general propositions may be inferred; he does not present the theories themselves, as the scientist does. Because the human condition is especially poignantly and precisely exemplified in works of art, fictive relationships frequently lead to such inferences.

Moreover, not only do poignant situations such as those presented in *King Lear* or *Volpone* and memorable characters such as Coriolanus or M. Jourdain encourage such inferences, but they significantly change the ways in which we comprehend and conceptualize human existence. From this point of view, works of art are related to truth not merely in a "passive" way—in the sense that they are congruent with our general experience of the world—but in an "active" way because, like other phenomena in the world (only perhaps more so), they profoundly affect our perception, comprehension, and experience of existence. In this respect, then, art is indeed comparable to science. For, just as our experience of the sun rising over the horizon is radically influenced by

---

are. Of course, biographies make the claim that their subjects really lived. But that claim is a historical one and has nothing to do with what is called *artistic truth*. If it were discovered that Dr. Johnson never lived, Boswell's *Life* would cease to be his biography, and tests of historical accuracy would become irrelevant. The genre of the work would presumably change: it would probably be considered a fictive biography.

This raises the interesting question of the difference between a true biography and a fictive one. I suspect that the fundamental difference lies in our understanding of the probabilities of existence. When a work is known to be a real biography or history, the accuracy of the representation is, so to speak, guaranteed by the genre. Consequently, the reader is prepared to accept events and relationships that might have seemed absurd and wildly improbable in a fictive representation of a "realistic" sort. Put differently, the creator of a fictive account must use his art to make the improbable credible, while the biographer or historian must employ his craft to make the credible coherent, imparting form to happenstance.

our knowledge of heliocentric theory, so our perception of the sea is changed by our familiarity with Turner's paintings, and our understanding of human behavior is modified by Shakespeare's plays.

Once formulated, scientific theories become phenomena in the cultural world. As such they may be subjects for further inquiry in other areas of learning—for instance, in philosophy or in history. Like other phenomena such as sunsets, chess games, and works of art, theories may be the occasion for aesthetic delight. Expressing sentiments similar to those of Hildebrand (quoted earlier), C. P. Snow observes that "the scientific edifice of the physical world [is] in its intellectual depth, complexity and articulation, the most beautiful and wonderful collective work of the mind of man."[29] And the presence of such aesthetic pleasure may be one reason why the analogy that I have been trying to confute is so prevalent and seems so plausible.

But prevalence and plausibility cannot compensate for a lack of consistency and precision. If the relationships among disciplines and fields of endeavor are to be ordered in ways that are comprehensible, coherent, and fruitful, then scientific theories must be compared not to presentational patterns but to other theories—specifically to those devised by humanists to explain works of art.

2

Like phenomena in the natural world, works of art may be the subject of scrupulous inquiry. One important goal of the humanities is to discover and define the relationships presented in a work of art and to explain how such relationships are comprehended and experienced by competent listeners, viewers, and readers. Thus it is the humanist, not the artist, who is comparable to the scientist. But even this analogy is not exact. The discrepancies between the two are revealing because they not only account for the difficulties of the humanist's task but at the same time suggest why his studies have not achieved, and in some respects cannot achieve, the rigor and certainty possible in science—and why, as a result, humanistic inquiry has not as a general rule been cumulative. To make both the parallels and the differences clear, I must now consider the nature of humanistic studies at some length. I first differentiate understanding and explaining and then distinguish three interrelated areas of humanistic inquiry: theory, style analysis, and criticism. Finally, I contrast the role of the critic with that of the creative artist, on the one hand, and the scientist, on the other.

29. Snow, *Public Affairs,* 21.

A

To explain something is to make a perceived, experienced relationship the object of conscious and explicit conceptualization and to account for the relationship in terms of some general principle or hypothesis, however informal or unsystematized. Explanation thus depends upon understanding. For, unless something is understood to *be* a relationship, there is nothing to be explained. But the converse does not hold: although cognition (i.e., mentally relating perceptions to one another in some way) is invariably involved, we can understand—in the sense of responding appropriately, making reasonable inferences, or performing skillfully—without the need or even the ability to explain. Indeed, something can be understood correctly but explained incorrectly. To use Michael Polanyi's expression, we often know (or understand) "tacitly." [30]

Examples illustrating that understanding is possible in the absence of explanation come readily to mind. Men have understood—have known how to use and respond to—language since there have been men; but only now are we beginning to be able to explain how and why language works. For almost as long, men have used fire and constructed buildings without being able to account for combustion and without knowing the principles of force and elasticity, stress and strain. Bicycles have been ridden for almost a century; but only recently has a theory explaining their stability been proposed. Chinese medicine has used acupuncture effectively, as Western medicine has used aspirin beneficially; yet the basis for their palliative power remains to be discovered. Even one who is especially accomplished in some field may be at a loss to account for his skill. For instance, Zobrist and Carlson observe that "a grand master might be quite unable to explain the reasoning behind a particularly brilliant move." [31]

And so it is in the arts. One can understand a play or a poem, a painting or sculpture, a symphony or a tone poem without being able to explain it. Indeed, one can write, paint, or compose without conceptual knowledge of stylistic-grammatical rules or of the psychological principles involved in creative activity. Consider the situation in music.

Ardent listeners sometimes avow that they are devoted to and delight in music but don't "understand" it. This is, however, most unlikely. People are

30. Michael Polanyi, *Personal Knowledge* (Chicago, 1958).
31. A. L. Zobrist and F. R. Carlson, "An Advice-Taking Computer," *Scientific American* 228, no. 6 (June 1973): 100–101.

seldom devoted to what they do not understand. Rather, because it threatens a powerful need for psychic security, what is incomprehensible is generally abhorred and avoided: witness the intense hostility often evoked by avant-garde music in audiences accustomed to the syntax and structure of tonal music.

What such listeners mean when they assert that they don't understand music is that they cannot read it, identify or conceptualize technical procedures, or explain its ability to delight and move them. But understanding music depends neither on literacy nor on conceptual knowledge. If it did, audiences, past and present, for the music of Bach and Brahms, Mozart and Mahler would have been very small indeed.

Enjoying a Bach fugue or a Mahler symphony does not require being able to name and explain kinds of cadences, contrapuntal devices, or formal structures any more than enjoying *Hamlet* involves being able to name and explain grammatical or prosodic means, dramatic procedures, and the like. Being a competent listener, viewer, or reader is not a matter of knowing *about* works of art in the sense of being able to explain them. To paraphrase what Bertrand Russell said of language, it is a matter of habits and skills—of tacit knowledge —correctly acquired in oneself and properly presumed in another, that is, in the creative artist whose work is being attended to.

More radically still, artists and performers may not, and need not, be able to explain their own works. To take a particularly striking example, Albert Lord, a student of folk literature, went to Yugoslavia, where poet-musicians still improvise folk epics in the manner of Homer. Lord discovered that these poets, whose chief claim to fame is the use of words, lines, and poetic devices, often did not know what a word was and could not tell where a line began or ended.[32] That is, they neither consciously classified nor explicitly conceptualized the poetic relationships they employed, and, in consequence, they could not explain what they did. Yet they were accomplished creative artists.

Perhaps, however, this sort of situation prevails only in folk or in primitive cultures. Cultivated artists in the East as well as the West often do discuss, analyze, and explain their works. But, when they conceptualize about technical and aesthetic matters, such artists generally do so in terms of the theoretical and philosophical formulations already current in their culture. Consequently, their speculations are relevant to those aspects of their work that are most traditional, rather than those in which they have been most innovative. For, since

32. Albert Lord, *The Singer of Tales* (Cambridge, Mass., 1960), 25.

they are for the most part devised to account for already existing styles, forms, and genres, theories have not as a rule preceded practice but followed it. Sophocles did not begin with a theory of drama and then write *Oedipus;* he began with traditions and habits, models and norms. Aristotle formulated a theory of tragedy, using Sophocles' drama as the central example. Similarly, the composers of the Renaissance did not begin with a theory of triadic structure and then apply it in their compositions. Rather, as Richard Crocker describes it: "After 1450 this sound [the triad] appeared with increasing frequency, until by 1550 it accounted for the overwhelming majority of sounds in the average piece. . . . Around 1550 Zarlino *gave theoretical recognition* to this group of three tones—the triad—as an entity" (emphasis added).[33]

To put the matter bluntly: creative artists—composers, painters, and writers—are not necessarily knowledgeable, or even reliable, explainers of what their skills have wrought. The artist, like God, is a creator. But, as with God, the comments of artists on their work are often cryptic and inscrutable. They know how to invent and shape patterns that intrigue and affect us but may be at a loss to explain how and why we—*and* they—comprehend and respond to a work of art as we do.

This is not to contend that education, which often does involve conceptualization and explanation, cannot enhance understanding and hence enjoyment. By calling attention to relationships, by analyzing processes and structures that might otherwise have escaped notice or been misunderstood, education refines the aural, verbal, or visual imagination and increases the awareness and sensitivity of the cognitive ear and eye. But, were explanation a prerequisite for understanding, Bach might not have been able to compose or Shakespeare to write. For, while both supremely *understood* what they were doing, they might not have been able to *explain* it. In short, composers, writers, and artists are especially sensitive, skillful, and imaginative understanders of tonal, verbal, and visual relationships and of how people (including themselves) will respond to such relationships. But much of their knowledge is tacit rather than conceptual.

A further question arises. If they are not necessarily expert explainers, how are creative artists able to teach effectively? To answer this, we have only to remind ourselves that teaching a skill need not involve explaining the basis for the skill. All of us have taught our children to read, ride a bicycle, or play

---

33. Richard Crocker, *A History of Musical Style* (New York, 1966), 223.

tennis without being able to explain the skill ourselves. We say, "Listen: *th* sounds like this"; or, "Look: stand sideways to the net, and sweep your racket evenly." We teach by example and admonition, establishing proper habits that are the basis for the skill. And artists teach in the same way. If a student comes to his composition teacher with a problem, he will be told: "Well, why don't you try doing it this way," and the teacher writes down a possible solution. Or he may refer the student to similar situations in the works of other composers. The composer-teacher might not be able to say *why* a particular solution works. But he can do it. And, by doing it, he teaches his student. It is because creative artists usually teach in this way that they use the apprentice method rather than formal classes for their instruction.

Scientists, too, must acquire tacit knowledge—become skilled in perceiving relationships and in formulating, as well as testing, hypotheses. Consequently, particularly on the graduate level, they often teach by admonition and example. But even here, as earlier discussion suggests, surface similarities mask a more basic difference: broadly speaking, the skill of the creative artist involves synthesis, while that of the scientist involves analysis. The artist begins with internalized rules, the norms and procedures of some style, and employs his tacit understanding to combine and coordinate the variables of his art— in music, for instance, melody, harmony, rhythm, texture, and so on—in order to form a specific phenomenon, a work of art. The scientist, on the other hand, begins with particular phenomena (natural events) and, by isolating variables and analyzing their interactions, seeks to discover the general principles that underlie and govern their structure and process.

Many scientists are not only competent listeners but skilled performers as well. As a rule they are also experienced readers and viewers. Perhaps possession of these competencies has encouraged them in the belief that they are analogous to artists. But even though scientific research undoubtedly depends upon tacit knowledge—intuitive understanding and skill, which the scientist may himself be at a loss to explain—the result, a scientific hypothesis, is not tacit. It is an explicitly formulated conceptual proposition. C. P. Snow's comparisons, for instance, indicate a confusion between understanding and explanation:

> Once or twice I have been provoked and have asked the company [of non-scientists] how many of them could describe the Second Law of Thermodynamics. The response was cold: it was also negative. Yet I was asking something which is about the scientific equivalent of: Have you read a work of Shakespeare?

> I now believe that if I had asked an even simpler question—such as, What
> do you mean by mass, or acceleration, which is the scientific equivalent of
> saying, *Can you read?*—not more than one in ten of the highly educated
> would have felt that I was speaking the same language.[34]

But the questions are by no means equivalent. To take the simpler first, the
proper analogue of such concepts as mass and acceleration is another concept
—not a skill, like reading. A proper analogue to the question "What do you
mean by mass?" is "What do you mean by rounded-binary form?" or "What
is chiaroscuro?" And one wonders how many highly educated scientists could
respond. Conversely, the correct analogue of "Can you read?" is not a concept but a skill: for instance, "How far can you throw a ball?" Similarly, what
is comparable to reading and understanding a play of Shakespeare is not familiarity with a propositional theory like the second law of thermodynamics.
Rather, it is observing and comprehending the kinds of relationships in the
natural world that led to the formulation of the law. The equivalent of "Have
you ever read a play of Shakespeare?" would be something like "Have you
ever noticed that, if a cup of hot coffee is allowed to stand, it will cool off,
reaching the same temperature as the surrounding air?" And most of us have
done that—just as we have thrown balls with varying degrees of skill. The
appropriate analogue to the second law, then, is not a play of Shakespeare but
a conceptual theory about the ways in which plot and character, diction and
setting are related to one another and to the audience's experience and comprehension of them. It is not *King Lear* but Aristotle's *Poetics*.

From this it appears that, just as humanists have for the most part been
content to appreciate and tacitly understand nature rather than explain it, so
most audiences—including those made up of scientists—have been satisfied
to appreciate and tacitly understand works of art. The mistaken parallels suggested by Stent, Snow, and many others indicate that scientists tend to know
as little of serious humanistic inquiry—of studies such as those of Tovey and
Schenker in music, of Gombrich and Wölfflin in the visual arts, and of countless literary theorists and critics from Aristotle on—as humanists are alleged
to know of science.

If comparisons are to be convincing, the relationships both within and between disciplines must be as precise and palpable as possible. It is important,
therefore, to distinguish among different facets of humanistic inquiry.

---

34. Snow, *Public Affairs,* 22.

B

Every explanation must ultimately rest upon some general principle that commands assent. To explain why stones fall or prices rise, why species evolve or governments decline, a hypothesis must be devised and tested. Similarly, to account for the ways in which works of art are understood by and affect competent audiences, hypotheses must be formulated that relate the processes and patterns in works of art to human cognitions and responses. Three kinds of hypotheses, used to explain works of art, may be distinguished: *(a)* general laws, which are presumed to be constant over time and space; *(b)* restricted principles, derived from and applicable to the norms and procedures of a specific style; and *(c)* ad hoc reasons, which, as we shall see, are necessary adjuncts to the first two types when particular works of art are being explained.

The general principles used by humanists may be "theories" in the sense of being related to one another in logical, deductive ways. Such systematic formulations may be developed by the humanist himself—as, for instance, in the work of Heinrich Schenker, Kenneth Burke, or E. H. Gombrich. Or they may be based, wholly or in part, upon hypotheses derived from some other discipline—as, for instance, in the work of I. A. Richards, Rudolf Arnheim, and my own studies. That is, just as many of the hypotheses used to explain biological phenomena come from closely related fields such as chemistry, so those employed by humanists may be borrowed from closely related fields such as psychology, acoustics, or systems analysis. Relating such principles to his own observations—and, in so doing, often extending them—the humanist-theorist attempts to construct a more or less coherent and consistent conceptual framework for the explanation of his own art.

Humanists also employ commonsense reasons. Although these are general propositions, they are "informal" in the sense of being unsystematized. That is, they are not related to one another as part of a more comprehensive theory but are essentially discrete and independent propositions to which we assent because of our cultural beliefs and our own everyday experience. For instance, instead of explaining Michelangelo's *Moses* in terms of a formalized theory like Freudian psychology, it might be pointed out that our sense of its indomitable force and irresistible authority is in part the result of its colossal size. Similarly in music, the extension of a phrase might be explained by observing that, had the cadence come precisely as expected, it would have seemed obvious and uninteresting. Or, to take an example from history, which in my view is essentially a humanistic discipline, explaining the turmoil in England in 1831, Trevelyan writes that "unemployment and starvation urged desperate deeds." [35] It should be noticed that, while these commonsense reasons are not stated as general principles, they can easily be put in that form; for example, because we tend to compare other sizes and masses with our own —particularly if the other is or represents a human being—large-scale phenomena create an impression of commanding power; similarly, what is highly predictable is flat and tedious; or, starving men will do almost anything to get food.

Humanists generally make liberal use of such unsystematized, commonsense reasons—often in conjunction with principles of the more formal sort. They do so because there is no viable empirical basis for a rigorous theory of the arts. Psychology, the science upon which such a theory must ultimately be founded, has not been able satisfactorily to explain how even simple patterns are perceived, comprehended, and remembered or how such cognitive behavior is related to intellectual and affective experience. What experimental data exist are for the most part concerned with the effects of more or less discrete stimuli, short successions of single variables, or broad behavioral responses that cannot easily be related to specific characteristics of the stimulus that generated them. But works of art present enormously complex patterns in which the variables are organized in different ways, on a number of hierarchic levels. At present, psychology offers little help in explaining how a competent audience's experience is shaped by such intricate, subtle patterns.

Nor are the prospects for significant progress very encouraging. In addition to the difficulties arising from the complexity of works of art, there are major methodological problems. Human cognitive and affective processes can seldom be directly observed. Behavioral responses to works of art can, of course, be studied. But, because behavior is itself made up of a complex set of responses, its interpretation is problematic; that is, the several facets of behavior cannot readily or rigorously be related to specific characteristics of the particular pattern. Introspective reports by subjects about their own mental or affective responses are equally difficult to interpret and, in addition, are notably unreliable because they tend to be biased by personal idiosyncrasies and by culturally determined modes of conceptualization.

It may well be that a solid empirical basis for a theory of the arts will not be established until the biochemical functioning of the nervous system can be

35. G. M. Trevelyan, *British History in the 19th Century and After* (New York, 1966), 237.

related to human cognitive and affective behavior. For only then will it be possible to explain subjective mental events in objective physical terms. But as Jean L. Marx has observed: "The ultimate goal—the explanation of human behavior in terms of cellular biochemistry—may not be achieved in the foreseeable future. . . . There is no way to correlate these biochemical changes with the behavior, including learning and memory processes, of the living animal." [36] If this is correct, psychology should perhaps pay more attention to the arts and to humanistic inquiry. For works of art constitute unequivocal, objective data for studying the ways in which the human mind organizes diverse variables into complex, comprehensible patterns. And, despite their limitations, the theories developed by humanists may provide, or suggest, hypotheses useful in the explanation of cognitive behavior.

The possibility of formulating a comprehensive theory of the arts is remote for reasons other than methodological ones. Even if all the arts were found to be based upon a single set of fundamental principles yet to be discovered, many of the principles would have to be qualified and restricted in application. They would be qualified because the several arts use different materials; they would be restricted because significant stylistic differences may exist within a single art. The need for qualification can be easily explained: there is no guarantee that the neurophysiological-cognitive processes involved in the creation and comprehension of language, music, and visual patterns are precisely the same. Indeed, there are good reasons for believing that, in some respects at least, they are quite different—perhaps not even comparable. For instance, memory obviously plays a crucial role in our understanding of musical events, while its importance is relatively slight in our experience of the visual arts. Represented subject matter is significant for an understanding of most literature and visual art, but its role in most music is ancillary. If the several arts are comprehended and experienced in somewhat different ways, then whatever basic principles there are must be qualified if relationships in a particular art are to be explained.

Styles in each of the arts vary from culture to culture and change from one epoch to another within the same culture. Consequently, although there *may* be invariant laws applicable to all styles of a particular art, both general principles and commonsense reasons must be reinterpreted in restricted ways when applied to a specific style. In practice, however, inquiry works the other way around. Style analysis begins by identifying, describing, and classifying

36. Jean L. Marx, "Cyclic AMP in the Brain: Role in Synaptic Transmission," *Science* 178 (15 December 1972): 1188.

characteristics common to a number of works of art—usually ones that are similar in syntax or form, genre or subject matter. For instance, it describes and classifies the characteristic features of late Baroque music—its typical textures, harmonic progressions, melodic patterns, formal organization, and so on. Or it may concern itself with traits common to some genre—landscape painting or religious architecture, detective stories or pastoral poetry. Insofar as they merely describe and classify, the formulations of style analysis are to general principles as the taxonomy of species is to a hypothesis about their evolution or a theory of their physiology.

From such taxonomies, the humanist attempts to derive and formulate principles governing the syntactic processes and formal patterns characteristic of a specific style. The theories thus discovered may be restricted, not only in the sense of being applicable to a single style, but in the sense that they may explain the functioning of only one variable. The theory proposed by Rameau, for example, is restricted both to the syntax of tonal music and to the parameter of harmony. Not only may the syntax of a particular variable change from style to style—the harmonic syntax of tonal music is very different from that of late medieval music—but the relationships among the several variables, including their relative importance in the articulation of structures, do not remain constant. Consider a case in which natural and artistic phenomena are analogous. Like physical or biological structures, musical patterns are hierarchic—tones combine to form motives, motives join to form phrases, and so on. The articulation of such structures depends upon the existence of "forces" whose internal cohesiveness, relative to their connection with larger units, creates closure. In chemistry, the ways in which atoms combine to form molecules and, in biology, the ways in which molecular structures combine to form cells remain constant throughout time and space. But the variables articulating the closure of, say, a musical phrase may function quite differently in the musics of different epochs and of different cultures. Harmonic syntax, for example, is of central importance in creating closure in Western tonal music, but it plays virtually no role in articulating the structure of serial music or that of Indonesia.

It is as though the laws—the syntax—of nature were variable: not the same in Java as in Japan; different in the fourteenth century than the twentieth century in Europe. It is not a question of theories varying from one hierarchic level to another—as between the statistical behavior of subatomic particles and the nonstatistical behavior of "ordinary matter." This kind of variability also occurs in works of art: for instance, the principles governing the syntax of sentences in a novel are not the same as those controlling the organization of its paragraphs and chapters. Rather, it is that on one and the same hierarchic level different principles have governed the structuring of a particular art at different times and in different cultures. Because the principles ordering relationships in the music of Mozart are different from those shaping the music of Machaut or Boulez and the principles underlying a haiku are different from those governing a poem written in heroic couplets, humanistic studies have seldom transcended the inductive taxonomies of style analysis. And, because those that have transcended taxonomy are as a rule restricted, theories in the humanities are not only plural but discrete in the sense that they are not logically related to one another—either directly or through some more comprehensive conceptual scheme.

It is also important to recognize that the relationship between phenomena and the theories explaining them is different in the humanities and in the sciences. Because works of art (the phenomena) are created by men, they can be affected by explanatory theories. For example, based upon the compositional practice of Haydn, Mozart, and Beethoven, but also influenced by contemporary beliefs about artistic necessity, organic unity, and dialectic change, a theory of sonata-form structure was formulated during the early years of the nineteenth century. The theory in turn had a significant effect on the musical thinking and procedures of later composers. At times, concepts borrowed almost without change from other disciplines may affect artistic creation: witness the importance of Freudian theory for surrealist painting. More recently, structuralism, developed primarily by anthropologists and linguists, has had a significant effect upon literature, particularly in France.

In the natural sciences, however, there is no "feedback" from theory to phenomena. Newton's laws of motion, Darwin's theory of evolution, and Mendel's principles of heredity do not affect the relationships they were designed to explain.[37] Human behavior cannot alter the fundamental principles of

---

37. This is not to say, of course, that such knowledge does not affect other realms of human endeavor. Genetic theory, for instance, has had a significant influence on a variety of fields such as agriculture, marriage counseling, and so on. But the principles governing the laws of heredity have not thereby been changed, any more than the laws of motion have been affected by journeying to outer space. Quite the opposite: their successful use has helped confirm their validity.

Kuhn emphasizes the importance of the "unparalleled insulation of mature scientific communities from the demands of the laity" (*Scientific Revolutions,* 163) in fostering progress in the natural sciences, as distinguished from the social sciences and philosophy. But the fact of "feedback" from theory to behavior seems to me at least as important in explaining the lack of progress in these fields. Indeed, this may be the chief difference between theoretical inquiry in the natural sciences, on the one hand, and the social sciences and humanities, on the other.

nature as it can change those governing works of art. Consequently, although scientific theories have a history and an ethnography, the principles underlying them do not. A scientist studying physical chemistry or molecular biology need not be concerned with how elements combined to form atoms during the late Middle Ages or how nucleic acids function in Indonesia. Nor, as we have seen, need he study the history of scientific theories.

For the humanist, the opposite is the case. He must be a historian—not only because works of art do not supersede one another as scientific theories do, or because the arts of different epochs are explained by different theories, but because the explanation of a given stylistic practice may involve understanding how theory and practice interacted. And, in addition, as interest in the arts of other cultures grows, the humanist will have to be an ethnologist as well.

Stylistic diversity enormously complicates the studies of the humanist. It is difficult enough to formulate coherent and consistent theories when the relationships they are to explain are invariant. When they are not, the task becomes formidable indeed. The complexity of works of art, the variability of their structural principles, the problems of verification, and the lack of a validated psychological theory of human cognitive-affective behavior—all help explain why theories in the humanities have failed to achieve the certainty and universality possible in the sciences—and why, in consequence, humanistic theories have not for the most part been cumulative.[38]

C

The critic, as distinguished from the creative artist, the performer, and the audience, is crucially concerned with explanation. In this respect he is akin to the scientist—and to the humanist-theorist as well. While the phenomena to which they attend and that they analyze are different—the critic explaining the works of man, the scientist the work of "God" (nature)—they are similar in a number of ways. Both select from phenomena, separating the essential from the accidental, in order to exhibit significant relationships; both are moved by a desire for consistency and elegance; both often work by trial and error; both reason and argue in basically the same way; and both often

---

38. To these observations it should be added that theoretical and taxonomic studies in the humanities have been less fruitful than might otherwise have been the case because humanists have tended to isolate their disciplines from the natural and social sciences, which might have been sources, if not of verified theories, at least of new concepts, models, and methods.

begin with informed intuition. But there is a vital—one is tempted to say critical—difference in their ultimate goals.

The scientist is primarily concerned with developing general hypotheses and laws that account for some relationship discovered in the natural world. In order to do so, he isolates, limits, and controls the several variables producing the phenomenon. Thus it is the humanist-theorist, not the critic, who is analogous to the scientist. The critic, on the other hand, attempts to understand and seeks to explain how the patterns and processes peculiar to a specific work are related to one another and to the aesthetic experience that they shape. Criticism, in other words, is concerned with what is idiosyncratic about a particular composition, painting, or literary work. Employing, yet at the same time passing over, theory and taxonomy, it asks, How is this work of art different from all others, even those that are the same in style and form, subject matter and genre?

In music, for instance, criticism is concerned not with the *nature* of cadences and motivic relationships, or with sonata form and imitative counterpoint, but with the specific cadences and motivic relationships, the singular form and texture of the patterns in this particular movement—and with the ways in which these are understood by and affect the competent listener's experience. To put the matter somewhat crudely, the scientist discovers and formulates general principles governing how and why things fall; the critic, using such general principles as well as commonsense reasons and taxonomic ones, attempts to explain how and why this apple fell at this particular moment on the head of this specific scientist. One further example will perhaps help make the contrast clear.

Suppose that on Monday, 8 February 1587, after watching her execution, you had asked the medical examiner why Mary Queen of Scots died. He might well have replied: "Why? because she 'ad 'er 'ead chopped off!" (Or, wanting to be more scientific, he might have said: "Because her cervical vertebrae were severed.") And, coming from a medical man, the answer is satisfactory: he sees Mary's death as an instance of a general class of recurring events. But had you asked a historian the same question—and historians are analogous to critics in that they are concerned with explaining particular phenomena in all their individuality—such an answer would have been inappropriate, and you might well have concluded that your respondent was being evasive or indulging in a kind of macabre humor. Nor would you have been satisfied with a "social science" answer—for instance, one asserting that "pretenders to thrones who lack power, who panic and act rashly, frequently suffer catastrophic consequences." (Or, tautologically: those who lose their heads often lose their heads.) When you ask a historian why Mary Queen of Scots died, your interest is not in a class, pretenders to thrones, but in this particular one—Mary Queen of Scots. What you want recounted is her story in all its individuality. And so it is with works of art. Criticism seeks to discern the secret of the singular—to account for the relationships peculiar to this drawing of Daumier, this novel of Dickens, this motet of Josquin des Pres.

The lawlike principles and general typologies needed by the critic to explain particular works of art come, for the most part, from the inquiries of humanist-theorists and style analysts. At times, as we have seen, they may be derived from related disciplines such as psychology. Frequently, they have to be developed by the critic, temporarily assuming the role of theorist. But the discovery of such hypotheses is not his primary goal—as it is for the scientist and the humanist-theorist. To put the matter succinctly: theorists and style analysts use particular works of art as exemplars—as data—for the discovery and formulation of general principles and for the description of the characteristics typical of some style; the critic, working the other way around, uses the general principles and taxonomies thus developed to explain and illuminate particular works of art.

But, no matter how complete, rigorous, and systematic they may be (or may become at some future time), such general principles and taxonomies cannot, I believe, ever fully account for the relationships that constitute a specific work of art and shape our experience of it. This is because every individual relationship—of whatever kind and hierarchic level—is the result of a *non*recurring interaction among all the variables that make it the specific phenomenon that it is.

Because the goal of criticism is the explanation of individual relationships in all their particularity, no variable can be ignored; nor can any be considered constant and be set aside with qualifications such as "other things being equal. . . ." From this arises one of the central problems of criticism. For what theories and taxonomies refer to and can explain are repeatable relationships and recurring classes. To be repeatable and recurring, relationships and classes must be limited—whether with respect to subject matter or genre, means or manner, mode of organization or the syntax of particular parameters. There are innumerable instances of landscape painting, chiaroscuro, and linear perspective; of revenge tragedies, metaphor, and blank verse; of dance suites, harmonic sequences, and imitative counterpoint. What are not, and cannot be, repeated from one work of art to another are the precise—the unique—relationships among the diverse variables: their relative weightings and specific interactions.

There are many examples of antecedent-consequent structures, in common time, the minor mode, and with homophonic texture, whose melodies begin with an upbeat skip to the fifth of the scale and then descend to the tonic. But there is only one such combination of relationships that is Chopin's Prelude no. 4 in E Minor. Because they are not repeated, the myriad of individual relationships, resulting from the interactions of the variables, cannot be the basis for—cannot be subsumed under and explained by—general principles or classlike regularities. Any attempt to do so would fail because the result would necessarily lack what any theory or taxonomy must have—namely, generality. Consequently, while criticism depends upon the existence of adequate theories and taxonomies (fields of humanistic endeavor in which there is undoubtedly room for improvement), these must be complemented by special ad hoc reasons that are explicitly devised by the critic in order to explain the ways in which variables act in relation to one another and thereby shape the processes and structure peculiar to a particular work of art. In short, general principles and style analysis can explain only those aspects of a work that, given the nature of the human mind and the characteristics of some style, are normal, probable, and recurring. Ad hoc reasons are required to account for those aspects of a work that are idiosyncratic.

Because this matter is important to an understanding of what is special about the critic's task, let me state it in another way. In *The Ghost in the Machine*, Arthur Koestler points out that every skill—in this context, that of the creative artist—has a fixed aspect and a variable one. The fixed aspect

> is determined by its canon, the "rules of the game," which lend it its characteristic pattern—whether the game is making a spider's web, constructing a bird's nest, ice-skating, or playing chess. But the rules permit a certain variety by alternative choices: the web can be suspended from three or four points of attachment, the nest can be adjusted to the angle of the fork in the branch, the chess-player has a vast choice among permissible moves. These choices, having been left open by the rules, depend on the lie of the land, the local environment in which the holon operates—they are a matter of strategy, guided by feedbacks. Put in a different way, the fixed code of rules determines the permissible moves, flexible strategy determines the choice of the

actual moves among the permissible ones. The larger the number of alternative choices, the more complex and flexible the skill.[39]

In the arts, psychological constants, such as the nature of human perceptual and cognitive processes, and the characteristics of particular styles constitute the "rules of the game." Such rules, which may be only tacitly known by the artist, determine the kinds of patterns he creates. Making explicit the rules that artists have actually employed and formalizing them to the extent possible are the province of theory and style analysis. The idiosyncratic actualization of such rules as a particular work of art depends upon what Koestler calls "flexible strategy." It is the goal of criticism to explain such strategies— that is, why a general rule or principle was actualized in a specific way. For example, in the last movement of Mozart's Symphony no. 39, the main melody of the second key area is interrupted just before what would have been its closing cadence. The rules of the game tell us how this sort of melody— an antecedent-consequent pattern—*should* have been continued. The strategy to be explained is this particular realization—or, rather, nonrealization —namely, why did Mozart interrupt the melody at this particular point? Because rules do not *determine* strategies, ad hoc reasons must be advanced if what is unique about a pattern is to be explained. They bridge the gap between rule and realization.[40]

Devised to account for those aspects of a work of art that are neither lawlike nor recurring, ad hoc reasons do not form a coherent order as do hypotheses that complement and reinforce one another. Rather, such reasons remain discrete insights or aperçus. This suggests that good criticism requires that the insights provided by ad hoc reasons be balanced by the rigor and coherence created by theory and taxonomy. For when ad hoc explanations merely follow one another seriatim, instead of complementing a consistent pattern of reasoning based upon general principles, the result is an impromptu collection of unconnected aperçus. Conversely, of course, when theory and taxonomy are employed to the exclusion of ad hoc reasons, the result is pedantic criticism that explains only what is routine and regular about works of art.

39. Arthur Koestler, *The Ghost in the Machine* (New York, 1968), 105.

40. When theoretical formulations are inadequate, commonsense reasons may be advanced to account for an observed relationship in a work of art. Often such reasons seem like ad hoc ones. But there is, *in principle,* a difference. For "true" ad hoc reasons are consequences not of theoretical inadequacies but of the necessities attendant upon the explanation of the idiosyncratic.

Ad hoc reasons must be both credible and persuasive. Their credibility depends upon their conformity with the basic beliefs, attitudes, and modes of argument sanctioned by the culture. For instance, an ad hoc explanation that ascribed the interruption mentioned above to the positions of the planets at Mozart's birth would doubtless be rejected as incredible, while one that related the interruption to some event in Mozart's sex life would be received with considerable skepticism by all save the most devout followers of Freud. The persuasiveness of those reasons that are considered credible depends upon their congruence with our own experience—our tacit understanding—of the relationship being explained. They must illuminate what our imagination felt but left unformulated. In Pope's words, "Something, whose truth convinc'd at sight we find, / That gives us back the image of our mind."

To more than match the comprehension of the competent audience, the critic must be especially sensitive to the delicate interplay among the variables and particularly perceptive in discerning how specific patterns are related to both proximate and remote parts of the work being analyzed. Not only must his insights be imaginative, but his explanations must be intelligent. These qualities in part may be inborn, but they must be developed and refined through repeated encounters with, intense concern for, and deep devotion to works of art.

The critic, then, occupies a middle state—between the scientist and the creative artist. Like the scientist, he strives not only tacitly to understand but explicitly to explain. Like the artist, what he does depends upon acute comprehension and discriminating taste, which are the products of extended and varied, yet trenchant, experience. Thus it would appear that, although humanistic theory and taxonomy may legitimately aspire to the universality characteristic of the natural sciences, criticism cannot do so. The need for ad hoc reasons in the explanation of the idiosyncratic precludes cumulative development; criticism is, therefore, and will remain, an art—albeit one founded upon explicitly formulated principles.

D

Because the ultimate goal of the sciences is to formulate general theories about recurring phenomena, it is not surprising that no distinct discipline corresponding to criticism is explicitly recognized. The sciences are, however, occasionally concerned to account for historical change. In such cases, even the carefully confirmed theories of the natural sciences must be complemented, as in the criticism of works of art, by ad hoc reasons or hypotheses. Let us take an example from the physical sciences: although his account of the evolution of the Andes is based upon a formidable array of geological theory, David E. James employs what seem to be ad hoc reasons (which he significantly characterizes as "speculations") in order to account for those aspects of the evolution that appear to have been anomalous:

> It is significant that the Cretaceous arc lies on the continent side of the older Jurassic arc because it has usually been supposed that . . . the trench and arc will migrate oceanward. Quite the contrary is true in the Andean region: during the course of Andean evolution the axis of the volcanic arc has marched ever inland, away from the sea. . . .
>
> It is therefore possible to speculate with some basis in fact that the position of the Benioff zone has not changed greatly with time. If that is so, the eastward migration of the arc over the past 200 million years implies that the position in the mantle at which the oceanic crust melts has been pushed to progressively greater depths. It may well be that in the Andes the continued underthrusting of the cold oceanic slab into the mantle under the continent has gradually cooled the surrounding mantle rocks, so that the temperature at which melting occurs in the descending plate is attained only at greater and greater depths.[41]

Similarly, naturalists explaining a particular ecological development often employ ad hoc hypotheses: "Species ancestral to the troglobites occupied cool, moist forests. They *could* have become widespread in surface habitats during the periods of glaciation, gradually being restricted to forested ravines, sinkholes, and caves as the ice sheets retreated and temperatures rose. For a period of time they *could* have colonized caves and existed as troglophiles, but with increasing temperatures and decreasing precipitation they *would* have become extinct in the forest floor, surviving only as cave isolates" (emphasis added).[42]

The comparability of criticism and history was mentioned earlier, particularly in connection with the Mary Queen of Scots example. History is analogous to criticism in that it too seeks to explain particular events in all their specificity. To do so, it employs general theories formulated by the social sciences and, because these are often far from satisfactory, generalizations based upon common sense and ordinary experience. For instance, a history of the United States in the 1930s would almost certainly explain some events in

41. David E. James, "The Evolution of the Andes," *Scientific American* 229, no. 2 (August 1973): 66, 69.

42. Thomas C. Barr, "Refugees of the Ice Age," *Natural History* 82, no. 5 (May 1973): 30–32.

terms of the law of supply and demand. But historical explanation must also employ ad hoc reasons. As in the case of criticism, these bridge the gap between general rules and particular realization, explaining how the weighting of and interaction among variables shaped the course of events in this specific instance. And it is not irrelevant to observe that, in history, as well as in criticism, a large proportion of the disagreements among scholars result from differences about the relative weightings of the variables being considered.[43] In terms of the events leading to the execution of Mary Queen of Scots, for instance, what was the relative importance of dynastic rivalries, religious differences, political ambitions, national feeling, the personalities of the chief protagonists, and so on?

Over the past three hundred years, invention has become increasingly associated with science. As a result, it tends to be thought of as a consequence of scientific discovery; or, more specifically, science is considered to be the foundation on which invention depends. But, as suggested earlier, the invention of new generic principles for structuring human existence is not confined to the manipulation of the natural world. Concepts such as justice and love, institutions such as the Catholic Church and the Congress of the United States, ceremonies such as puberty rites and academic convocations, symbol systems for musical notation or formal logic, and artistic techniques, forms, and procedures like fresco, the limerick, and double counterpoint—these are just as much inventions as are the wheel and transistors, crop rotation and penicillin. The enumeration calls attention to two points. First, the origins of many inventions (particularly those basic ones so taken for granted that they are not thought of as inventions: the alphabet, numbers, money, etc.) are veiled in the obscurity of prehistory; others such as the British Constitution or sonata form evolved over a considerable period of time and were the result of contributions by a host of "inventors," many of whom are unknown.[44] Sec-

43. One sign of the importance of the weighting of variables in the explanation of specific cases is the common use of so-called counterfactual statements. For what such assertions do, rhetorically, is to emphasize the contingency of events and the role of a particular variable in affecting their outcome. For instance, Trevelyan emphasizes that Wellington's intransigence played a part in the events leading to the passing of the Reform Bill of 1832 by describing his actions in counterfactual form: "If the Duke had made a declaration promising a peaceful and liberal policy towards France and Belgium, and a small measure of Parliamentary Reform, he could have rallied these men around him and stayed in office" (Trevelyan, *British History*, 230).

44. Because we tend to identify *discovery* with the intentional act of specific individuals (often scientists), technological innovations that occurred during the anonymity of prehistory or that were the result of gradual change are not customarily thought of as "inventions." The telephone is thought of as an "invention" because we know who devised it. But to characterize the wheel, selective breeding, or rhyme as inventions seems somewhat strange because their discovery can-

ond, invention does not depend upon theory and does not presuppose scientific discovery. While science has in recent times frequently led to inventions such as plastics or the atom bomb, inventions such as the city-state and epic poetry, the compass or the use of limes to prevent scurvy were not the result of theories. Even today inventions are effectively employed—aspirin and shock therapy come to mind—that have yet to be satisfactorily explained.

Especially when the result depends upon the complex interaction of a number of variables, ad hoc insights as well as theoretical knowledge and factual information may be indispensable in making decisions. Consider, for instance, the case of medicine. The theoretical study of the etiology of human disease is a "science." The diagnosis of the specific symptoms of a patient, involving the explanation of an idiosyncratic pattern, is analogous to criticism. Repeatable means available for treatment—vaccination, antibiotics, surgical operations, and so on—are essentially inventions. And the treatment of the diagnosed disease entails choosing to prescribe or apply some specific means. When diagnosis and treatment are the focus of attention, we tend to think and speak of medicine as an "art." It is to ad hoc insights that depend upon experience, to almost intuitive tacit knowledge, that Kerr L. White evidently refers when he observes:

> Decisions about the severity, complexity and urgency of the patient's illness are based on a probabilistic system, not a deterministic one. The decision maker needs to be skilled in eliciting information from the patient and in interpreting vast amounts of data on the prevalence and patterns of clinical manifestations in general populations. . . . The task of the primary physician requires judgment, wisdom, compassion, patience and common sense, not more hardware. Decision making in medicine is rarely simple even in so-called simple cases. . . . It is rare that specific decisions for individual patients can be found in books or made by computers.[45]

Similar considerations are pertinent in other realms. In business, too, making the right decision depends upon having a sense of how all aspects of a specific pattern of events function. This is why conventional wisdom (which is often wiser than it is given credit for) has tended to denigrate "book

---

not be attributed to a particular person. The same is true of those inventions—the bathtub, the British Constitution, and sonata form—that evolved gradually through a succession of incremental changes.

45. Kerr L. White, "Life and Death and Medicine," *Scientific American* 229, no. 3 (September 1973): 29. The reader cannot have failed to notice that the same terms that were used to describe criticism are used in this quotation, e.g., *skill, interpretation, patterns, judgment, common sense* (here probably meaning ad hoc hypotheses), *specific decisions*.

learning." For, although hypotheses and facts are indispensable, they must be complemented by experience, which is the basis for perceptive ad hoc insight—for sound judgment. The importance of experience in another realm, politics, was put succinctly by Sam Rayburn, when Lyndon Johnson, then vice president, waxed enthusiastic about the brilliance of the men surrounding Kennedy—Bundy, McNamara, Rusk, et al.: "Well, Lyndon, you may be right and they may be every bit as intelligent as you say, but I'd feel a whole lot better about them if just one of them had run for sheriff once."[46]

The contrast between the formulation of a theory and its application is revealing. Earlier it was pointed out that scientists sometimes disregard factual discrepancies for the sake of the elegance and explanatory power of a theory. This is possible because, as we have seen, the goal of science is the formulation of a proposition *about* the world: a progression from the particular to the general. But moving in the opposite direction, from general principles to particular results, all the evidence must be considered and evaluated and all interactions among the variables scrutinized. Because unique interactions are not "covered" by general theories, ad hoc insight must play a part in choosing a specific course of action. As in the case of medicine, our ordinary way of speaking seems to reflect this sort of distinction. For, when theories are being formulated, we speak of "political *science*"; but, when a particular decision is in question, we speak of the "*art* of politics."

The behavior of Kennedy's advisers, as described in *The Best and the Brightest,* lends support to this analysis. Throughout the book Halberstam emphasizes their "belief that sheer intelligence and rationality could answer and solve anything."[47] It is also made clear that a lack of political experience was complemented by a strong commitment to general principles that posited, for instance, the threat of monolithic communism, the obligations of the United States as leader of the free world, the ability of technology to achieve "results," the efficiency of air power, and so on. In Kenneth Galbraith's words, "They were men who had not traveled around the world and knew nothing of this country and the world. All they knew was the difference between a

46. Quoted in David Halberstam, *The Best and the Brightest* (New York, 1969), 41. Actually, Bundy had run for office—and been defeated. When the tempering effect of experience and the insights it begets are wanting, reliance on principles increases until, in the extreme case, they become the sole basis for decision making. Then theory tends to become dogma. There is nothing like commitment to principles—the expression *blind commitment* is precise—to prevent us from seeing discrepant facts.

47. Ibid., 44.

Communist and an anti-Communist."[48] According to the hypothesis proposed here, lack of experience tended to preclude insight into the idiosyncratic, and a consequent commitment to principles led them to disregard or reject discrepant evidence and counterargument.

Because they seem objective, unambiguous, and trustworthy, general principles provide a relatively easy and efficient way to reach agreement. Evaluations of specific circumstances, on the other hand, not only are more personal but are marked by complexity and doubt, contingency and nuance. Agreement about them is generally harder to achieve. Consequently, when consensus is an important goal, adherence to principles tends to take precedence over reliance on ad hoc hypotheses.[49]

But consensus is a mistaken goal. It is characteristic of totalitarian, not democratic, forms of government. Democracy neither seeks nor depends upon national unanimity. Quite the contrary. It is an invention (of laws and institutions, customs and procedures) whose special virtue lies in its ability to elicit public decisions from private disagreement. Consider the Congress, for instance. Although no two members are likely to be in full agreement—one favoring, another opposing, some principle; one stressing the importance of a particular variable, another discounting its significance—the product (legislation, resolution, etc.) is the result of something analogous to an ad hoc judgment: as if a single individual, reasoning and debating with himself, had considered the relevant principles, studied the evidence, and weighed the variables before reaching a decision. (Of course, group decisions, like individual ones, may prove to be mistaken.) This suggests that the phrase *the collective wisdom of Congress,* though sometimes used facetiously, is no misnomer and that what is most remarkable about democratic forms of government is that

48. Quoted in ibid., 60. No doubt these men were both rational and intelligent. But rationality (which is by no means incompatible with myth) does not ensure realism. Nor does intelligence guarantee wisdom. Recognition of the hazards of moving from the general to the particular fosters humility, prudence, and skepticism, which are the bases for realistic appraisal; actual experience with such hazards refines intelligence and, transmuting it into wisdom, makes perceptive ad hoc insights possible. This is not to imply that lack of experience was the sole cause of the myopic mistakes in Vietnam. Halberstam's account makes it evident that social background, education, and personality were also important. So, too, perhaps, was belief in the desirability of common, group decisions.

49. Note that, since the sciences are concerned with the formulation of general theories, consensus is not only a possible but a necessary goal (see Kuhn, *Scientific Revolutions,* chap. 13). For this reason group inquiry may be more fruitful in the sciences than in the fine arts, criticism, or the applied sciences and arts, which are concerned with creating, explaining, or producing an idiosyncratic pattern.

they enable groups to make ad hoc judgments so that insight bridges the gap between general principles and specific application.

One tangential observation: It is sometimes suggested that all students should study the sciences so that they can make intelligent judgments about public issues involving scientific questions—for example, whether to build the hydrogen bomb or the SST, whether "saving" the environment depends upon slowing technology or reducing the birthrate, whether to continue space exploration, and so on. This view is, it seems to me, essentially mistaken.[50] From a practical standpoint, when knowledgeable specialists such as Teller and Szilard disagree about these matters, it seems implausible to believe that a few years of undergraduate science will provide the basis for expert judgment. But the important point is that, even among experts, disagreements are about the weighting of variables, only some of which—and usually *not* the decisive ones—are "scientific." For example, the variables that seem to have weighed most heavily in Teller's advocacy of the hydrogen bomb were political: his belief in the evils of communism, the aggressive intent of the Soviet Union, and so on. In short, if the goal is making reasonable judgments about such issues, then students should be required to take more courses in history, political science, and moral philosophy rather than in the natural sciences.[51]

As the perceptive reader will have noticed, there is one glaring omission in this survey of fields and disciplines, particularly since the arts have been central to the discussion—namely, the field of performance. In a broad sense, of course, all who employ a skill to accomplish some end might be considered performers; that is, they "perform" some action. Thus it is customary to say that surgeons perform operations and that scientists perform experiments. Yet

50. C. P. Snow evidently makes this error when he suggests that Hitler's "total lack of scientific comprehension was fortunate for the world" (*Public Affairs*, 135). But the crucial thing that Hitler lacked was not *comprehension* of science but an *appreciation* of its significance, an appreciation resulting from traditions in the social sciences and the humanities. Stanley Baldwin, whom Snow commends for appointing Tizard to the Committee of the Scientific Study for Air Defense in 1934, could scarcely have had much "scientific comprehension." But he had learned a set of cultural beliefs and attitudes that fostered respect and appreciation for scientific inquiry. His was the tradition of British philosophical empiricism; Hitler's was that of German metaphysical speculation.

51. Courses in the natural sciences should, I believe, be required of all college students—not because such courses will enable them to make expert judgments about public issues that involve science and technology but quite simply because an educated person is one for whom many different kinds of experience and realms of inquiry are interesting and, in the best sense of the term, entertaining. To be interesting and entertaining—in the current jargon, *relevant*—the ideas and issues of a discipline, or the style and syntax of an art, must be comprehended with a reasonable degree of skill and competence.

clearly we do not think of surgeons and scientists as being performers. A performer, as the term is usually used, is not someone who seeks to accomplish some practical result—setting a fracture or testing a hypothesis—but someone who uses his skill to animate and delight, affect and amuse an audience.[52]

But what about games, like bridge or chess? or sports: tennis, football, bicycle races? They certainly delight and amuse; but they are not generally thought of as performances. It might at first appear that performances are different because they make use of a score, a text—or at least an oral tradition. But improvised works of art, such as jazz or folk poetry, have neither score nor text; and games and sports have traditions—often venerable ones. The distinction seems to lie neither in the means nor in the form of the activity but in its goal—what Aristotle would have called its *final cause*. In games and sports, that goal is winning (for oneself or one's team), even if the resulting pattern lacks elegance and coherence. But, in performance, the presentation of a pattern to an audience is crucial. The difference can be illustrated with a mundane example. Had you watched an Olympic wrestling match on television, you would probably not have said of it: "That was a great performance!" But having watched one of the fixed, professional matches, which are patently presented for your amusement, you might reasonably observe: "Well, that was quite a *performance!*" In performances, as in the works of art they present, there is no winning or losing; nor is there confirming or disconfirming. There is only well, or poorly, done.

Although it has no precise analogue, a comparison of performance with criticism and with the applied sciences and arts is not without interest. Performance and criticism deal with works of art in complementary, perhaps even opposite, ways. The performer presents idiosyncratic patterns; the critic endeavors to explain them. In the familiar case, both begin with a score or text[53] and with a tradition for "reading" it. The score, however, provides only potential patterns. It does not fully specify what the performer shall do; rather it guides him.[54] Similarly, the critic must interpret the composer's notation in the light of performance traditions. Then, explaining the relationships latent

---

52. The performer may, of course, be his own audience when he plays or recites for his own enjoyment. Notice, incidentally, that performing is distinguished from practicing, whose goal is the exercise or improvement of some skill (practicing medicine or the piano) for the sake of a practical result rather than to entertain.

53. For the sake of simplicity, music will for the most part be used to illustrate this discussion.

54. Earlier, when works of art were said to be presentational, a competent "reader"—one familiar with the appropriate performance tradition—was taken for granted. Even the silent reading of a novel presumes knowledge (usually tacit) of how to "perform" the text. And one reason

in the score, the critic suggests how phrases should be articulated, forms defined, and character delineated. In so doing, every criticism implies a range of
possible performance.[55]

If criticism is a kind of inaudible performance, performance may be regarded as criticism made palpable. Like the critic, the performer interprets the
composer's score in the light of performance traditions. But, instead of explaining relationships, he literally performs, and thereby presents, them. Although the performer's understanding is often tacit (and in this respect he is
akin to the composer), his performance is the audible exemplification of an
"explanation." That is, he articulates, defines, and delineates sound patterns
and, in so doing, shapes the listener's comprehension and experience. Thus
he transforms a range of possibilities into a particular idiosyncratic event. And
this step from score to specified sound pattern is in many ways comparable
to the hazardous move from principles to particulars in the applied sciences
and arts.

                               *

    Stent and Snow are "on the side of the angels" in that both want to
bring the various kinds of human activities and pursuits closer together. So
do we all. But mistaken analogies, however commendable the motive behind
their advocacy, will not unite disparate disciplines or join noncomparable ways
of knowing. One way of comprehending all knowledge is through metadisci-
plines such as history and philosophy. The difficulty with these modes of in-
tegration, at least for me, is that, the more encompassing they are, the more
obscure and vaporous they become. Instead of the clarity and concreteness of
scrupulous observation and the precision of rigorous argument, we are given
elusive "spirits" and untestable speculations clothed in abstruse language.

    Tenable analogies *do* exist among the natural sciences, social sciences, and
humanities. And I have sought to show that when parallels are justly drawn
—that is, in terms of comparable kinds of inquiries and activities—similar
methodological problems and shared conceptual concerns emerge. Questions
having to do with the need for, and characteristics of, ad hoc hypotheses unite

---

why poetry is not often read today may be that few people know how to perform (recite) it skillfully, even to themselves.

55. The fact that a score or text permits a number of somewhat different interpretations does
not mean that any performance is acceptable. Some may simply be wrong. This point, as well as
the relationship between performance and criticism, is discussed in my *Explaining Music: Essays
and Explorations* (Berkeley, Calif., 1973), esp. chap. 2.

fields as diverse as music criticism and medical diagnosis, political history and ecological analysis. The nature of inventions and their role in the natural and social sciences, the arts, and the humanities are another area of commonality. So, too, is the problem of translating general principles into specific practice in the applied sciences and arts.

Equally important is the existence of equivalent areas of theoretical inquiry. One of these, mentioned earlier, will serve as an example. Hierarchic structures are encountered as frequently in works of art as in natural phenomena and social organizations. Just as protons and electrons combine to form atoms and atoms combine to form molecules—the process continuing until the highest level of patterning is reached—so in music, for instance, tones combine to form motives, motives cohere forming phrases, and so on, until the highest structural level (that of the movement or work as a whole) is reached. The nature of such structures—the problem of the bonding of parts, the relation of parts to whole, the mechanisms of articulation, etc.—is a subject for objective inquiry in a wide variety of fields. In areas such as these, the natural sciences and the humanities—as well as the social sciences—are precisely and explicitly comparable. And it will be from such legitimate liaisons that fertile concepts and productive inquiry will spring.

II

Music, Perception, and Process

2

Grammatical Simplicity and Relational Richness: The Trio of Mozart's G-Minor Symphony

In "Some Remarks on Value and Greatness in Music," I argued, among other things, that complexity was at least a necessary condition for value.[1] The appeal of simplicity was acknowledged, but its attraction was attributed to its association with childhood remembered as untroubled and secure. This view now seems to me, if not entirely mistaken, at least somewhat confused. Schubert's song "Das Wandern," cited in that essay as an instance of simplicity, certainly appears to be uncomplicated and straightforward.[2] It employs familiar melodic materials, regular rhythmic/metric organization, and normal harmonic progressions. But, as I have shown in a more recent study, the syntactic relationships that arise from these unassuming, conventional means are rich as well as elegant.[3]

Relational results must, then, be distinguished from material means.[4] When this is done, it is evident that what is essential in the evaluation of music are not the foreground (note-to-note) successions of pitches, durations, harmonies, and other musical parameters but the higher-order patterns created by these palpable means. What is crucial is relational richness, and such richness (or complexity) is in no way incompatible with simplicity of musical

Reprinted from *Critical Inquiry* 2, no. 2 (1976): 693–761.

The suggestions and comments of several colleagues have found their way into, and improved, this essay. I am specially grateful for the help of Professors Philip Gossett, Janet M. Levy, and Barbara Herrnstein Smith.

1. "Some Remarks on Value and Greatness in Music," in *Music, the Arts, and Ideas* (Chicago, 1967), chap. 2.

2. Ibid., 37.

3. *Explaining Music: Essays and Explanations* (Berkeley, Calif., 1973), 152–57.

4. The "richness" that results from manifold relationships created by a small set of patternings ("qualitative" richness) needs to be distinguished from that which results from diversity of components ("quantitative" richness). Cohn and Dempster seem to have the latter kind of richness in mind in their discussion of hierarchic unity (R. Cohn and D. Dempster, "Hierarchic Unity, Plural Unities: Toward a Reconciliation," *Indiana Theory Review* 13, no. 1 [Spring 1992]: 178).

vocabulary and grammar. That value is enhanced when rich relationships arise from modest means is scarcely a novel thesis.[5] Indeed, the "Value and Greatness" essay suggested it in passing: "Evidently the operation of some 'principle of psychic economy' makes us compare the ratio of musical means invested to the informational income produced by this investment. Those works are judged good which yield a high return. Those works yielding a low return are found to be pretentious and bombastic."[6] But, like most writers, I failed to show how this general principle might apply to a particular piece of music. In order to demonstrate how simplicity of means gives rise to relational richness, this essay will analyze a relatively brief excerpt, but one that is complete in itself, with as much precision as the present writer can command.

*

Few will, I think, doubt that the Trio from the Minuetto movement of Mozart's G-Minor Symphony (K. 550) seems simple, direct, and lucid—even guileless (see ex. 1).[7] Its melodies are based upon common figures such as triads and conjunct (stepwise) diatonic motion.[8] No hemiola pattern, often encountered in triple meter, disturbs metric regularity. With the exception of a subtle ambiguity (discussed below), rhythmic structure is in no way anomalous. There are no irregular or surprising chord progressions; indeed, secondary dominants and chromatic alterations occur very infrequently. The instrumentation is quite conventional, and no unusual registers are employed. Nor, as the following prefatory "sketch" makes clear, is its structural plan strange or eccentric.

Like countless other compositions, or parts of compositions, written during the eighteenth and nineteenth centuries, Mozart's Trio is in rounded-binary form:

Part I	Part II
: A :	: B–A' :

---

5. See, e.g., G. D. Birkoff, *Aesthetic Measure* (Cambridge, Mass., 1933).

6. Meyer, "Some Remarks," 37.

7. Although only short scores of the Trio are given, instrumentation is specified where necessary.

8. Because this essay was published in a journal whose readers were not necessarily acquainted with the terminology and concepts of music theory, terms and relationships are explained that might not have been so in a periodical addressed to specialists. This is also the case in essays 1, 4, and 5.

Part I, or Section *A* (mm. 1–18), consists of two phrases and a codetta. The first phrase (mm. 1–6) presents the motives (labeled *m* and *n*) that are the basis for most subsequent melodic patterns. Harmonically, the phrase moves from the stability of the tonic triad (I), built on G, to the complementary tension of the triad built on the dominant (V), D. A return to tonic harmony in

Example 1

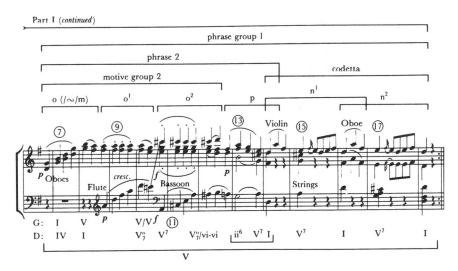

(continued on page 58)

Example 1 *(continued)*

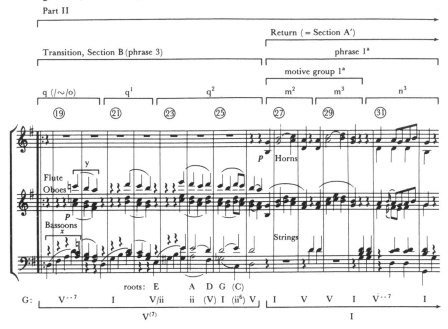

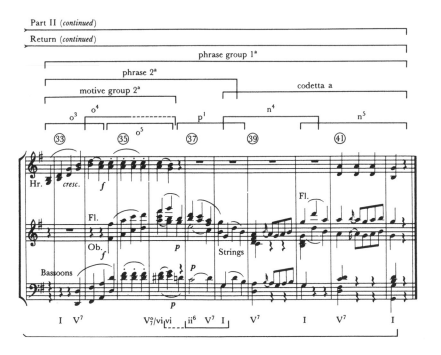

measure 4, as well as melodic structure, creates provisional closure, making the first four measures a subsidiary event, motive group 1, within the larger phrase. A complete cadence (ii$^6_5$–V–I^6) follows and confirms the key of G major as the tonal center of the Trio.[9]

The second phrase (mm. 6–14) builds upon and extends the patterns presented in the first[10] and modulates to the dominant (D major). After a deceptive cadence (V$^0_7$/vi–vi), which creates provisional closure and defines a subsidiary pattern (motive group 2), the second phrase closes with a traditional cadential gesture *(p)* that is related to the opening motive *(m)*. Although the cadence is harmonically complete, closure is only partial: first, because it is in the "wrong" key, the dominant rather than the tonic; second, because, as the brackets over example 1 indicate, the beginning of the codetta (mm. 14–18), marked by the entrance of the first violins, overlaps the end of the second phrase. That is, the first beat of measure 14 is a beginning as well as an end. Despite this elision, measures 14–18 are understood as an "added," concluding event—a kind of miniature coda. For not only do they follow a complete cadence; they consist of the regular repetition of an authentic cadence together with a melodic motive that is familiar both because it is borrowed from the end of the first phrase and because it is an archetypal closing figure in this style.

The first phrase of Part II, the *B* section (mm. 18–26) of the rounded-binary form outlined above, is a *transition* back to the tonic. Taken as a whole, it can be considered to be a prolongation of the dominant harmony with which it both begins (mm. 18–20) and ends (m. 26). The prolongation is elaborated by a sequential progression (mm. 22–25) through a series of harmonies whose roots are a fifth apart: E–A–D–G–(C). Though harmonic instability is minimal, the progression serves to heighten the feeling of goal-directed motion and, hence, the sense of arrival created by what follows. The melodic patterns of the transition are related to those of the second motive group of Part I and, in this way, to the opening motive: that is, *q/∞/o/∞m*. However, unlike *m* and *o*, motive *q* is divided into submotives *x* and *y*. This change, together with other modifications, gives rise to subtle rhythmic/

---

9. The term *complete cadence* will be used to designate one in which a progression from the dominant to the tonic is preceded by subdominant harmony (ii or IV). Because a key or tonal center is defined by a progression from the subdominant to the dominant rather than by one from dominant to tonic (as is often supposed), a complete cadence creates more decisive closure than one that is merely "authentic" or "full"—i.e., V (or V^7)–I.

10. The symbols "*o(/∞/m)*" in ex. 1 mean that "*o* is similar to *m*."

metric ambiguity, making the passage less stable than harmonic analysis alone
would suggest.

Section A' (mm. 26–42) is a *return*—both to the patterns presented
in Part I and to the Trio's central tonality, G major. This "rounding out" of
the binary form enhances high-level closure. Despite manifest similarities,
there are significant, if sometimes seemingly slight, differences between
Sections A' and A. Some of these can be attributed to the fact that no modulation takes place in A'. For instance, since this section remains in G major,
closure at the end of phrase 1^a (mm. 26–32) is harmonically less decisive than
in Section A (mm. 4–6). The cadence is authentic, not complete. A complete
cadence occurs only at the end of phrase 2^a. As though to compensate for the
tension previously created by modulations (mm. 7–12), motive group 2^a
(mm. 32–36) involves compression. That is, the imitative entrances of the
horns (o^3), bassoons (o^4), and upper woodwinds (o^5) now occur after only
three beats instead of six, as in the parallel passage in Part I. Once again an
elision links the forceful cadence at the end of the second phrase to the
codetta. But now closure is in the tonic.

What engages, delights, and moves us, then, is neither the novelty of the
Trio's form nor the singularity of its musical vocabulary and grammar. Rather,
the competent listener[11] can comprehend and respond to its complex processes, its shadings of similarity and difference, and its structural subtleties
precisely because these arise out of uncomplicated, unassuming tonal means.
That the Trio's means are simple cannot be proved but will be obvious to
anyone familiar with the style of Classic music. That its relationships are rich
can be demonstrated by exhibiting them in a scrupulous analysis of the work
itself.

The analysis that follows is, alas, not only detailed but intricate and
lengthy. In two respects this was unavoidable. First, because explanations are
almost always longer than the phenomena they account for. A splendid sunset is over in a few minutes; a decisive battle may last little more than an hour.
But a scrupulous explanation of such events is likely to be complicated and
protracted. Particularly so if, as in the case of works of art, what is to be explained are not merely typical, classlike characteristics and the principles
thought to govern relationships but what is peculiar—even unique—about
the structure and process of the work. Second, because this essay is addressed

11. As argued in essay 1, a competent listener is one who understands the style of a work, not
in the sense of knowing about—of conceptualizing—grammatical means, syntactic structures,
or formal procedures, but in the sense that he has internalized the probabilities of the style as a
set of perceptual, cognitive habits of discrimination and response.

to the interested amateur as well as the professional music theorist, terms and concepts have been defined and relationships explained that might not otherwise have been so. In addition, references to the musical examples are made as clear and explicit as possible.

The analysis is difficult and extended for another reason. Every explanation must be based, whether expressly or intuitively, upon general principles of some sort—upon hypotheses about how the relationships latent in the work might be understood by a competent listener, including the first listener, the composer, as well as subsequent ones, performers, critics, and members of an audience. Throughout I have tried to argue, with as much care and precision as I can command, from such principles. The explication of theoretical premises and of their application is also partly responsible for the length and complexity of what follows. In this respect, the essay is doubtless somewhat self-indulgent. For it has been used to demonstrate (to myself as much as to others) that hypotheses and methods developed in my earlier studies have genuine explanatory power: that they are able to account, with considerable rigor and specificity, for the ways in which the several parameters of music interact with one another on different hierarchic levels to form the relationships peculiar to a particular composition.[12] Not infrequently it may seem that a detail—for instance, why a particular phrase mark makes sense and how it affects other relationships—has been discussed at inordinate length. Perhaps. But details are not trivialities, and subtleties may be signs of significant connections.

Part I

Phrase 1 (Mm. 1–6)

The patterns presented in the first phrase are the basis for much of the relational richness of the Trio. They are the main source for what follows: for motivic development, for incongruities subsequently resolved, and, above all, for implicative processes whose elaboration and realization create continuity, coherence, and closure.[13] Though inextricably connected with what comes later, the first phrase is nevertheless patently separated from the second. All parameters—harmony, melody, rhythm, texture, and instrumentation—combine to make this separation clear.

12. Though not discussed in this essay, richness is a result not solely of relationships actualized in a work of art but of those possible, even probable, but not actualized. In this connection see essay 7, pp. 274–75.

13. As observed later in this essay, any particular implication is a matter of the probability of the various possible alternatives.

Example 2

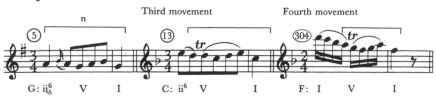

Harmonic closure is emphatic (ex. 1). Except for the cadence in measures 37–38, that in measures 5–6 is the most complete in the Trio.[14] Nor is there any doubt about the function of motive *n*. It is a typical closing figure—a motion from the second degree of the scale, through a turn (usually ornamented by a grace note or a trill), to the tonic—encountered time and time again in the music of the period. For instance, virtually the same motive occurs in the third and fourth movements of Mozart's String Quartet in F (K. 590) (ex. 2). The characteristic shape of motive *n*, and consequently its function, is especially apparent because it is clearly differentiated from what precedes and follows (see ex. 1). It is differentiated from what precedes it by the relative coherence and partial closure of the first four measures (see pp. 65–66 below) and by a marked increase in the rate of harmonic motion—from one harmony per measure in motive group 1 to at least two harmonies per measure. Texture, too, changes. For the first time there is contrapuntal interaction among four more or less independent parts,[15] and this change in texture results in a concomitant change in sonority.

The beginning of the second phrase (ex. 1, mm. 6–14), too, helps make the closure of the first unmistakable. Paradoxically, not only the differences between the two, but similarities, heighten the sense of disjunction. The beginning of the second phrase is distinguished from the end of the first in texture, sonority, and harmonic motion. The contrapuntal texture of measures 4–6 is followed by a return to the simplicity of parallel triadic motion with its attendant sonority, and the rate of harmonic change slows to one chord every two measures. These differences are emphasized by the change in instrumentation: the first phrase was played by the strings; the second is begun by the

14. The parallel cadence in mm. 31–32 is authentic but not complete; the closure produced by the complete cadence in mm. 13–14 is only provisional because it occurs in the dominant, D major, rather than in the tonic, G major.

15. Until the cadential gesture begins on the second beat of m. 4, the texture really consists of a single melodic strand, that of the first violins, doubled for the sake of harmony and sonority by the second violins. The D in m. 2, played by the violas and celli, serves mainly to mark the beat and to complete the harmony—making manifest what was already latent.

Example 3

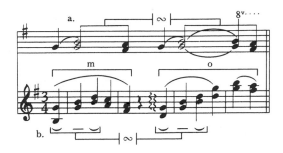

Example 4

oboes. The contrast is especially clear because what the oboes play is related to, and derived from, what the violins played earlier.

This brings us to the disjunction created by similarity. The opening of the second phrase is related not to the closing motive *(n)* but to the opening of the first phrase (ex. 3). Because pitch level, texture and intervals, and higher-level melodic structure (graph *a*) as well as foreground melodic/rhythmic shapes (graph *b*) are similar, motive *o* is understood as a varied repetition of motive *m*.[16] As a second "beginning," the new phrase confirms unequivocally that the preceding one is closed. For, until this varied repetition takes place, it is possible that the first phrase will be extended in some way—for instance, by a repetition of the closing motive (ex. 4). Indeed, because the end of the first phrase is shorter than the initial motive group leads us to expect—that

16. Repetition on the same hierarchic level creates separation; return (remote "repetition") creates coherence and closure (see pp. 80–81 below). Often modest differences between the original presentation of a pattern and its repetition act as signs that the function of the repeated passage is changed. In this case, orchestration is different: oboes replace violins; and the passage begins with a perfect fourth (D below G) between first and second oboe rather than with a minor sixth (B below G) between violins. Although the latter change may have been made because

Example 5

is, two measures instead of four—such extension seems not only possible but probable (see pp. 72–73 below).

Melodically, the tonic, G, has been strongly implied from the beginning of the first phase, and closure is considerably enhanced by the realization of this goal in measure 6.[17]

This implication is generated by a number of interdependent melodic relationships (ex. 5).

the oboe of Mozart's time could not easily play the low B, it nevertheless helps the listener recognize that this phrase has a different function—that it begins the departure from the home key.

17. An implicative relationship is one in which a musical event is patterned in such a way that reasonable inferences can be made both about its connections with preceding events and about the ways in which the event itself might be continued and reach closure and stability. "Reasonable inferences" are those that a competent listener—one familiar with, and sensitive to, the style of the composition—would make. A single event—on whatever hierarchic level: a motive, a

1. The first accented, structural tone of the phrase is the third degree of the scale, B. Of the tones of the tonic triad, the third is the least stable. Its mobility implies conjunct (stepwise) motion through the second degree of the scale, A, to the tonic (graph 1*a*). When the second degree, A, arrives on the same structural level as the B, the implicative inference is strengthened.

2. The motion from B to A is implicative for another reason as well. Namely, it is a general rule in the formulation of implicative inferences that, once an orderly process (particularly one that is stylistically established) is begun, it tends to continue until a point of stability is reached on the same structural level. The motion from B to A generates such a process and, consequently, implies continuation to a point of tonal stability, which is not realized until the G arrives in measure 6 (graph 1*b*).

3. The implication of descending conjunct motion is particularly strong because the structural B in measure 1 is preceded by a skip from the upbeat, G. This skip creates a *gap* that implies that the notes skipped over will eventually be presented and that the pattern will return to its initial pitch, which will function as a goal on the same level as the first structural note. In short, the gap-fill pattern represented by graph 2*a* also implies linear motion to the tonic, G.

But the arrival of a structural G is delayed. Instead of moving directly to G, as it might have done (see pp. 66–67 below), motive *m* is restated (*m*^{1}) a step higher beginning on A. This varied repetition in turn generates implications some of which suggest continuation to G.[18]

4. The fourth degree of the scale (C), which is the first structural tone of motive *m*^{1}, is even less stable than the third degree, and its mobility is enhanced not only because it functions as the seventh of a harmonically goal-directed dominant chord but because it is preceded by a gap (A–C). When

---

phrase, or a period—may imply a number of alternative continuations and goals. Some of these will usually be realized proximately; others will be realized only remotely (after intervening events have taken place). Implicative relationships are often understood in prospect, as events are unfolding; sometimes, however, what was implied by an event can be comprehended only in retrospect—by discovering what the event actually led to, what it was connected with. Implications can be generated by parameters other than melody—e.g., by harmony, rhythm, instrumental timbre, texture, and so on. Frequently several parameters reinforce one another in defining a specific implicative relationship. When this is the case, the parameters are said to be *congruent*. At other times parameters are noncongruent: e.g., melody may make for closure and stability, while harmony and rhythm produce continuation and mobility.

18. As we shall see (p. 79 below), other aspects of the higher-level patterning (*m* + *m*^{1}) imply continuation to D.

the C moves to B in measure 4, the seventh is resolved, and the realization of the fill is begun. The fill is completed when A is reached in measure 5. But, because the A, too, is melodically mobile and is part of a forcefully goal-directed cadential progression, the linear motion (C–B–A) generated by the gap-fill process (graph 2*b*) has a tendency to continue downward to the stability of the tonic. The G in measure 6 is, thus, the goal of several complementary and converging implicative relationships, and its realization contributes significantly to the impression of closure at the end of the phrase.

Though the processes generated by motive *m*[1] ultimately move to G, it is important to observe that its closure on B in measure 4 is more forceful than is the parallel closure of motive *m* in measure 2. This is so because (1), as a note of the tonic triad, B is stable relative to A; (2) the B is harmonized as part of the tonic triad that functions as the resolution of mobile dominant harmony; (3) the first four measures create a familiar and relatively stable melodic pattern, namely, a changing-note figure (graph 3) in which A and C ornament a more stable B;[19] and (4) the coherence of the changing-note pattern is emphasized by the changes (already described) in texture, sonority, and rate of harmonic motion that follow it. Thus, as example 5, graph 4, indicates, the first phrase of the Trio can be understood as a prolongation of B, as part of tonic harmony, followed by a complete cadence in which A moves to G.

If the fundamental motion of the first phrase is from B through A to G,

---

19. The stability of the B in m. 4 is probably also somewhat strengthened because it is implied by the subsidiary gap, B–D, in m. 1. The first note filling this gap, the C, follows immediately; but return to B is delayed, and, before it occurs, the implication has been generated more forcefully by the A–C of motive *m*[1] (graph *a*). The comparable gap (C–E) in *m*[1] begins to be filled by the D that follows. But the D does not move to C:

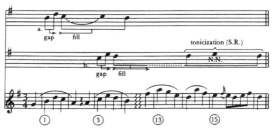

Instead, the D is transformed into a relatively stable goal when it becomes a temporary tonic in m. 14 (graph *b*). It can function as a provisional realization because of what Professor Eugene Narmour has called "substitution by rank" ("A Theory of Tonal Melody" [Ph.D. diss., University of Chicago, 1974]). In the return (mm. 26–37), not only does the D move through C to B, but the first subsidiary gap, B–D, becomes a primary one (see pp. 115–16 below).

then the first motive might have moved directly from the A reached in measure 2 to the closing figure *(n)*. This possibility, shown in example 6, calls attention to the relationship between motives *m* and *n* (graph *b*). For motive *m* consists essentially of a conjunct descent (B–A), preceded by a gap, and ornamented by C, which is an échappée (marked E in the example). (The validity of this analysis is demonstrated by what the horns play when this music returns at the beginning of Sec. *A'* [ex. 6, graph *c*].) Though motive *n* is not preceded by a gap, it too consists of a conjunct descent (A–G) ornamented by an échappée (E). Thus despite manifest differences, particularly in rhythm, motives *m* and *n* are melodically similar as well as implicatively connected.

Though grammatically simple and regular, the relationships both within and between the motives of the first phrase are complicated and in some respects even conflicting. The first motive *(m)* is related to the last *(n)* by implication (ex. 5, graphs 1*a*, 1*b*, and 2*a*) as well as by similarity of shape (ex. 6, graph *b*). The second motive *(m¹)* continues the first by repeating its shape on another step of the scale and, at the same time, completes it *(m)* by returning to the first structural tone (B) and the stability of tonic harmony. The second motive thus prolongs the first (ex. 5, graph 3) and, in so doing, delays the cadential figure that might have followed the first motive directly (ex. 6). Like the first motive, the second also implies motion to the tonic—not only because of its own patterning (ex. 5, graph 2*b*) and because the B in measure

Example 6

4 acts as a kind of surrogate for that in measure 1 but because of the tonal tendency of the third to move conjunctly to the tonic (ex. 5, graph 4).

The relationships thus far considered have been those contributing to coherence and closure. But clearly there must be others—ones that produce mobility, involve incompleteness, and transcend the limits of the phrase. Otherwise the remainder of the Trio would not follow *from,* but would merely come after, the first six measures. As we shall see, the motives themselves, as well as the connections between them, generate patterns and implications that influence and inform later events. Before considering these, however, it should be observed that, though closure is unmistakable, it is mitigated by elements of instability and incongruity.

Harmonically, the close of motive *n* is not as stable as it might have been. Though the cadential progression (ex. 7) is complete in the sense that the subdominant (ii⁶₅) precedes the dominant, closure is mitigated because the tonic chord is initially presented in first inversion (with B in the bass) rather than in root position (with G in the bass) as it might have been (ex. 7B). It should be observed, however, that harmonic instability is itself the result of the organization of another parameter—namely, texture.

The texture of motive *n* is compound. As a whole, it is homophonic: melody supported by accompaniment. But the accompaniment is contrapuntal. Not only does the suspension in the viola part contribute to mobility (see p. 69), but so does imitation between voices. The second violins begin

Example 7

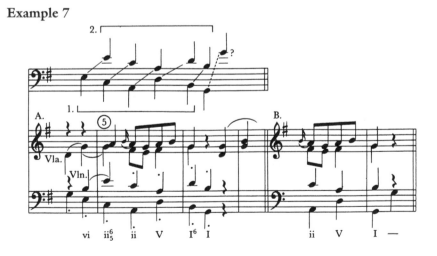

Example 8

Example 9

by mimicking the rising fourth played by the violas; however, they continue by following the celli in strict canon, beginning with the E in measure 5 (graphs 1 and 2). Though the canon is scarcely audible,[20] the relationship between parts creates momentum and affects the cadence. There its consequences are audible. Because they remain canonic, the second violins have a D on the first beat of measure 6. (They could have broken the imitation and played a B, as in ex. 7B.) In order to complete the triad, the celli must play the third (B)—which they do.[21]

Nor is rhythmic closure decisive. On the lowest level, the eighth-note motion at the end of measure 5 suggests that the grouping across the bar line is a closed, end-accented anapest (ex. 8). But the potential stability of this pattern is undermined by the mobility created by the weak afterbeat played by the violas and celli. Moreover, for harmonic and textural reasons, motive *n* is understood as a single composite event. On the subprimary level *(i)*, it seems to consist of a series of overlapping or pivoted groups (ex. 9). Despite its considerable ambiguity, however, the pattern is, I think, heard as a primary-level

20. Because the note values are the same in both voices, harmonic progression and the melody in the upper parts tend to mask contrapuntal relationships.

21. One admittedly speculative point: The G, which begins the oboe passage on the third beat of m. 6, might be thought of as a continuation of the canon. That is, though displaced an octave and played by a different instrument, G is the scale tone that would have followed the B played by the second violins on beat 2 of m. 6. There is no canon in the parallel passage in the return (ex. 1, mm. 31–32), and, as a result, the cadence can occur in root position.

Example 10

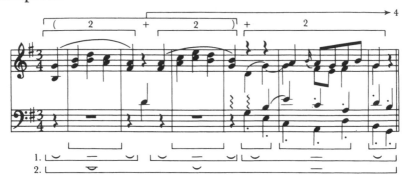

(1) amphibrach—albeit a complex one. It is so not only because of the tendency to continue the palpable amphibrach grouping[22] established by motives *m* and *m*¹— 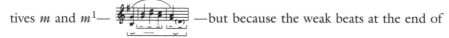 —but because the weak beats at the end of measure 4, and especially the suspension in the viola part, make the fifth measure seem "accented" relative to the sixth. On the highest level (2), motive *n* acts as a stable goal for the preceding measures (ex. 10). However, though the phrase is end-accented, its closure is not satisfactory because it is too short. The sense of morphological incongruity is the result of prior organization.

The first motive *(m)* is a structural entity on the lowest hierarchic level. But its closure is tenuous. Melodically, it ends on one of the most mobile tones of the scale, the second degree (A); harmonically, it stops on an unstable dominant chord; and, rhythmically, the motive is an amphibrach that closes on a mobile weak beat (ex. 10). Thus motive *m* is defined as a formal event not primarily because it is syntactically closed but because its varied repetition *(m*¹*)* a step higher makes its extent clear.

Though it is a separate shape in which implicative possibilities are embedded, motive *m* is incomplete. It has no end—only a beginning and a middle. Though more closed, motive *m*¹ too is incomplete. It has a middle and an end but no beginning. When the motives are combined, however, they complement one another. The result is a coherent, though low-level,

---

22. This is a corollary of the hypothesis, mentioned earlier, that once begun a process tends to be continued to a point of stability.

syntactic structure whose integrity and closure are not contingent but a consequence of melodic patterning (ex. 11, line *a*, the changing-note motion around B) and harmonic progression (ex. 11, line *a*, the movement from tonic to dominant and back). Rhythmic relationships are quite subtle. The first four measures function both as a coherent syntactic structure and as a *sequence* of motives. Understood in the first way (ex. 11, graph *a'*), the melodic return to B and the authentic cadence foster rhythmic closure, suggesting a trochee pivoted to an end-accented anapest. Understood in the second way (graph *b*), motive m^1 functions as a mobile, ongoing event on the second rhythmic level (2). Put differently: retrospectively the structure articulated at measure 4 is relatively stable and closed; prospectively there is minimal articulation—motives *m* and m^1 begin a sequence that is mobile and implicative, though their implications are not realized by what immediately follows.

Whether understood in prospect or in retrospect, however, these measures establish an unambiguous morphological length of four (2 + 2) measures that acts as a standard for subsequent syntactic structures. Consequently, when the strong cadential figure of measures 5 and 6 proves to be only two measures long—and the beginning of the next phrase leaves no doubt about this—it seems aberrant. The pattern "should" have been four measures long. Two somewhat different continuations seem possible.

The phrase following motive m^1 might have been a single, basically undivided gesture. The result (illustrated by the hypothetical version given in ex. 12) would have been a bar form of 2 + 2 + 4 measures. Because in the

Example 11

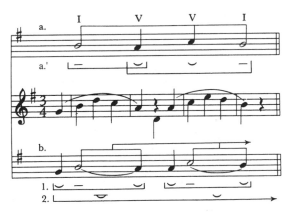

prospective view the sequence of motives *m* and *m*[1] is additive, it seems to suggest this possibility. Notice that closure is strengthened not only by the morphological "fit" with the first four measures but by the high-level rhythmic structure that is end-accented on levels 2 and 3. In addition, the whole seems integrated because, as implied, the sequence continues to D, the relatively stable fifth of the scale, after which there is a return to the tonic. As we shall see, something similar to this sort of patterning does occur when Section *A* returns in Part II of the Trio.

Motive *n* might also have been lengthened by simple repetition. The result (illustrated in ex. 13) would have been more additive: a countercumulative pattern of $4(2 + 2) + 2 + 2$. Because in the retrospective view the first four measures form a cohesive event, this sort of continuation seems appropriate. Notice that this "normalization" is more open not only because the implied D is not realized but because on the second level (2) the phrase ends on a mo-

Example 12

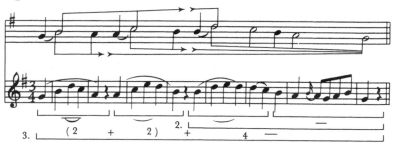

Example 13

bile weak beat. Moreover, because the morphological structure is counter-cumulative—that is, $4 + 2 + 2$, rather than cumulative, $(2 + 2) + 4$—the effect is one of passive subsidence rather than of active termination.

As the reader will recognize at once, the repetition of motive n is precisely what concludes the first part of the Trio (mm. 15–18) in the dominant and the second part (mm. 39–42) in the tonic. In short, the discrepancy between the four-measure length established by the motive group ($m + m^1$) and the two-measure closing figure creates an incongruity—a kind of morphological "dissonance."[23] This dissonance is "resolved" in the codettas that, from this point of view, are consequences of the brevity of the phrase in relation to the structure of the motive group.

Phrase 2 (Mm. 6–14)

The closure of the first phrase is less than decisive for other reasons as well. First of all, there simply hasn't been enough music. It is not just that, given the scope and proportions of the symphony and of the Minuetto movement of which this Trio is a part, the phrase is much too short to create convincing closure. If the six measures were played seven times (making a length of forty-two measures—that of the whole Trio, without repeats), the result would not be an enhanced sense of completeness but boredom followed by irritation. Nor is the sense of incompleteness solely a matter of familiarity with music in the Classic style—a familiarity that makes the competent listener aware that trios are usually in rounded-binary form and that at measure 6 such form remains to be realized. What is required for convincing closure is the development and resolution of more urgent, higher-level instability: harmonic, melodic, formal, or rhythmic, or some combination of these. Such tension occurs in the second phrase and subsequently.

Second, implications generated by the opening measures remain to be actualized. One of these was generated by the very first notes of the Trio. In addition to shaping the gap-fill relationships already discussed (ex. 5, graph 2a), the first three notes form a familiar schema in tonal music—namely, a triad. The same principle, mentioned earlier in conjunction with linear patterns, applies to disjunct, triadic ones. That is, once an orderly process is begun, it tends to be continued as a mode of organization until a point of relative stability and closure is reached.

The nature and probability of such continuation depend upon the dis-

23. There is no incongruity on the foreground level because the motives are all the same length.

Example 14

Example 15

position of all the parameters involved: for instance, the position of the triad (whether it begins with the root, the third, or the fifth of the scale), the harmonization of the several pitches, the rhythmic/metric structure of the pattern, and so on. Mozart's String Quartet in F Major (K. 590) also opens with a root-position triadic pattern (ex. 14). But because the fifth (C) is an accented goal—a point of relative stability—the pattern is quite closed, and further motion to a stable, structural high F is not strongly implied.[24] Notice, too, that in this case the triadic pattern is the main motive and that its metric placement is straightforward.

In the Trio from the G-Minor Symphony, however, the relationships between the triadic pattern and the motive of which it forms a part, and between the metric and melodic structure of the triad itself, are more complicated. Although almost immediately subsumed within the larger structure of the gap-fill process of motive *m* (ex. 15*a*), the coherence and familiarity of the triad suggest—perhaps only subliminally—that it is a potentially independent

24. Nor is one presented until late in the movement (at m. 174), and then it is a consequence of other pattern processes.

Example 16

rhythm:	⌣ — ⌣			⌣ — ⌣			⌣ — ⌣		
meter:	3	1	2	1	2	3	3	1	2
pitch:	1	3	5	1	3	5	3	5	8(=1)

shape. Given the metric designation (3/4), a kind of covert amphibrach rhythm arises (ex. 15*b*).

Though the first three notes of motive *m* are scarcely unusual, they involve a subtle incongruity. The triad begins on its most stable pitch—the root, G (ex. 16*a*, pitch). But the rhythmic group begins on a mobile weak beat (ex. 16*a*, rhythm). The patternings are, so to speak, "out of phase." Since pitch relationships are fixed, the discrepancy can be resolved only by a change in rhythmic/metric patterning. For this reason, as well as because it is the first note of the Trio, there is a slight tendency to perceive the G as being the beginning of a metric unit—to understand it as being a virtual accent (ex. 16*b*). Put the other way around: because a stress placed on an accent ties the following weak beat to the accent, had the B (the downbeat of m. 1) been emphasized by articulation of any sort—for example, by a change in texture or harmony, dynamics or instrumentation—the following D would have been less mobile and ongoing. This helps explain why no accompanying harmony marks the first beat of measure 1.

To the extent that such subliminal adjustments are made, the mobility of both the actual accent (B) and the following weak beat (D) is enhanced. As a result, the implication that triadic motion will continue is strengthened.[25] This implication is regenerated and realized at the beginning of the second motive group.

Except for a striking change in orchestration (oboes rather than violins)

25. In the opening measures this incongruity merely enhances what was already latent in motive *m*. But, when an analogous and related patterning occurs at the beginning of the transition (mm. 18–23), the ambiguity becomes manifest and significantly affects our understanding of melodic and metric relationships (see p. 95 below). Compatibility might also have resulted if the first pitch of the triad had been mobile—e.g., the third of the scale (ex. 16*c*). From this point of view, the discrepancy is *really* resolved through sequential motion; i.e., the sequence of motives—*m*, *m*[1], etc.—ultimately moves to *o*[3] (mm. 32–34), and there (as well as in the main closing motive at mm. 36–38) pitch and rhythmic and metric patterns are congruent.

Example 17

and a slight change in harmony,[26] the second phrase begins like the first. But, instead of being deflected down from D to C and A, the triadic motion continues upward through G to high B. Thus the implications latent in the first phrase are remotely realized (cx. 17, graph 1*a*), and those regenerated in the second are proximately realized (graph 1*b*).[27]

The high B in measure 8 is at once the goal of the extended triadic motion and a mobile appoggiatura that resolves to A on the second beat of the measure. This observation calls attention to the dual—almost punning—function of these measures. For motive *o* is both a realization of implications la-

26. The first interval between the oboes is a perfect fourth rather than a minor sixth (see n. 16 above).

27. The equivalent triadic motion (A–C–E) at the beginning of motive *m*[1] does not strongly imply continuation to the upper octave. This for a number of reasons. Because it is the first event of the Trio, motive *m* can be understood initially *only* in terms of its own internal relationships. Its foreground, triadic patterning is, therefore, a focus of attention. (Significantly, when motive *m* returns at mm. 26–27, the same continuation does not follow.) Motive *m*[1], on the other hand, is understood not primarily as an event in its own right but rather as a varied repetition of motive *m*. More important, from the first it is comprehended as part of a larger process—the relationship between motives. That is, as we have seen (ex. 11, graphs *a* and *b*), motive *m*[1] not only complements motive *m* but is a sequential continuation of it. These higher-level, and more forceful, processes tend to mask foreground patterning. In short, what motive *m*[1] implies is the continuation of relationships *between* motives rather than those within them.

Example 17 *(continued)*

tent in motive *m* (graph 1*a*) and a variation of motive *m* (graph 2).[28] Both motives consist of a gap from an upbeat, G, to an accented B (prolonged through deflection in the case of motive *m* and through triadic extension in the case of motive *o*), followed by an A that begins the fill.

But these similarities should not be allowed to obscure significant functional differences (see analysis under ex. 17). In motive *m*, B is a structural tone, accented on both the subprimary (i) and the primary (1) levels; and A, though accented on the subprimary level, is mobile on the primary level. In motive *o*, however, the first B (m. 7), though accented and structural on subprimary levels (ii and i), is part of a larger anacrustic motion to measure 8 on the primary level (1). There, transferred an octave, it becomes a mobile, nonstructural appoggiatura. Though it is unaccented, the A in measure 8 is the goal of the overall motion and an important structural tone. Conse-

28. It will be recalled that the sign "/∞/" means "similar to."

quently, while both motives could be analyzed as amphibrach patterns, their proportions, and hence their purports, are very different. Because the primary-level accent of motive *m* is longer (three beats) than the weak beats that precede (one beat) and follow (two beats), it is rhythmically quite stable. Motive *o*, on the other hand, consists of a very short accent (one beat) preceded by a long anacrusis (four beats) and followed by a short weak beat. As a result, the accent is quite mobile. The extension of the gap by an octave, the strong anacrustic motion to the high B (emphasizing its instability as an appoggiatura), and the striking change from rising disjunct to falling conjunct motion—all heighten the sense of goal direction and imply that the fill, which the A begins, will continue to descend, reaching the structural tone from which it began (the B in m. 7) and perhaps ultimately the tonic, G.

Though complemented and even crossed by the flute part, the gap-fill process generated by the oboe—and continued by it—dominates the melodic structure (ex. 17, graph 3*a*). The linear fill descends from A to G in measure 10 and from G to F♯ in measure 12. The oboe continues to E in measure 13, and as before this structural tone is preceded by an appoggiatura (F♯). But, in this cadence to D, the oboe is joined by, and somewhat subservient to, the flute, which plays the main melodic strand in parallel thirds above the oboe. Though the essential linear motion is never in doubt, assurance is made doubly sure. For, when the oboe plays the final cadential figure (mm. 16–18), the descent from E to D is patent and unequivocal (ex. 17, graph 3*b*).

The D in measure 14 is a strong point of arrival and one of considerable stability. It is so for a number of reasons. Most obviously, because a change of tonal center has occurred (ex. 17, graph 5). When the harmony in measure 9 (first understood as the dominant of G major, which preceded it) is followed by its own dominant, A major (mm. 10–11), the progression begun in measure 7 is reinterpreted in retrospect. For the harmonic progression can be more simply understood as a succession of primary harmonies in the key of D major than as one involving secondary dominants in the key of G. This interpretation is strengthened by the deceptive cadence in measure 12[29] and is confirmed by the complete cadence (ii^6–V^7–I) in measures 13 and 14. Thus, though the linear fill begun on the A in measure 8 (ex. 17, graphs 3*a* and 3*b*) remains to be completed (it is so after the double bar, moving through C to B, then to A, and ultimately to G), D is a point of provisional stability because

---

29. Were G major the tonal center, the deceptive cadence would have to be interpreted as V/iii–iii, which is a very improbable progression in the harmonic syntax of Classic music—at least in the major mode. The interpretation V/vi–vi in D major is much more probable.

it has been tonicized. That is, D functions as a goal by what might be called harmonic fiat.[30]

The D in measure 14 is, however, the intrinsic and "natural" goal of another implicative relationship established in the first phrase but mentioned only in passing (ex. 17, graph 4*a*). On the highest level, that of two-measure groups, the motion from B (m. 1) to C (m. 3) generates a linear pattern. Once begun, this pattern implies continuation to a point of relative stability. Even in the key of G major, D, the fifth of the scale, is more stable than the third (B) or the fourth (C). And, of course, the stability of this goal is enhanced because, when it arrives (m. 14), the D is a temporary tonic. It is partly the convergence of the rising linear process (graph 4*a*) and the descending fill (graph 3*a*) in a common goal that makes the D such a strong point of arrival.

That the relationship between the process generated in the first phrase and the D in measure 14 is more than an analytic fiction is indicated by orchestration. For, just at this point of arrival (the D), the violins that generated the linear process (graph 4*a*) return after an absence of seven measures. In other words, the instruments that began the process participate in the realization of its goal.

Throughout the Trio, the scrupulous handling of orchestration makes clear, and thereby confirms, the connection between the generation, continuation, and realization of implicative relationships. This applies not merely to the kind of instrument(s) employed but to the register they play in. The D implied by the linear process in the violins (mm. 1–4) is not only played by them but in the right octave. Similarly the extended gap-fill process, begun in measures 6–8 and provisionally stabilized on the D's in measures 14 and 18, is continued (and in the proper register) by the oboes (mm. 19–26), the instruments that generated the implicative relationship in the first place (see pp. 89–90 and ex. 22, graph 1*a*, below).

Even the octave doubling in measures 17–18 is not simply a result of Mozart's "sense of sonority." It is a consequence of relationships established earlier. In actualizing the triadic continuation latent in the opening motive (ex. 17, graphs 1*a* and 1*b*), motive *o* activates a second registral region, an octave above that established by the violins (mm. 1–6).[31] Just as the oboe moves down to the D in "its octave," so the first violins, after actualizing the implied D at measure 14, move through the triad (m. 16) to the low E and D in measures 17 and 18, playing the closing figure in octaves with the

---

30. See n. 19 above.

31. As in the case of "echo" repetitions, the distinctness of the registers is emphasized by the similarity between motives *m* and *o* (see graph 2).

oboe.[32] Thus the bilevel registration created by the octave transfer of the oboes in measures 6–8 plays a part in shaping the instrumentation and registration of the cadence at the end of Part I.

The goal-directed momentum of the main melodic pattern of the second phrase (mm. 6–14)—that is, the gap-fill process begun and continued by the oboes (ex. 17, graphs 3a and 3b)—is reinforced by the organization of other musical parameters. The gradual crescendo, resulting both from the designation in the score and from the addition of instruments (first flute and then bassoons),[33] creates a sense of destination. So does the concomitant increase in richness of sonority and density of texture.

The motives (o^1 and o^2) played by the flute and the bassoons not only imitate but complement and specify relationships latent in the main melodic process. Harmonically, goal-directed motion is enhanced because the progression through a circle of fifths—IV (G major)–I (D major)–V (A major) (see ex. 17, graph 5)—suggested by the thirds in the oboes, is specified by the triads played by the flute and the bassoons. Moreover, the rising disjunct intervals in the flute and the bassoons contrast with, and thereby emphasize and make more urgent, the conjunct descent of the oboe's "fill." Though not intervallically exact, the imitation is unmistakable because melodic similarity is complemented by rhythmic identity.

Rhythmic identity contributes to the goal-directed character of the second phrase on both foreground and higher levels. On the foreground level, ongoing motion is perpetuated by the varied repetition of motive o. As we have seen, the relative length of that motive's anacrusis (ex. 17, level 1), as well as the mobility created by its rising triadic pattern, generates considerable momentum. As a result, the first beats of measures 8, 10, and 12 are, potentially, emphatic accents. But, when these prove to be unstable appoggiaturas, the accumulated momentum is transmitted to the following weak beat. The normal mobility of the weak beat is increased not only by the momentum it acquires but by its harmonic function. For, since the circle of fifths moves upward, the first two weak beats are mobile dominants in relation to the chords that precede them, while the third (m. 12) is a deceptive resolution. Though the impetus of each motive becomes attenuated by the prolongation of its

32. In so doing, the violins continue the motion begun in the first phrase (ex. 17, graph 4b). For the linear descent presented in the first phrase is processively strong (see ex. 5, graphs 1a–1b, 2a–2b, and 4), and, since there is no explicit reversal of these processes in the first phrase, there is some tendency (despite the strong cadence in mm. 5 and 6) for the linear descent to continue.

33. Moreover, there is a tendency not only for rising lines to be performed "crescendo" but for higher pitches to be perceived as being louder, even though intensity is not increased.

final pitch (e.g., the repetition of the oboe's A following the closure of motive o), it is renewed by the momentum created by its varied repetition: that is, motive o is renewed by o^1, and motive o^1 is renewed by o^2.

On the next level, that of the succession of two-measure motives, rhythm is at least as mobile and goal-directed (ex. 17, level 2). Because it begins the phrase, motive o is presumed to be stable and accented. However, when it is followed by a similar pattern (motive o^1)—one that is characterized by increasing intensity, richer texture and sonority, and ongoing harmony—motive o is understood in retrospect as unstable.[34] For, when similar events (such as motives o and o^1) follow one another in a context of syntactic mobility, they do not as a rule form a single, cohesive group.[35] Rather they tend to be understood as discrete, though coordinate, events implying a more stable event to which both can be related as parts of a larger, integral pattern.[36] Both for this reason and because it is cadential (moving from V^7 through V^0_7/vi–vi), the next event (motive o^2) is first understood as the accented goal of the preceding groups.

But it is so only initially: stability is partial and closure provisional. This, for a number of reasons. First, the cadence in measure 12 is deceptive (ex. 17, graph 5); that is, instead of continuing to the new tonic, D major, the harmony moves through an incomplete dominant seventh (V^0_7/vi) to a chord built on B (vi) that acts as a surrogate for the tonic—but one that is not conclusive. Harmonic mobility is emphasized by rhythmic instability: for the deceptive resolution occurs on a weak beat. Second, the D played by the flute in measure

---

34. When signs for rhythmic functions occur together, as they do under motive o ($\smile$), the upper sign represents the initial interpretation of the pattern, and the lower sign represents a retrospective interpretation of its function.

35. When the context is one of stability, however, repetition does not create goal-directed motion. For example, because it follows the cadence in m. 14, prolonging the stability it establishes, the repetition of motive n in the codetta produces relaxation and gradual subsidence.

36. The first line of Blake's "The Tyger" seems a comparable phenomenon in verse:

In general, the more alike two successive events are, the more separate and discrete they seem to be, and the stronger the implication that they will be followed by a differentiated event in terms of which they can be grouped. This is so because relationships (such as antecedent consequent or weak beat and accent) can arise only if there is some difference—as well as some similarity—between successive events. The ticks of a watch, e.g., provide no objective basis for rhythmic patterning.

12 is an octave higher than that implied by the patterns generated in the oboes (graph 3*b*) and in the violins (graph 4*a*). Last, motive *o*² is too short fully to absorb and resolve the ongoing motion of the preceding measures.

Though its stability is partial and its closure provisional, the deceptive cadence in measure 12 is nonetheless consequential. As such cadences usually do, it signals the approach of more complete harmonic closure. In addition, it provides time for the dissipation of accumulated momentum and, in so doing, prevents the complete cadence (mm. 13–14) that follows from seeming abrupt. As a result, the closure of the second phrase is more effective than it might otherwise have been.

Equally important, the momentum itself is damped by a break in the prevailing sequence. The break, or *reversal of process,* involves changes in both harmonic progression and melodic patterning (ex. 18). Harmonically, the de-

Example 18

ceptive cadence ends the progression through the circle of fifths; instead of continuing to a chord based on E, which would have been the next in the sequence (graph 1*a*), the bassoon moves, as we have seen, to a chord built on B (graph 1*b*). This change, marked and emphasized by the chromatic motion from A to A♯ to B (the first such motion thus far), breaks the established gap-fill pattern. Observe that, had the pattern been regular, the B played by the bassoon would have occurred just as it does in Mozart's music (graph 2). But this "normalized" continuation would not have reversed the process.[37] Not only would sequential continuation have been more strongly implied, but the separation and integrity of the following cadential gesture would have been less apparent, and closure would, in consequence, have been somewhat less decisive.

Melodically, the flute also fails to conform to the appoggiatura figure presented by the oboes in measures 8, 10, and 12 and by the flute in measure 10. The pattern is broken; instead of falling a whole step, the flute rises a half step. In this, its motion parallels, and thereby emphasizes, the crucial chromatic motion in the bass (graph 3). Notice that the flute might easily have followed the established pattern; that is, it might have descended from C♯ to B (graph 4*a*).[38] But, had the flute moved down in this way, no reversal would have occurred; rather, continuation would have enhanced momentum.

The rhythmic structure of the second phrase is also affected by the deceptive cadence. Because harmonic and melodic closure prove to be provisional, motive o^2, at first presumed to be accented, is subsequently understood as mobile on the second rhythmic level (ex. 17, level 2). Though mitigated, goal-directed motion is not terminated. Compelling closure is still to come.

37. While the parallel motion between the first oboe and the bassoon resulting from this normalization is not ideal, it is not grammatically wrong. More problematic is the lack of a leading tone, A♯, to make the dominant function clear. But this tone might have been played by the flute. For instance:

38. From a harmonic point of view, this would have produced a more normal doubling—that of the root of the triad rather than the third. And this suggests deliberate avoidance of the prevailing pattern.

Example 19

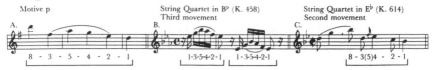

Example 20

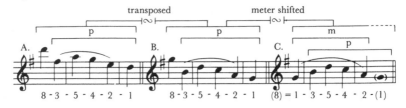

The closure created by the cadence that follows (ex. 18, motive *p*) is unequivocal—or virtually so. Its integrity and identity are assured not only by the process reversal just discussed but by a drop in register (from the high D to F♯ below), which, together with a marked change in dynamics from *forte* to *piano,* suggests movement toward the repose of closure. Harmonically the cadence is complete: a progression from subdominant (ii⁶) to dominant seventh (V⁷) to the tonic (I), here in root position.[39] The syntactic function of motive *p* is unmistakable. It is an archetypal cadential gesture in this style, as similar motives from other compositions by Mozart show (ex. 19). Even the skip from the upper tonic (8 = 1) down to the third (3) is not uncommon (ex. 19C).

Motive *p* is an appropriate close for the second phrase not only because it is typical but because it combines characteristic features of motives *m* and *o* that, as we have seen (ex. 3), are related to one another. Motive *p* is like motive *m* in intervallic structure. If the high D at the end of motive o^2 is included, the succession of scale degrees is the same (ex. 20) except that the tonic does not follow motive *m* immediately.[40] But the motives are not alike in metric placement: the tonic occurs as the second beat of motive *p* but as the third

39. As distinguished from the resolution of the complete cadence in m. 6.
40. As noted earlier, however, motive *m* strongly implies continuation to the tonic that does follow after four measures (see ex. 5, graph 2*a,* and ex. 6). From this point of view, motive *p* might be regarded as realizing a potential latent in motive *m*.

Example 21

beat of motive *m*. To make the similarity between motives unmistakable, in part *C* of example 20 the barring of motive *p* has been changed to that of motive *m*.

Metrically—and, consequently, in terms of melodic function—motive *p* resembles motive *o*. Both consist of a skip of a third from an upbeat to an appoggiatura whose resolution begins the fill implied by the skip (ex. 21). But instead of being an ending, as it is in motive *o*, the gap-fill pattern begins motive *p*, and, continuing beyond the rhythmically weak resolution characteristic of motive *o*, the pattern moves to closure on a tone that is melodically and rhythmically stable (ex. 17, levels i, 1, and 2).

The relationship of the high D in measure 12 to what follows is equivocal. In terms of intervallic structure, it can be considered part of the following cadential gesture. Orchestration, too, fosters connection: the flute moves down and participates in the performance of the gesture. Nevertheless, there is an impression of incompleteness. Because of its rhythmic and harmonic mobility, yet its importance as a goal, and because of the patent change in register and dynamics, the high D seems to be "left hanging"—to be only incidentally connected with, not significantly related to, what follows. By separating the resolution of the deceptive cadence from the beginning of the complete cadence, Mozart's phrasing emphasizes disjunction. The disjunction is important because it suggests that the high D is essentially related not to the proximate gesture that follows but to processes still to come.[41]

Codetta (Mm. 14–18)

Part I closes with a codetta (ex. 17, mm. 14–18) that, though elided with the preceding cadential gesture, is nonetheless understood as a separate event. Unlike earlier phrases, however, it generates no new implicative pro-

---

41. These more remote processes occur in the second part of the Trio. There, played by the same instrument and in the same register, the high D moves down through C (m. 24) to B and A (mm. 25–26)—and eventually to G (see pp. 87–93 and ex. 24, graph 2, below).

cesses. Rather, because of its own internal patterning, and because of its relationships to preceding events, it facilitates closure.

Internally, a slower rate of harmonic change—compared to measures 12–14 (see ex. 17)—reduces the level of activity, while the repetition of a progression from dominant seventh to tonic not only confirms closure in D but, by prolonging the provisional stability reached in measure 14, allows time for ongoing motion to subside still further. Nor is there new melodic motion. The typical closing figure (ex. 2), borrowed from the end of the first phrase, is simply repeated with registral extension to the lower octave.[42] Texture, too, fosters closure. No contrapuntal process, such as the canon in measures 4–6 (see ex. 7), creates ongoing motion. A simple figure (melody)/ground (accompaniment) relationship enables harmonic and melodic closure to be fully effective. Differences in both texture and harmony help explain why motives n^1 and n^2 are considered to be relatively closed, iambic groups (ex. 17, level 1), while motive n (mm. 5 and 6), which is melodically identical, was analyzed as a more mobile amphibrach group (see p. 69 and exx. 8–10 above). For in the absence of contrapuntal motion—particularly the suspension, G (mm. 4–5), which emphasized the beginning of motive n—the eighth-note pattern in measures 15 and 17 and the dominant-seventh harmony in those measures suggest motion *to* the measure that follows, making the groups seem end-accented. In addition, because there is no canon (ex. 7) in the codetta, the tonic chord of the new key is in stable, root position.

Relationships between the codetta and preceding events also contribute to closure. As we have seen, several implicative processes generated in the first two phrases are at least provisionally realized in the codetta: (1) The continuation of the oboe's conjunct fill (mm. 8–12) through E to D, which was masked by the flute in measures 12–14, is audibly actualized in measures 16–18 (ex. 17, graph 3*b*). (2) The D played by the first violins in measure 14—and prolonged through a neighbor-note motion (D–E–D) and an octave transfer—is the realization of a goal implied by the high-level linear motion begun by the violins in the first four measures of the Trio (ex. 17, graph 4*a*). (3) In measures 16–18, the registral relationship implicit in motives *m* and *o* is explicitly affirmed as the violins and oboes play motive n^2 in octaves (see pp. 79–80 above). (4) The possibility that the two-measure length

---

42. Because this repetition is "postcadential," its effect is not to enhance goal-directed motion (see n. 35) but to diminish kinetic tension.

of motive n might be extended and "normalized" through repetition (see pp. 72–73 above) is actualized in the codetta. (5) Finally, and perhaps most fundamental of all, because they rhyme with the figure that closed the first phrase, motives n^1 and n^2 are understood as a "return," and the psychic satisfaction of such return considerably enhances the formal completeness and closure of the first part of the Trio.

Part II

In the second part of the Trio the processes begun in the first, and provisionally stabilized at its close, are resumed and satisfactorily completed. In what follows, the continuation of those processes in the transition and the return will be considered first. Then subsidiary relationships generated within the transition and completed in the return will be discussed. And, last, the return will be analyzed, with special attention to the differences between it and Section A (= Part I), which it restates in modified form.

The Transition (Mm. 18–31)

In the prefatory "sketch" of the structural plan of the Trio, the transition was described (pp. 59–60 above) as an elaborated prolongation of dominant harmony linking the close of Section A with the beginning of the return (Section A'). But to say no more than that is both to ignore the subtle way in which the interaction among parameters shapes events within the section and to overlook important relationships between the transition and the return. At the beginning of the transition, for instance, what seems to be a continuation of the high-level melodic process (begun by the oboe in the second phrase) is artfully undermined and deflected by rhythmic/metric ambiguity. A new, but subsidiary, melodic process is generated (see pp. 105–6 and ex. 28 below). This process is continued in the return. There it affects the significance of the high G in measure 36. Instead of being the mobile middle of a patterning—as the comparable high D in measure 12 was—the G is the relatively stable goal of the subsidiary patterning begun in the transition. It is only toward the end of the transition that the main melodic process is actually resumed. Its gradual emergence from the subsidiary process is a fascinating example of how the intricate interplay among melody and harmony, meter and rhythm, texture and phrasing shapes the listener's understanding of musical events.

Phrase 3 (Mm. 18–26)

The relative stability achieved at the end of Part I is undermined at the very beginning of the transition (ex. 22). The C♮ of submotive *y* (m. 19) transforms the D-major harmony reached in measure 18 from a stable, if temporary, tonic into a mobile dominant-seventh chord. For several reasons, motive *q* suggests that the gap-fill processes generated by the oboes and the flute in motive group 2 have been resumed. (1) Like motives *o* and *o*¹, motive *q* consists of a rising triad followed by descending conjunct motion. Because of this similarity, there is a tendency to associate the later pattern *(q)* with the earlier one *(o)* in function as well as shape. (2) The C at the start of submotive *y* can be understood as the continuation of two earlier descending fills: namely, that begun by the oboes in measure 8 and provisionally stabilized in measure 18 (ex. 22, graph 1*a*) and that begun by the flute in measure 10 but deflected and "left hanging" in measure 12 (ex. 22, graph 2). (3) Furthermore, submotive *y* is played by the same instruments, oboes and flute, and in the same registers as was the case earlier. (4) Last, the sonority, dominated by the thirds in the oboes, is not unlike that characteristic of the earlier descending fill.

But the resumption is provisional at best—an intimation, perhaps, of more satisfactory realization. It is so for two reasons. In motive group 2, conjunct fill occurred on the level of the measure or higher, that is, A (mm. 8–9), G (mm. 10–11), F♯ (m. 12), E (m. 13), and D (m. 14). To be satisfactory, the resumption of this process must take place on the same hierarchic level or on a higher one.[43] Submotive *y* does not fulfill this condition. It moves on the level of the beat (C–B–A, within the measure); and, when it is restated a step higher (*y*¹) rather than a step lower, the provisional nature of the resumption is patent. Equally important, the appoggiatura-resolution figure so characteristic of the earlier descending fill (particularly in the oboes in mm. 8, 10, 12, and 13) is missing. In short, though the C♮ in measure 18 and submotive *y* as a whole may serve as signals of impending realization, their main function is not the resumption of processes already begun but the generation of new, albeit subsidiary ones.

The gap-fill processes begun in motive group 2 are continued not at the beginning but toward the end of the transition (ex. 22, graphs 1*a* and 2).[44] There the oboe D of measure 18 and the flute D from measure 12 move in

43. See the discussion of the law of hierarchic equivalence in *Explaining Music*, 134–35 and passim.

44. Precisely how the rhythmic/metric structure of the transition moves from intimation to realization of the appoggiatura-resolution figure is discussed below (see pp. 97–98).

Example 22

(continued on page 90)

Example 22 *(continued)*

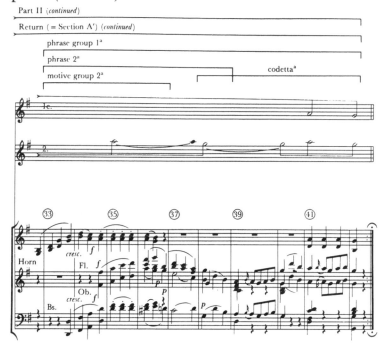

their respective registers through C (m. 24) and B (m. 25) to A (m. 26). And this descending motion not only occurs at the level of the measure but is realized as an appoggiatura-resolution figure.

The transition ends in measure 26. As we shall see, rhythm plays an important part in this articulation: the high-level structure is a closed, end-accented group of 6 + 6 + 12 quarter notes, and, as metric placement becomes "normalized" in measures 24–26, the appoggiatura-resolution figure latent in measures 19–22 is actualized. What follows the cadence in measure 26 makes closure unmistakable. It is not merely that melody, rhythm, texture, and orchestration are significantly different, or that the patterning is more stable and regular, but that there is a *return* to relationships presented at the beginning of the Trio.

Though unmistakable, the closure of the transition is by no means definitive. Both the foreground rhythm, which ends on a weak beat, and the harmony, which cadences on an unstable dominant chord, create mobility. More important for present purposes, however, the processes resumed in measures

24–26, as well as those generated within the transition itself (mm. 19–23), are incomplete. The descending fill has reached its penultimate pitch, A, but return to the stability of the tonic—the full completion of the fill—is still to come.[45] In theoretical terms, there is a bifurcation of form and process. That is, processes generated as far back in the piece as measure 7 transcend the articulation that divides the Trio into formal entities (Sec. *B* followed by Sec. *A'*).[46]

In the return (mm. 26–42), the process begun by the oboes in motive group 2, and resumed by them in the transition, is continued and completed by the French horns. This change in the instruments performing an established process—one of the few such changes in the Trio—is probably made partly for registral reasons.[47] That is, in the relatively low register of measures 26–42, the sound of the oboes would be quite weak. The music played by the horns will be discussed in more detail later. For the present, it need only be observed that, though they begin by doubling and "clarifying" what is played by the violins (mm. 26–32), it is reasonable to regard the horns as surrogates for the oboes. For, when they are given the main melodic material (mm. 32ff.), their music is similar to that performed earlier by the oboes (mm. 6ff.). However, while the oboes reached only partial closure (in an authentic cadence in the dominant) and provisional realization (through substitution by rank) at the end of Part I, the horns achieve both full stability and satisfactory realization. For, at the end of the Trio, an authentic cadence in the tonic establishes full stability, and, as they move on structural tones from A to G, the horns complete both the gap-fill process they regenerate in the return and that begun by the oboes in measure 6 (ex. 22, graphs 1*a* and 1*c*).

The gap-fill process begun by the flute in measures 9–10 is also continued in the transition (ex. 22, graph 2). After provisional motion to C (m. 19), the

45. Observe that the oboe's A in m. 26 can be construed not only as part of the long descent begun by the large gap in mm. 7–8 but as the fill of the smaller gap from G in m. 6 to the structural B in m. 7—as ex. 22, graph 1*b*, shows. Looked at in this way, mm. 6–26 combine comparable processes on two registral levels into a single extended motion. From another point of view, both these gap-fill processes are analogous to that which opens the Trio. They are, so to speak, motive *m* "writ large."

46. The point seems worth making because it emphasizes that, contrary to the views of some critics and aestheticians, form and process are distinguishable and sometimes independent aspects of structure. Observe that a similar bifurcation occurred between Sec. *A* (of Pt. I) and Sec. *B*.

47. The change is not inappropriate because the oboes have, from one point of view, completed part of their task. For, since the B in m. 8 is an appoggiatura, the first structural tone in the oboe's descending fill is the following A, and, when it reaches the lower structural A in m. 26, it has sounded in conjunct succession all the tones of the G-major scale. Or, to put the matter differently, the oboe part consists of a linear prolongation of A.

Example 23

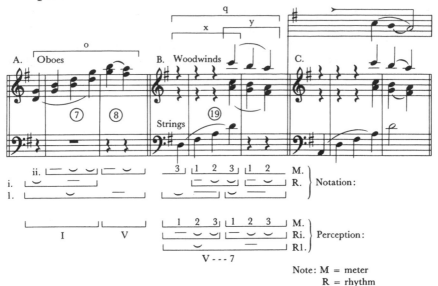

Note: M = meter
R = rhythm

high D "left hanging" in measure 12 functions (appropriately) as an appoggiatura that resolves to C (m. 24), and this pattern of descent is continued to the A in measure 26, where the flute part ends temporarily. But in the return no surrogate instrument completes its process. The flute continues; the structural A reached in measure 26 is picked up in measure 35 and, after an excursion through F♯ and G in the upper octave (see pp. 106–7 below), moves to G (m. 38), completing the descent from D.[48] Closure is reinforced as the flute joins in the performance of the codetta figure in the final measures of the Trio.

Before considering the larger structure of the transition, discussing the implicative processes generated within it, and following these to their realization in the return, subtle, low-level rhythmic/metric relationships must be analyzed in some detail.

To illuminate these subtleties, motive *q* will be compared with motive *o*. Their similarity was mentioned earlier: both consist of a rising triadic motion followed by conjunct descent (ex. 23, parts *A* and *B*). But there are

48. Although the gap has not been completely filled (the flute does not return to the structural D in m. 9), substitution by rank here creates satisfactory closure because it occurs on the tonic. In addition, it might be argued that the horns complete this process, moving down conjunctly from D in m. 34 to G in m. 42.

important differences between them. Motive *o* is essentially a single gesture. Though it can be divided into parts, these are cohesive because they are functionally related as gap to beginning of fill. Melodic integrity is reinforced by harmonic progression, as tonic (mm. 6–7) moves to dominant (m. 8). Furthermore, a single instrumental timbre, that of the oboes, connects the parts of the motive and links its two registral levels. Motive *q,* on the other hand, is made up of patently separate, almost independent, parts: submotives *x* and *y* (ex. 23, part *B*). The parts are differentiated by instrumental color, strings followed by woodwinds, and by registral contrast, bass followed by treble winds as well as bassoons.[49] Though the submotives overlap (the winds enter before the strings finish) and are related to one another in a kind of "statement/response" dialogue, no implicative melodic process welds them together. They are not understood as gap and fill. Nor does the mere addition of the seventh (C) create enough harmonic change to ensure cohesive connection.

These melodic differences have a significant effect upon rhythmic/metric organization. Motive *o,* as we have seen, consists of an extended anacrusis followed by an appoggiatura-resolution figure that functions as a relatively short, but emphatic, accent (see analysis under ex. 23*A*). Motive *q* has also been analyzed as an end-accented group on the primary level (see ex. 23*B*, Perception, R-1). This analysis is based partly upon the prevalence of end-accented groups on the primary level at the end of Part I (see ex. 17), partly upon the tendency of rising disjunct patterns to be understood as mobile and goal directed, and partly upon the fact that the change in register and instrumentation makes the woodwind entrance seem stressed. However, even though the last two notes of motives *o* and *q* are identical in pitch and metric position (B and A on beats 1 and 2), the impression of end-accented grouping is much weaker in motive *q.*

The accent is weak because the B in measure 20 does not function as an appoggiatura. No articulation in phrasing, no change in dynamics or timbre indicates such function. No harmonic change marks the beginning of the measure, making the B into an accented dissonance—as might have been the case (ex. 23*C*). Put differently, the B is a "potential" appoggiatura, but its actualization *as* an appoggiatura is delayed until the very end of the transition

---

49. Though the bassoons are not in a markedly different register, submotive *y* is nevertheless understood as separate and "high" because it is dominated by the sound of the upper winds. For the sake of convenience the bassoon part is not given in the "short" scores.

(see ex. 24, level i). Moreover, had actualization occurred in measure 20, the continuation of the descending conjunct fill assigned to the oboes and flute (ex. 22, graphs 1*a* and 2) would have been unsatisfactory because, although the A would have been structural on the proper (equivalent) level, the preceding C and B would not (ex. 23*C,* graph).

Though it *should* function as an appoggiatura—its metric position and its relation to previous patternings suggest this role—the B sounds more like a passing tone. It does so because, despite its notation, its metric role is ambiguous. This ambiguity is present from the beginning of motive *q.*

According to the notation, the low D that begins the transition should be understood as a mobile upbeat to the following F# (ex. 23*B,* Notation). At least in retrospect, however, its metric placement is equivocal. For it seems to function partly as the accented beginning of a metric unit (ex. 23*B,* Perception). This anomaly is the result of the organization of the several parameters:

Example 24

1. Since submotive x consists of a single ascending triad, played in unison by one group of instruments (double basses), harmony, texture, and orchestration do not articulate the first beat of measure 19. The absence of stress on this beat weakens the impression of meter.[50] To the extent that F♯ is understood as accented, it is so because the prevalent metric organization is continued in the mind and motor behavior of the listener.

2. The triad is phrased as a single unbroken event. Put counterfactually, had Mozart written [musical notation] rather than [musical notation] the change of bow after the D would have placed a slight stress on F♯, making the notated meter more palpable.

3. When a triadic pattern begins on the root, there is a tendency for the root to be perceived as the beginning of a metric unit (see pp. 74–75 and ex. 16 above as well as ex. 23B, Perception). Because in this case no articulation is created by the other parameters (unless, of course, the conductor requires his performers to place special stress on the F♯, which, as we shall see, would be a mistake), the D is most readily understood as an accent—as the beginning of a metric unit.[51] The relationship between melodic pattern and metric placement is more normal at the beginning of the next submotive (x^1) because the first note is the fifth (D), rather than the root (G), of the triad: [musical notation]. But it is too late to dispel or alter the sense of metric placement that has, in the meantime, been reinforced by the patterning of submotive y.

4. All parameters cooperate to suggest that the first notes of submotive y may be the accented beginning of a metric unit. Because it transforms the preceding triad from a provisional tonic into a dominant-seventh chord, the C renews the harmonic impulse and thereby emphasizes the beginning of the submotive. Both the change in instrumentation and the separation in register incline the listener to perceive the third beat of measure 19 as the beginning

50. To see the difference that texture and harmony can make, compare the first beat of m. 19 with the F♯ played by the bassoons on the first beat of m. 34. Although the triads (beginning on D in mm. 18 and 33) are the same, the F♯ on the first beat of m. 34 is stressed and its metric function unambiguous because the appoggiatura in the horns makes the rhythmic structure crystal clear. But nothing articulates the first beat of m. 19.

51. From this point of view, the beginning of the transition is similar to the beginning of the Trio and may be said to intensify the ambiguity latent in the triadic pattern of motive *m*. Note, however, that in motive *m* the second violins skip up a minor sixth, from B to G, and the resulting emphasis on the note following the skip (G) probably helps articulate the meter. So, of course, does what follows.

of a new metric unit. Equally important, no parametric articulation differentiates the first beat of measure 20 as the accented beginning of the meter. For instance, there is no change in phrasing at this point. In short, the simplest way to perceive the patterning of these submotives is to make the meter begin on notated third beats.

The force of the metric disturbance should not, however, be exaggerated. Because the metric placement prevalent in Part I continues to affect the listener's mental and motor behavior, and because the appoggiatura-resolution figure explicit in that placement is latent in the patterning of submotive *y,* the shift in the position of the perceived (vs. the notated) meter is not unmitigated.[52] As a result, the original metric placement could have been reestablished easily. But this does not happen. Let us consider what does take place.

A new stage in the transition begins at the end of measure 23 (ex. 24). In what follows, the rate of harmonic motion virtually quadruples: instead of two chords in twelve beats (mm. 18–22), two chords occur in only three beats (mm. 24–26). Texture, motivic pattern, and instrumentation are also altered. Instead of a dialogue between contrasting submotives played by different instrumental groups, one submotive *(y)* is the sole melodic material in a quasi-contrapuntal texture played by a single group of instruments: the woodwinds. Yet, despite these manifest modifications that signal the close of the transition, rhythmic/metric changes are gradual.

The metric ambiguity established at the beginning of the transition is supported by the pattern begun by the oboes and flute on the last beat of measure 23, and, as a result, the ensuing group is beginning-accented (ex. 24, level i). But the bassoons suggest the possibility of change: because it is twice as long as the note that precedes it, the half note at the beginning of measure 24 is an agogic accent, and, responding to this durational emphasis as well as to the notated meter, the bassoonists will probably place some stress on the longer note, making it seem like the beginning of a metric unit. In addition, the half-note harmony makes the notes played by the upper winds into a proper appoggiatura that is properly resolved. Since appoggiaturas normally occur on the first beat of a metric unit, this also indicates that perceived meter and notated meter are becoming congruent.

But only "becoming." For the potential influence of the appoggiatura-

52. Thus, though the third beats of mm. 19 (C), 21 (D), and 23 (E) will be analyzed as structural tones (see ex. 27, graphs 3*a* and 3*b,* below), they are provisionally, rather than definitively, so.

resolution figure is undermined by phrasing. Instead of making the figure patent, as it might have done (ex. 24, graph *A*), the actual phrasing ties the appoggiatura/resolution both to the preceding E and to the following D. Because it begins a varied repetition of submotive *y*, the E is understood as the beginning of a metric unit. As a result, it preempts the middle-level accent (ex. 24, level i) and relegates the appoggiatura-resolution figure to a very subsidiary rhythmic level (level iii). By transcending the closure of the figure on C, the phrasing to D obscures the presence of the figure and, consequently, the accent characteristic of it.

The phrasing beyond C to D (m. 24) is important for other reasons as well. As part *B* of example 24 shows, the motivic structure of measures 23–26 is potentially very regular. Submotive *y* is simply restated sequentially three times—though the third time (y^a) the first motivic tone (C) is preceded by a grace note (D). Had the phrasing emphasized this uniformity by repeating that in measures 19–22 (ex. 22) or one such as that given in part *A* of example 24, continuation would have been strongly implied, and the cadential closure in measure 26 would have seemed abrupt—even jolting. Mozart's phrasing ruffles this potential regularity so that, instead of being the beginning of y^{1a}, the D (m. 24) functions as an extension of y^2. Similarly, in measure 25, phrasing disturbs uniformity and tends to obscure the presence of familiar submotives.[53]

Because the D at the end of measure 24 is phrased with what precedes it rather than with what follows, the appoggiatura figure at the beginning of measure 25 is not subsumed within submotive y^{1a}, as it might have been (ex. 24*B*-1). Instead, phrase and figure begin together. By enhancing the articulation of the appoggiatura, phrasing emphasizes the rhythm of the figure and makes its function more palpable; it is now understood as an event on levels ii and i. Here perceived meter and notated meter become congruent again.

But the appoggiatura figure, though now manifest, is not yet fully realized as an event in its own right. It is the accented beginning of a compound

rhythmic group on level i ♩ ♩ ♫ but not an integral, stable goal. It becomes

---

53. Although they contravene the previously established, and probably more basic, motivic organization, the phrasings in mm. 24 and 25 do not create disordered patterns. Rather they give rise to a kind of substitute regularity: a neighbor-note motion of D–C–D/C–B–C (ex. 24*B*-2).

so in the following measure (m. 26). Not only are the two eighth notes at the end of measure 25 a mobile afterbeat coming *from* the accented beginning of the measure (as the phrasing indicates), but, because they are separated from the second beat (B) by a skip and are shorter than the notes surrounding them, the eighth notes also function as an upbeat to the appoggiatura figure in measure 26.[54] Thus, on the subprimary level (i) part, and on the primary level (1) all, of measure 25 acts as an anacrusis to measure 26, which is a stable goal. Here the integrity and function of the appoggiatura figure are fully realized.

One important consequence of the metric displacement, discussed at such length, is now apparent. It makes possible the progression, mentioned earlier, from veiled potentiality to patent actuality. Let us briefly review this change.

Though no proper appoggiatura figure is embedded in submotives y and y^1 (ex. 22), their notated metric placement and the similarity of motives q and q^1 to o and o^1 subtly intimate such patterning.[55] Submotive y^2 is the middle term, or link, in what proves to be a mirror pattern (ex. 25).[56] Appropriately, therefore, while an appoggiatura figure is unquestionably contained in y^2, its function tends to be subsumed and its identity masked by the dominance of the submotive as a whole. As the motivic patterning is weakened by the phrasing, the appoggiatura figure gains in strength and prominence until, as we have seen, it is fully actualized in measure 26. This progression is evident in

54. The inverted bracket in ex. 24 suggests that the upbeat is only latent—partially realized. But it is somewhat stronger than this because the eighth-note motion from D to C is itself a low-level appoggiatura figure that makes the third beat stressed (') and thereby strengthens its anacrustic function.

55. Performance should not, however, make this possible patterning palpable—e.g., by stressing notated accents. For then the sense of progression and of ultimate realization would be weakened.

56. The mirror structure suggests that the transition should be analyzed as a prolongation of the dominant harmony with which it begins and ends. Possibly. But it should be observed that only motivic structure is organized in this way. Harmony, rhythm, texture, and instrumentation do not exhibit this sort of symmetry. Moreover, even motivic structure is varied in reflection because submotives y^{1a} and y^a are functionally different from their earlier counterparts. More generally, some prolongations are nonprocessive, e.g., declarative and normalizing prolongations, parentheses, and those that, allowing time for respite of process, might be called *composed fermatas*. (An instance of composed fermata occurs in the first movement of Beethoven's String Quartet in B♭, op. 130, mm. 37–40.) In the transition of Mozart's Trio, however, new processes are generated, old ones resumed, and kinetic motion enhances directionality.

Example 25

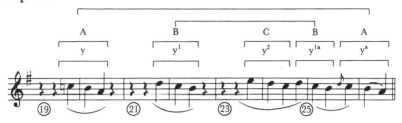

the analysis of rhythmic structure (ex. 24). When the figure first appears (m. 24), it is "buried" on subprimary levels (iii and ii); as it becomes manifest (m. 25), it shapes the structure of the next levels (ii and i); and, finally, when it is fully realized, it participates in the organization of the highest levels (i and 1).

At the same time that it shapes events within the transition, the progression from potentiality to actuality brings about the resumption of other implicative processes—ones that, as we have seen, extend beyond the confines of the transition. For the actualization of the appoggiatura figure makes it evident (partly perhaps in retrospect since actualization is gradual) that what was merely intimated in the first half of the transition (mm. 18–23) is consummated in the second (mm. 24–26). Namely, the descending fill, begun by the oboes and flute in period 1 (and completed by the horns and flute in period 2), has been resumed and continued on the proper hierarchic level (ex. 22, graphs 1*a*, 1*c*, and 2).

The end of the transition is a result of the momentary stabilization of strongly goal-directed processes. Though rhythm is most important in creating closure, modest inflections in other parameters contribute to the articulation of the cadence even as they signal its approach.[57] The regular harmonic

---

57. The structure or form of a composition is something that the competent listener *infers* from the hierarchy of closures that it presents. The strength of any closure depends upon the degrees of closure articulated by the several parameters. Sometimes all parameters join in creating closure; then they are said to move congruently. At other times, one or two parameters will foster closure, while others make for continuation of process; then they are said to be noncongruent. In the case of the close of this transition, the parameters are scarcely congruent. Rhythm, as we shall see, is relatively closed and stable, but melody stops on one of the most mobile notes of the scale. For this reason, closure at the end of the transition is quite weak.

Example 26

progression through chords whose *roots* are a fifth apart—E (V^6/ii), A (ii), D (V^6), G (I)—is deflected in measure 25 (ex. 26*A* and the harmonic analysis).[58] Instead of continuing the cycle of fifths by skipping down a third to E (as the bass of a first-inversion triad built on C), there is a larger skip to C (as the bass of a triad built on A). This change produces a higher-level disjunction (ex. 26*B*). The fourth-species counterpoint, implicit in the relationship between bass and treble (mm. 24–25), is modified when the bass, which might have continued descending by step to F♯ (the first beat of m. 26), skips

58. An *x* in an example signifies a disjunction or break in process.

down to D. Melodically, the skip of a third from B to D (m. 25) breaks the prevailing conjunct motion (ex. 26*C*), and the break is emphasized because eighth notes, rather than quarters, fill the gap thus created. These slight discontinuities not only damp ongoing motion and presage closure but transform potentially uniform processes into a function-confirming gesture—an archetypal semicadence.[59]

Such changes would not have created convincing closure, however, were it not for rhythm. Although the foreground patterning ends on a mobile weak beat, middle-level rhythmic closure is unequivocal, and it is strong enough to impose upon the other parameters a stability they would not otherwise possess. Reinforced by the eighth-note motion at its close, measure 25 is, as we have seen, anacrustic to measure 26 on the primary level (exx. 24 and 26, level 1). On the next level (ex. 26, level 2), the grouping is end-accented—a closed anapest. The organization is understood in this way not only because other parameters, including low-level rhythm, weld measures 23–26 into a cohesive event but because the first four measures of the transition imply this sort of structure. That is, the varied repetition of motive *q*, like that of motives *m* and *o* in Part I, makes it probable that a longer group, an accent to which the essentially equivalent motives can be related (see pp. 80–81 above), will follow. When motive q^2 begins on a new step of the scale (E rather than D), it seems the beginning of such a cohesive event. And this surmise is confirmed by what follows.

Though rhythm creates sufficient closure to articulate the end of the transition, the sense of goal-directed motion is by no means diminished. For, despite the contribution to closure made by the disjunctions mentioned above, the other parameters remain open and ongoing. The harmonic progression (ii^6–V) at the end of the transition implies continuation to the tonic. Melodically, the descending line of appoggiatura resolutions (C–B–A), which resumes processes begun in Part I, stops on one of the most mobile notes of the scale, and the tendency to move to the tonic, G, is very strong. Moreover, melodic processes generated within the transition remain to be realized. These kinetic patternings affect the rhythmic structure of the highest

59. As, e.g., that in the fourth measure of the theme from Mozart's A-Major Piano Sonata (K. 331):

level, making the whole transition function as an anacrusis to the return
(ex. 26, level 3).

The sense of goal-directed motion is high not only because inhibition
(resulting from rhythmically imposed closure) intensifies inclination but because an increase in psychological tempo, or pace, heightens the sense of ur-
gency. It was pointed out earlier that, by obscuring the uniformity of motivic
structure, phrasing facilitates closure. Paradoxically, the same phrasing that
tempers a tendency toward continuation produces a kind of composed accelerando. That is, the phrase groups at the end of the transition become progressively shorter (ex. 26D)—from four beats, to three, to two. As a result,
events seem to occur more rapidly.[60]

Though the degree of closure is such that the transition is understood as a
separable event, the presence of strong syntactic processes prevents it from
functioning as an independent, formal entity. Rather it is a contingent one,
calling for a section in which tension is resolved, stability established, and processes satisfactorily concluded. This dependence seems to be reflected in the
morphology of the Trio. It will be recalled (ex. 1) that the first part of the Trio
consists of two main events: the first, phrase 1, is six measures long; the second,
phrase group 1, is twelve measures long. The ratio of the events (1:2) suggests
that the third morphological length might be twice the second, making the
succession of lengths 6–12–24.[61] A twenty-four-measure unit does follow,
and it proves to be not a section within but all of Part II. Moreover, since the
transition is eight measures long, the proportions of Part II are the same (1:2)
as those of Part I. These proportional relationships seem to indicate that (1)
what is morphologically equivalent to Part I is not the return (though the return is motivically and syntactically so) but the whole of the second part[62]

---

60. The change of pace itself acts as a sign of impending closure. See, e.g., the more extended
"accelerando" toward the end of the development section (mm. 134–64) in the first movement
of this symphony. In both cases, pace increases because our sense of tempo depends to a considerable extent upon the rate at which differentiated events—more or less closed patterns—follow
one another.

61. Another consistent succession would, of course, be 6–12–18.

62. The fact that the proportions of the sixteen-measure return (6 + 10) cannot easily be related to others in the Trio also seems a sign of the morphological integrity of the whole second
part. It might be suggested that the "stretto" in mm. 33–35 represents a compression of a more
commensurate length. But, if this sort of argument is allowed, anything can be made to fit—and
often is. It should perhaps also be mentioned that the Trio is the same length as the Minuetto
proper—i.e., forty-two measures.

and (2), though it is a separable entity, a cohesive bar form of 2 + 2 + 4 measures (ex. 26*F*), the transition is morphologically as well as functionally subordinate.

The transition is functionally dependent—open and mobile—partly because implicative melodic processes remain to be realized. One of these, that resumed toward the end of the transition and continued in the return, has already been discussed (see pp. 81–91 and 98–100 and also ex. 22, graphs 1*a*, 1*c*, and 2, and ex. 27, graphs 1*a* and 1*b*). The other, begun in the first half of the transition, is the result of the rising linear motion whose structural tones are C (m. 19), D (m. 21), and E (m. 23). Once established, this pattern, too, implies continuation to a point of relative stability and closure—probably by conjunct motion through F♯ to G (ex. 27, graphs 3*a* and 3*b*). Thus, though both patterns imply continuation to the tonic, they move in opposite directions. The primary process, resumed in the second half of the transition, suggests motion *down* to G; the secondary process, generated in the first half of the transition, suggests motion *up* to G.[63]

The structure of the secondary pattern is crucially dependent upon the metric ambiguity discussed earlier. For, had there been no metric disturbance at the beginning of the transition, the C, D, and E would probably have functioned as mobile anacruses to appoggiatura figures.[64] In that case, the structural tones of the transition would have consisted of an unambiguous succession of appoggiatura resolutions—that is, a conjunct motion from A to C and back again (ex. 27, graph 2*a*); and the whole section might have been understood as little more than a prolongation of A (ex. 27, graph 2*b*). But meter is disturbed. As a result, the beginnings, at least as much as the ends, of submotives *y*, *y*^{1}, and *y*^{2} are structural.[65] However, because meter is equivocal (see pp. 96–97 above), the tones defining the ascending melodic line are structurally somewhat tentative. Appropriately, the continuation of this process is less decisive than that of the primary one.

---

63. The process resumed at the close of the transition is considered primary not only because it plays a central role in the melodic structuring of the Trio from m. 6 on but because its tones are unequivocally structural—are congruent with the prevalent (and notated) meter. The process begun in m. 19 is considered secondary both because it plays an auxiliary role in the larger structure of the Trio and because its structural tones are somewhat tentative.

64. As, e.g., in ex. 23*C* (treble clef).

65. Submotive *y*^{2} acts as the common term, or link, between the different melodic processes. That is, its first note (E) belongs to the secondary ascending motion; its last note (C) is the first structural note in the resumption of the primary descending process.

Example 27

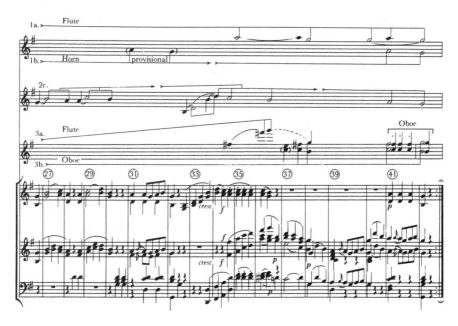

Example 28

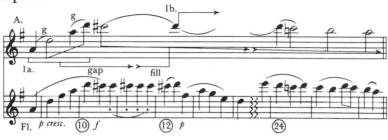

The continuation takes place in measure 36 of the return. There the flute, one of the instruments that generated the process, moves in the right register through F♯ (emphasized by motion from the lower octave) to the high G (ex. 27, graph 3*a*). Even though the G is accompanied by a deceptive cadence, the realization seems satisfactory. It does so partly because it is the tonic and partly because (1) it is the goal of the secondary process and (2) the tones generating the implicative pattern were themselves only "tentatively" structural.

Once again Mozart's phrasing is illuminating. The high G in measure 36 is comparable to the high D in measure 12 (ex. 28) but with significant differences. The D is considerably less stable than the G. It is not the tonic but part of a cadence within a modulation toward the dominant. Nor is it the goal of a process. Rather it is a transient upward deflection toward the beginning of a descending fill defined by unequivocal structural tones (ex. 28, graph 1*a*). As a result, the D in measure 12 is mobile; it seems, as mentioned earlier, to be "left hanging." It can be "left hanging" because it will be picked up and continued in the transition, where it descends through C♮ and B to A.[66] Not

---

66. The deflection may even be connected in retrospect with the rising motion of the subordinate process.

only is the high G in measure 36, on the other hand, a more stable goal, but, because it occurs in the final phrase of the Trio, remote continuation is unlikely. That is, it will not be picked up, as the D is, and move on to a further goal. Phrasing reflects these differences. Instead of ending the phrasing on the G, leaving it "hanging" and implying the possibility of continuation (as was the case with the high D), Mozart explicitly connects the G to the B that follows, fusing the deceptive cadence to the complete one that follows, and connecting high and low registers in a single gesture (ex. 28, graph 2*b*).[67]

The role of the oboes in the return is auxiliary (see ex. 27):[68] they play in octaves with both the flute (mm. 34–35) and the horns and then rejoin the flute in the performance of the cadential gesture (mm. 36–38). Consequently, analyzing their continuation of the secondary process is problematic. However, the contrapuntal connection between the last notes (m. 23) of their generative pattern and the final cadence of the Trio seems clear enough to make this move to closure a reasonable candidate for realization (ex. 27, graph 3*b*).[69] If this is correct, then it seems plausible to suggest that the movement from F♯ to G (and C–B) of the complete cadence (mm. 37–38) is understood—at least in retrospect—as a preliminary realization of the process begun by the oboes in the first half of the transition.

The Return

The return creates high-level closure both because tonic harmony is reestablished after a relatively extended departure (mm. 6–26) and because the melodic/textural patterns of Part I are re-presented—though with significant modifications. The modifications are important because they not only ensure that the whole section (*A'*) remains in the tonic but, as we have seen, make possible the realization of implications generated in preceding sections. Equally important, the changes are so designed that newly generated pro-

---

67. The phrasing of the first oboe part, whose conjunct descent from B (m. 36) through A (m. 37) to G (m. 38) is unmistakable, breaks as before; and the overlap of the flute and oboe phrasings assures that the motion from the last beat of m. 34 to the first beat of m. 38 will be understood as one pattern.

68. As we have seen, the primary process, begun by the oboes in m. 6 and resumed by them in m. 24, is assigned to the French horns.

69. Particularly since the oboes play the same rhythm as, and complete the harmony of, their surrogates, the French horns. For the sake of clarity, the oboe part is given in the analytic graph rather than in the short score.

cesses as well as those regenerated by repetition are realized within the confines of the return.

Phrase 1ª (Mm. 26–32)

Modifications are present from the beginning of the return (ex. 27). In the first four measures the violins restate what they played at the beginning of the Trio. But now they are reinforced by the French horns— except that the horns omit the second beats of measures 27 and 29.[70] This apparently slight qualification of tone color results in changes in syntactic emphasis. Though the implicative relationships discussed in connection with the analysis of the first phrase (pp. 64–68 and 70–73) are implicit in what the violins play, some are significantly strengthened by the addition of the horns, while others are considerably weakened.

To appreciate the ways in which the horns affect implicative relationships, the patterns generated by the violins must be briefly reviewed.[71] Though seemingly little more than a detail, the D in the violin part in measure 27— and, analogically, the E in measure 29—influences the musical patterning in a number of ways. Melodically, the D (1) forms part of the triadic motion, making it unequivocal (ex. 29, graph 1); (2) creates a subsidiary gap, B–D, which the C begins to fill (ex. 29, graph 2); and (3), by forming this subsidiary gap-fill pattern, obscures the échappée function of the C (ex. 29, graph 3). Rhythmically, the D enhances the stability of the C and contributes to the mobility of the preceding B (ex. 29, graph 4). The stability of the C is enhanced because, as the goal of the subsidiary gap, it is slightly stressed ('). As a result, the dactyl within the measure is a bit more closed than would otherwise be the case (ex. 29, graph 4, level i). Though it is an accent, the B has some mobility—both because it is the same length as the notes that precede and follow it (it is not agogically defined) and because, since it occurs in the middle of a coherent and familiar pattern (the triad), its stability is weakened by continuation to an ongoing afterbeat. Consequently, there is, as we have

---

70. Note that the entrance of the horns is "prepared" by the bassoons (mm. 23–26), which not only establish the durational pattern (♩ | ♩ ♪) played by the horns but, because of similarity of tone color, are commonly associated with and act as substitutes for the horns in this period of music history.

71. For the sake of clarity and convenience, the violin and horn parts, though played together, are given in separate examples: the violins in ex. 29, the horns in ex. 30.

seen, a fleeting impression of amphibrach grouping (graph 4, upper bracket). Finally, if motive group 1 can be understood as a changing-note pattern (as suggested earlier), it is partly because the C (m. 29), like the B (m. 27), is relatively mobile (ex. 29, graph 5). For, though both are accented on the primary level (1), neither is strongly stressed or markedly stable relative to the primary-level weak beats, A and B, that follow. As a result, harmonic closure—the progression from dominant to tonic (mm. 29–30)—can influence structure, making the B in measure 30 a goal of modest, though temporary, stability.

Consider now how the relationships inherent in the violin patterns are strengthened, weakened, and even denied by what the horns play (ex. 30). The omission of the second beats in measures 27 and 29—that is, the D and the E—weakens the impression of foreground triadic motion (because

Example 29

Example 30

only the first two notes of the triad are presented)[72] and eliminates the sub-sidiary gap-fill process. As a result, foreground linear motion is considerably strengthened. It is not merely that competing processes are weakened or de-nied. The linear pattern itself becomes more palpable and more mobile. Not only is the motion from B to C (m. 27) and C to D (m. 29), implicit in the first violin part, spelled out (ex. 30, graph 3), but the third beats no longer have stability, however slight, as subsidiary melodic goals. Rhythmically, too, the third beats are less stable because a weak beat that follows a note of longer duration (horns: 𝅘𝅥 𝅘𝅥) is more mobile than one that follows notes of equal duration (violins: 𝅘𝅥 𝅘𝅥 𝅘𝅥).

---

72. Though a structural G is presented in the upper octave toward the close of the return (mm. 40–42), orchestral as well as melodic relationships indicate that this follows not from the rising triadic motion of the violins (mm. 26–27) but, as we have seen, from the descending lin-ear pattern of the flute (ex. 27, graph 1*a*).

The gap-fill pattern of the main motive is also strengthened. The elimination of the second beats of measures 27 and 29 makes the échappée function (E) of the third beats, which is only latent in the violin melody, manifest (ex. 30, graph 1). As a result, the fundamental structure of the motive—a gap-fill relationship ornamented by a nonchord tone—is more apparent (ex. 30, graphs 2*a* and 2*b*). Durational changes also serve to emphasize this relationship. For, when a short upbeat skips to a longer downbeat, as it does in the horn parts, conjunct fill is generally implied.[73]

Higher-level processes, too, are more emphatic as well as more mobile and goal-directed. The force of the main gap-fill patterns makes the relationship generated by their succession more patent (ex. 30, graph 4*a*). As a result, sequential continuation—probably to a longer phrase that begins with a skip from B to D—is more forcefully implied than it was in Part I. Rhythm also enhances mobility and strengthens goal-directed processes. It does so by weakening the closure of the motive group at measure 30. Let me explain. If the foreground trochees (♩ ♩) within measures 27 and 29 are to function as the accented parts of primary-level amphibrachs—♪ ♩ ♩|♩ —creating coherent motives, then downbeats must be slightly stressed.[74] If they are not so, then (given the durational pattern, ♩ ♩, and the absence of a subsidiary melodic goal such as that which closes the dactyls in the violins somewhat) the third beat of each measure will, despite Mozart's phrasing, probably be perceived as an anacrusis, producing a series of low-level iambs: ♩|♩ ♩|♩ . But, if the C in measure 29 is thus emphasized, then the B (m. 30) will seem relatively weak and mobile; as a result, it will be unable to function as a provisional goal.[75] To put the matter in another way, melodic and rhythmic mobility are so enhanced by what the horns play that the closure and stability provided by harmony (the cadence to the tonic in m. 30) are not sufficient—as they are in the first motive group of the Trio—to make the changing-note figure an audible alternative. Finally, it should be observed that the same emphasis that weakens the closure of the motive group, and in so doing masks

73. See Eugene Narmour, *The Analysis and Cognition of Basic Melodic Structures* (Chicago, 1990), chap. 12 and passim.

74. They will tend to be so both because phrasing calls for a new tonguing or attack on the downbeat and because the skip—particularly that played by the second horn—will probably cause the performer to make the first note of the measure just a bit louder. In addition, the relative length of the downbeat may make it "sound" louder.

75. Note, too, that since there is no subsidiary gap in m. 27, the B is deprived of whatever stability it might have had as a subordinate melodic goal (ex. 29, graph 2).

the changing-note figure, reinforces the impression of high-level conjunct patterning from B to C. And this pattern, which is embedded both in the foreground linear motion within measures 27 and 29 (ex. 30, graph 3) and in the sequential succession of motive *m*, implies continuation to D (ex. 30, graph 4*b*).

High-level rhythmic structure, too, is more emphatically mobile and goal-directed. In Part I, as we saw (pp. 70ff. and ex. 11), motives *m* and *m*[1] could be understood prospectively as a sequential succession implying continuation and retrospectively as a pair of complementary patterns provisionally closed by the stability of tonic harmony. In the latter case, the final B functioned as an accented goal. In the return, on the other hand, the force of the sequential succession is noticeably enhanced, while that of the complementary motive group is considerably diminished. The palpability of the sequential aspect of the patterning, together with the fact that the B in measure 30 is patently a mobile weak beat, calls attention to the similarity of the primary-level amphibrachs (ex. 30, level 1). Alternative ways of symbolizing the larger rhythmic structure are given in example 30. In the first, two levels are represented: the lower (2*a*) is analyzed as an open trochee, the higher (3) as a mobile anacrusis. In the second, only one level is represented: the first amphibrach on level 1 is symbolized as being understood initially as stable and accented and then, in retrospect, as mobile and weak. The second amphibrach is also anacrustic. But, no matter how the relationships are symbolized, continuation is implied—probably to a longer group that will serve as the accent in terms of which these similar groups can be patterned. The analysis indicates that such a group follows. But, as is the case with high-level melodic patterns, it does not do so immediately.

First, the proximate implications of the gap-fill processes are realized (ex. 31*B*, graphs 1*a* and 1*b*). Though this aspect of melodic patterning is essentially the same as in Part I (cf. exx. 31*A* and 31*B*, graphs 1*a* and 1*b*), the cadence is modified. The modifications, which can for the most part be attributed to subsequent changes in the return, affect the closure of the phrase, though not radically. Harmonically, the cadence (ex. 31*B*, mm. 31–32) is authentic (V[7]–I) but not complete. The decisive definition provided by subdominant harmony (ii⁶₅) in Part I is missing. So is the progression from the submediant (vi) through a series of harmonies whose roots are a fifth apart (ex. 31*A*, graph 2). Both changes are understandable in the light of what follows. Since no modulation occurs (as it did in Pt. I, mm. 10–14), the complete cadence in measures 37–38 is in the tonic. Had the earlier cadence (mm. 31–32) been complete, the articulative force of the later one would have been

Example 31

weaker by comparison. Similarly, had the progression moved through the submediant (vi), that harmony would be a bit less effective when it subsequently acts as the goal of the deceptive cadence (ex. 31*B,* m. 36).[76] In one respect, however, harmonic closure is more stable than it was in Part I; that is, the tonic chord on the first beat of measure 32 is in root position rather than in first inversion (ex. 31*A,* m. 6). This difference is related to the change in texture.

In the return, the texture of the first phrase (mm. 26–32) is wholly homophonic. The canon between the second violins and the celli (ex. 31*A,* graph 3), which led to the first-inversion triad on the downbeat of measure 6 (see pp. 68ff. above), is gone and with it the impetus of contrapuntal interaction and the mobility of harmonic inversion. A clear figure/ground relationship fosters stability and contributes to closure. Though probably a consequence of the harmonic considerations just described—it is difficult to say because the relation of texture to harmony is a chicken-and-egg affair—the change in texture can also be accounted for in terms of subsequent events. For, immediately following the cadence (m. 32), intensity increases as imitative entries occur at one-measure intervals (mm. 32–35) rather than following the length of the two-measure module prevalent elsewhere in the Trio. Had the cadential measures been contrapuntal, the ensuing intensification would have been less effective.

Rhythmic structure is significantly affected by these textural/harmonic changes. Because the suspension in the violas and the upbeats in the second violins and celli (ex. 31*A,* mm. 4–5) emphasize the downbeat of measure 5, the high-level rhythm of the cadence of the first phrase is an open amphibrach (see pp. 69ff. above). These are absent in Part II. As a result, the eighth notes at the end of measure 31 tend to be grouped with the accent that follows. The clearly end-accented accompaniment in the violas and celli (♪ ♩ ♩|♩), reinforcing this grouping, is the more emphatic because it "resolves" the ambiguity of the weak beats in the accompaniment figure of measures 28 and 30 (ex. 31*B,* graph 2). Are they afterbeats in a dactyl (♩ ♩ ♩) or upbeats in an anapest (♩ ♩ ♩|♩)? In short, despite the tendency of the strengthened amphibrach grouping of measures 26–30 to be continued as a way of patterning events, the rhythm of the cadence is more clearly end-accented—more closed—than was the analogous cadence in Part I.[77]

76. Because of the modulation in mm. 8–14, no anticipation occurs in Pt. I.

77. All symbolization, whether of harmonic, melodic, or rhythmic relationships, involves schematization and, hence, some degree of distortion. In this case, I fear, the symbolization of rhythmic relationships is even less adequate than usual.

On balance, changes in harmony, texture, and rhythm probably strengthen cadential closure. Paradoxically, melody, the parameter that seems least altered, is very influential. And it weakens the impression of closure. Because the middleground gap-fill patterns (ex. 31*B,* graphs 1*a* and 1*b*) are patent in the return, motion to G is clearly implied, and the realization of this goal enhances stability and closure. But the effect of realization is more than offset by the increased force of the sequential and linear processes discussed earlier (ex. 31*B,* graphs 3 and 4). These higher-level processes are important not only because of *what* they imply but because their realization affects the relationship between the first and the second phrases of the return, making them more cohesive than the comparable phrases in Part I.

Despite the connection created by foreground triadic motion in Part I (see pp. 73–76 above; also ex. 17, graphs 1*a* and 2), the phrase that follows the cadence in measure 6 is in important ways a new beginning. It is not merely that it is preceded by a complete cadence. Because the opening motive *(m)* is varied (motive *o*) *at the same pitch level* (ex. 31*A,* graph 4), the separation or discreteness of the phrases, rather than their continuity, is emphasized. The sense of a "fresh start" is, needless to say, reinforced by the striking change in orchestration—from strings to oboes.

In the return, on the other hand, what follows the cadence in measure 32 is understood more as a continuation than as a new beginning. Not only are implicative patterns begun or resumed in the transition realized after the cadence (ex. 27), but the sequential and linear processes regenerated at the start of the return are continued—and by the same instruments, the horns—immediately following the cadence (ex. 31*B,* graphs 3 and 4).[78] Though the continuation begins in a register lower than that of the generative process, octave transfer through the tonic triad ensures that the implicative relationships are perceptible. For the sequential continuation, B–D, occurs in both registers, and the motion to C (m. 34) makes it evident that the pattern is intact. Similarly, though the structural D (m. 33) is transformed into an appoggiatura when it reaches the upper register, the clarity of the octave transfer leaves no doubt that the high-level linear motion has been properly continued.

Though by no means as forceful as in the return (note the difference made by the horns!), both these continuations were potential in the first phrase of

---

78. This suggests another reason why the harmonic progression in mm. 31–32 is changed in the return; namely, a complete cadence would have weakened the impression of continuity between phrases. One other, minor, point: since it suggests that the second phrase may begin on G

the Trio.[79] Their delayed actualization, following regeneration, gives rise to the kind of satisfaction experienced when something only dimly discerned becomes clearly manifest.

Notice, too, that the foreground melodic/rhythmic patterns that were discrepant in motives *m* and *o* are now "in phase" (see pp. 74–75 above). That is, the first note of motive o^3 is now a mobile pitch (the third of the scale, B) as well as a mobile element in the rhythmic group. The equilibrium created by this congruence complements and enhances the sense of arrival created by the realization of melodic implications.

The continuation of high-level melodic processes calls attention to another, perhaps more debatable, relationship—one probably recognized largely in retrospect. Namely, the implication, or at least the possibility, that the subsidiary will become the primary. For, when the main gap-fill pattern continues sequentially, reaching B–D to C (mm. 32–34), what had been a low-level, subsidiary relationship in the violins (mm. 1 and 27) and eliminated from the horn part (m. 27) becomes part of the main gap-fill process (ex. 31*B*, graph 5*a*).[80] The parallelism is quite apparent. Just as the C (m. 1 or 27) implies and moves to the B (m. 4 or 30) after two measures of dominant harmony, so the C (m. 34) implies and moves to B (m. 36) after the intervention of dominant harmony. The transformation of a subsidiary process into a primary one is authenticated at the cadence (mm. 36–38) where the same gap-fill pattern begins the closing gesture (ex. 31, graph 5*b*).

Here a hypothesis suggested earlier (pp. 84–85) is compositionally confirmed. That is, that the opening motive *(m)* of the Trio and the closing gesture of the second phrase *(p)* are related by similarity.[81] But with this qualification: the closing gesture is directly related not to the main gap-fill pattern of motive m^2 but to the subsidiary one. The change in roles is symbolized in the cadence. There what had been subsidiary (the B–D to C gap fill)

<hr />

(see n. 21 above) rather than on B, creating sequential continuation, the canon in mm. 4–6 is also inappropriate in this cadence.

79. This analysis indicates that the continuation of the first violins to D in m. 14 (see p. 79 above) is only provisional—both because the D functions as the temporary tonic of D major rather than the fifth of G and because it does not follow from the sequential process. That is, though appropriate and hence satisfying, the D is in a sense the result of a happy coincidence: the violins simply "pick up" a note that really comes from a different processive relationship—the descending fill being played by the oboes.

80. In a sense, what was denied to the horns in the first phrase of the return is given to them in the second. Clearly it was denied not only for the reasons discussed earlier but because the horns could not have played the second subsidiary gap—the one from C to E (m. 29).

81. The relationship between motives *m* and *o* (see pp. 76–77) is "reconfirmed" by the sequential succession from m^2 to m^3 to o^3 (= m^4).

is the main melody played by the flute, and what had been primary (the G–B to A gap fill) is an accompaniment played by the oboe (ex. 31*B*, graph 3*b*).

Phrase 2ª (Mm. 32–38) and Codetta (Mm. 38–42)

The continuation of the main gap-fill process in the second phrase of the return, though unmistakable, is not exact. The size of the gap is increased and its structure modified by the appoggiatura figure in measure 34 (ex. 31*B*, graphs 1*a*–1*d*). As a result, the high-level processes (ex. 31*B*, graphs 3 and 4), which were derived from the succession of middleground gap-fill patterns, are ended—superseded by the extended fill that follows (ex. 27, graph 2*c*). As we have seen, the horns begin the larger gap an octave below the register in which the pattern was previously stated. Because of their range, this is un-avoidable if events in the return are to parallel (rhyme with) those in Part I. It is appropriate because the register reached after the octave transfer is the one required for proper process continuation. And it is desirable because the extension of the gap by an octave strengthens the implication of descending conjunct motion and, in so doing, makes further sequential and linear pat-terning improbable.

Continuation of these processes is doubtful for other reasons as well. (1) Because it is the fifth of the scale, the accented D (mm. 33 and 34) can easily function as both a termination point and a reversal point for the pre-ceding pattern.[82] (2) The possibility of termination and reversal of direction becomes a virtual certainty when, following octave transfer (m. 33), the D be-comes an appoggiatura implying resolution to C.[83] And (3) these local pat-terns only corroborate what is clear from the larger relationships within the Trio; that is, the parallelism between the return and Part I makes it almost cer-tain that an extended fill will follow the expanded gap of measures 32–34 as it did earlier in measures 6–12.

The parallelism continues as the bassoons and then the flute and oboe en-ter in modified imitation of the horns. But there are significant differences. The bassoons enter before the flute and first oboe (ex. 31*B*, mm. 33–35) rather than the other way around (ex. 31*A*, mm. 8–11), and imitation occurs

82. The fifth of the scale can be a terminal point because, since it belongs to both the dom-inant and the tonic triads, it is relatively stable and can function as a provisional goal. It often acts as a turning point in melodic patterns because continuing up beyond the fifth to the tonic (the next stable tone) requires special energy.

83. Moreover, insofar as motive o^3 is understood to be a sequential continuation of motives m^2 and m^3, it will probably be presumed to be the last event in the larger pattern. For sequences do not usually consist of more than three successive statements of a motive because a fourth tends to produce pairing—(2 + 2) + (2 + 2)—so that a higher-level duple pattern (4 + 4) is formed.

after only three, rather than six, beats. To explain these changes, relationships between sections as well as those within the return must be considered.

1. The entrances of the bassoons and then of the flute (together with the first oboe) are explicitly connected with the end of the transition, where these instruments stopped playing .(ex. 27). Though in a lower register, the bassoons begin their imitation with the same pitch and interval—an octave D—that they ended on in measure 26. After moving through the deceptive cadence (m. 36) and participating in the performance of the complete cadence (mm. 36–38), they reach satisfactory closure as they play the cadential figure with the first violins (mm. 38–40).[84]

It will be recalled that the flute is responsible for the continuation of two processes: the long-range descending fill begun in measure 10 (ex. 28A) and the subsidiary, rising conjunct motion generated in measures 19–23 (ex. 28B). The first note of its imitation, F♯, resumes the subsidiary process that, after an octave transfer, is completed by motion to the high G (ex. 31B, m. 36).[85] The second note of the imitation, the accented A, is part of the main process— the descending fill that was from the first defined by structural tones. And the same pitch (A) was last played by the same instruments (flute and first oboe) at the same interval (an octave) and in the same register where the main process "broke off"—that is, at the end of the transition.

Had the pattern played by the bassoons been given to the flute and oboe (with appropriate changes in register) and vice versa, these relationships would not have been preserved. Or, if the flute had entered a measure earlier (and the bassoons a measure later), the flute would have had to continue the high F♯ throughout measure 35. As a result, the G in measure 36 would have been less stable because, like the D in measure 12, it would have been unable fully to accommodate the momentum and tension of the long, leading-tone anacrusis. Put the other way around: the abbreviated anacrusis in the flute/oboe part reduces the mobility of the high G. It is perhaps partly for this reason that the G can be phrased with the following B instead of being "left hanging" as the D was.[86]

---

84. The bassoons' participation in the performance of the cadential figure in the return helps bind the codetta to the preceding phrases. In addition, it is appropriate—perhaps even necessary—because the "early" entrance of the bassoons' imitation entails a prolongation of goal-directed, dominant harmony (m. 35). And the increased momentum that results may not be adequately dissipated by the cadences in mm. 36 and 38.

85. Observe that, since it was generated on (notated) third beats, the subsidiary process is related to the F♯ at the end of m. 34 by metric placement as well as by the continuation of linear patterning.

86. The G is more stable than the D for other reasons as well (see below).

2. The stability of the deceptive cadence and hence of its resolution, G, is also enhanced by the change of distance between imitative entrances. This change can probably be attributed in part to the fact that no modulation occurs in the second phrase of the return. Only two chords, tonic and dominant, precede the deceptive cadence in measure 36. To compensate for the resulting loss of motion, previously created by modulation (ex. 31*A*, mm. 6–14), texture is intensified through a kind of "stretto." That is, though each motive (o^3, o^4, and o^5) is basically two measures long, imitation takes place after only one measure. The piling up of overlapping entrances creates the cumulative, goal-directed tension required.

The intensification of texture enhances not only goal-directed motion but, paradoxically, the stability and closure of both the deceptive and the complete cadences (mm. 36 and 38). This occurs because the change of distance between imitative entrances affects the morphology of motive group 2^a (mm. 32–36) as a whole. For, instead of being additive (6 + 6 + 6 beats) and relatively open, as was the equivalent passage in Part I (mm. 6–12), motive group 2^a is cumulative (3 + 3 + 6 beats) and somewhat closed. In rhythmic terms, the group is an end-accented anapest: ⌣ ⌣ —. The stability that results curbs the momentum developed in the preceding measures and thereby enables the closure created by other parameters to be more effective.

Harmonically, the cadences in Part II (mm. 36 and 38) are more stable than the equivalent cadences in Part I (mm. 12 and 14) because they are in the tonic.[87] Partly, stability is enhanced because textural intensity is "resolved" into congruent, homophonic motion. More important, stability and closure are strengthened because, as we have seen, melodic processes begun earlier are satisfactorily realized at these cadences. Let us review them briefly. In addition to the reasons already mentioned, the G in measure 36 is more stable than the comparable D in measure 12 because it is the goal of the subsidiary melodic process generated in measures 19–23 (ex. 28*B*). The D (m. 12), on the other hand, is a temporary deflection of the gap-fill pattern begun by the flute in measure 8 and resumed by it toward the end of the transition (ex. 28*A*). That pattern is continued and satisfactorily completed when the structural A (left in m. 26, picked up in m. 35, and renewed as an upbeat in m. 37) moves to G as part of a complete cadence.

Although the tonic is reached as part of a complete cadence, the Trio cannot end here. The formal parallelism—the rhyme—with the close of Part I is

---

87. Perhaps, too, the cadence in mm. 36–38 seems more closed because it is complete while the preceding cadence (mm. 31–32) is only authentic.

incomplete, and the four-measure length latent in the morphology of the first phrase of the return ([2 + 2] + 2) remains to be actualized.[88] Nor has the main melodic process begun by the oboes in measure 6 been satisfactorily closed (ex. 22, graphs 1*a*–1*c*). For, instead of moving directly through a structural A to G in measures 37–38, as they might have done (see below), the horns (the surrogates for the oboes) halt their conjunct descent at the deceptive cadence in measure 36. Because it is the structural tone with which the sequential motion of the return began, B is a plausible stopping place. That is, as example 32 (graph 1) shows, the structural tones of the sequence move from B (m. 27) through C (m. 29) to D (mm. 33–34) and conjunctly back to B (m. 36). On a high level, then, it might be argued that measures 27–36 are basically a prolongation of the third of the scale ornamented by double upper neighbor notes.[89] Though there is provisional closure on B, continuation is forcefully implied, both for reasons mentioned earlier— (1) the third of the scale is the most mobile note of the tonic triad; (2) once begun, the descending motion (D–C–B) implies continuation to a point of stability; (3) the B is harmonized by a submediant chord (vi) rather than the tonic (I)—and because at the end of the transition the main process had already moved beyond B to A.

The delay in the continuation of the horn pattern joins the final cadence of the Trio to the main gap-fill process and, in so doing, welds the codetta to earlier phrases.[90] It is interesting in this connection to note what Mozart does

88. See the discussion (pp. 71–73) of the comparable relationships in Pt. I.

89. Since the B in m. 27 is equivalent to that in m. 1, it might seem that all that follows the first structural B is a prolongation that moves at least through A to G. And this might in turn suggest to some that the analysis given here is derived from the theories of Heinrich Schenker. However, without in any way minimizing the debt owed to Schenker, there are fundamental differences between the implication/realization model employed in this essay and the *Ursatz* model developed by Schenker and his disciples. For the Schenkerites posit the existence of a single archetypal structure (the *Ursatz*) that is realized as a specific musical composition through a set of invariant transformations. The implication/realization model, on the other hand, is pluralistic with respect to style as well as structure. It assumes the progressive generation of alternative processes within different parameters. The realization of these alternative processes, often delayed through parametric noncongruence, need not be simultaneous. In the analysis presented in this essay, e.g., implications generated by the oboes in mm. 6–8 are ultimately realized by the French horns at the close of the codetta; subsidiary processes generated by the flute and oboes in the transition are completed by the flute in m. 36 and by the oboes in mm. 41–42. The listener's confidence in his own competence does not depend upon his comprehension of a single "deep structure." Rather, it receives periodic support from the provisional or full realization over time of a number of alternative patterns.

90. As noted earlier, the oboes complete their subsidiary pattern here (see p. 106). Since the close of the flute's primary pattern is reiterated in mm. 41–42, three alternative processes converge and are realized in the final cadence of the Trio.

not do. The horns could have joined in the performance of the complete cadence (mm. 36–38), as part *2a* of example 32 shows. But this anticipation not only would have detracted from the importance of the final cadence but would have weakened the bonding of the codetta to what precedes it. The horns might also have performed the closing figure in measures 41–42, as

Example 32

they did in measures 31–32 (ex. 32, graph 2*b*). But then the relationship between what the horns play at the final cadence and what they played earlier would not have been as clear. For the repeated cadential figure (ex. 32, graph 2*b*) would have been related to the earlier one (mm. 31–32) rather than to the descending fill that the horns continue and close.

The codetta of the return is more closely linked to preceding phrases than was that of Part I in other ways as well. By continuing beyond the cadence in measure 38, the bassoon, as we have seen, creates a structural and timbral coherence. The flute's participation in the final statement of the closing figure reiterates its descent from A to G and thereby reinforces the closure of the process it began in measure 8. As in Part I, there is an elision between the end of phrase 2 and the beginning of the codetta. The violins begin the closing figure at the same time that the upper woodwinds reach cadential resolution. But, whereas in Part I the violins played the D implied by the sequential process of the first four measures, they need not do so in the return because the D is realized by the horns at the beginning of the second phrase. The register in which the violins play indicates that the G reached in measure 32 is their ultimate goal. In the codetta, they serve to prolong the closing figure until the morphological length implied by the first phrase of the return is reached and, at the same time, act as a common term connecting the bassoon's performance of the closing figure with that of the flute.

*

Mozart's Trio consists, then, of a rich network of distinguishable, but interconnected, relationships: conformant, implicative, and hierarchic. Like the personae in a novel or a history, conformance—motivic, textural, or harmonic similarity—fosters coherence and provides the constancy in terms of which change can be comprehended. And, as in carefully constructed narrative, each of the alternative, yet complementary, processive strands is ultimately resolved and reaches satisfactory closure. The musical structure of the whole, however, is more formal and more patently hierarchic than is generally the case with most verbal narratives. This is so because, since music is not explicitly representational, pattern repetition and return are indispensable if tones are to form separable parts and parts are to combine into intelligible wholes.

Thus far nothing has been said about the emotional response elicited by these relationships. Nor has the ethos—the feeling tone or character—of the music been considered. These have received short shrift not because they are unimportant but because it is both difficult to describe and problematic to explain the affective experiences evoked by works of art. The difficulties, and perhaps the problems as well, are compounded when, as in the case of music, the personae and processive "plots" are without semantic content and, hence, nonrepresentational. For we tend not only to classify and describe but even to recognize and comprehend affective experiences in terms of the external circumstances in which they take place and that are thought to occasion them.

The problems are not, however, due solely to the inadequacies of language or to the absence of representation. They also stem from the uncertainties and confusions that continue to plague our understanding of affective experience—whether elicited by works of art or by events in "real" life. For present purposes, two different sorts of experience, often included under the general term *affective,* must be distinguished. The first, *emotional response,* which changes over time, is a direct result of (and consequently congruent with) cognitive activity. It involves intricate patternings of anticipation and tension, delay and denial, fulfillment and release. If we assume that cognition of the conformant, processive, and hierarchic relationships peculiar to a work of art evokes and shapes this facet of affective experience, then the analysis presented in this essay of implication and mobility, deflection and parametric noncongruence, closure and realization is analogically—or by extrapolation—an account of what a competent listener's emotional response to Mozart's Trio would be like.

Ethos refers to those aspects of affective experience that remain relatively constant over time and that are the basis for the characterization of all or part of a composition.[91] Mozart's Trio, for instance, has been characterized as a "moment of sunshine . . . calm, reposeful, pellucid, truly idyllic . . . charming . . . pure and calm . . . so Elysian a grace. . . ."[92] Clearly, the ethos that Saint-Foix describes is delineated by the absence of extremes (or abrupt contrasts) of tempo and register, dynamics and sonority, together with the use of simple, even commonplace, grammatical/syntactic means—melodies made up of easily grasped intervals, flowing rhythms without marked durational differ-

---

91. Broadly speaking, ethos is delineated both by the disposition of relatively stable parameters such as tempo and register, dynamic level and mode, and by foreground grammatical/syntactic organization (e.g., kinds of intervals, rhythmic figures, harmonies, and chord progressions). Particularly when these combine to form a conventional iconic gesture—as they do, e.g., at the beginning of Chopin's famous funeral march—poignant feelings may be evoked, even though process and form have yet to shape emotional responses.

92. G. de Saint-Foix, *The Symphonies of Mozart* (London, 1947), 119–20. Other writers consulted used the same or similar terms to describe the Trio.

ences, regular meter (with a touch of ambiguity at times), and common triads and chord progressions.

But affective experience is not, as these distinctions seem to suggest, really divided. Ethos and emotion invariably qualify one another. As a result, the foreground simplicity of Mozart's Trio is tinged with the tensions of relational richness. Patent goal-directed processes prevent "calm" from being complacence and "repose" from being indolence; delay and deflection qualify "grace" and "charm" so that the former is not merely facile and the latter not merely perfunctory. Throughout, relational richness keeps the "pellucid" from being obvious, the "idyllic" from seeming fatuous.[93]

The delineation of ethos is also a matter of context. The serenity, grace, and simplicity of the Trio are especially apparent because they are in marked contrast to the dynamism, irregularity, and complexity of the Minuetto that precedes and follows. The Minuetto is in the minor mode, the Trio in the major; the Minuetto's dynamics are generally *forte,* those of the Trio *piano;* the rhythm of the Minuetto is vigorous and syncopated, that of the Trio smooth and flowing; the Minuetto is largely contrapuntal, the Trio homophonic— and one could continue listing differences.

But there are similarities as well. The main motive of the Minuetto (ex. 33, motive *r*), like that of the Trio (motive *m*), consists of a triad that begins on an upbeat (ex. 33, graphs 1*a*–1*c*); and, as in the Trio, part of the triad functions as a gap that is subsequently filled (ex. 33, graphs 2*a*–2*d*).[94] In both, motives move sequentially.[95] The most patent similarity is between the second statement of the Minuetto motive (r^1) and the first statement of the Trio motive (*m*); except for the difference in mode, the pitch patterns are almost identical (ex. 33, graph 4). Because the last six measures of the Minuetto are based upon the first six, a slightly varied version of motive r^1 is followed directly by its counterpart in the Trio (ex. 34, graph 1). The relationship is made particularly clear because the coda of the Minuetto "prepares" the listener for the Trio through changes in dynamics, orchestration, texture, and

93. In general, if ethos is to "ring true," it must be justified by the larger syntactic structure. "Empty bombast" is emphatic insistence without relational support.

94. Observe that the gap of Minuetto motive r^1 (ex. 33, graph 2*b*) is equivalent to the subsidiary gap of Trio motive *m* (graph 2*d*). This subsidiary gap, it will be recalled, becomes the primary gap in phrase 2ª of the return (ex. 31, graph 5*a*), and this, in a sense, "prepares" for the repetition of the Minuetto.

95. But the Minuetto motive moves up disjunctly, by thirds, while the Trio motive moves up conjunctly (ex. 33, graphs 3*a* and 3*b*). Despite this difference, both patterns imply continuation to a D (in parentheses). This is so because the succession of structural tones is different; i.e., G–B♭–D in the Minuetto and B–C–D in the Trio.

Example 33

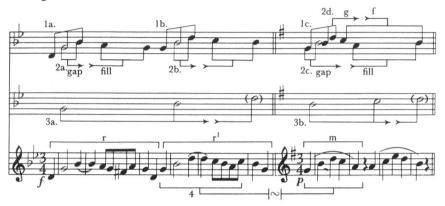

Example 34

sonority. Even the transformation of the second part of motive r^1 into a cadential gesture finds its parallel in the closing figure of the first phrase of the Trio (ex. 34, graph 2).[96] The juxtaposition of like motives emphasizes contrasts in the disposition and organization of those parameters most responsible for the delineation of ethos.[97] As a result, the ethos of the Trio is specified by its similarities to, as well as its differences from, the Minuetto.[98]

96. Because the Trio ends with the first closing figure played by the flute, there is a "rhyme" with the coda of the Minuetto. There are other reminiscences of the Minuetto in the Trio. For instance, the syncopated fourth played by the viola in mm. 4–5 of the Trio seems to recall the main motive of the Minuetto (ex. 34, graph 3).

97. Although changes at its close prepare us for what is to follow, the coda of the Minuetto remains, as it were, within the hegemony of the ethos of the Minuetto, as the presence of chromatic counterpoint and harmony indicate.

98. This suggests that motivic variation and transformation are important not primarily because they "unify" compositions but because motivic constancy makes differences in ethos more palpable. If this is correct, then it is not surprising that motivic development is especially characteristic of styles, such as those of the Baroque and Romantic periods, that stress the importance of ethos.

*

I am aware that there will be disagreements not only about particular points made in the preceding analysis but about fundamental premises. Alternative hypotheses are certainly possible, and these will undoubtedly call attention to and illuminate relationships I have failed to notice or have unwittingly neglected. Some differences will be matters of emphasis. For instance, it might be urged with some justice that matters of stylistic context should have played a more important role in my explanation of the relationships in Mozart's Trio. But, whatever the basis for disagreement, what seems crucial is that premises be made explicit and arguments from them consistent. This I have tried to do.

Others will find the whole enterprise repugnant—feeling that a tedious dissection has destroyed a fragile flower of the human spirit. Though no reply will allay such reservations, I have taken the liberty of quoting a paragraph from the preface to *Explaining Music*. It seems appropriate to do so since, as noted earlier, the present essay is in part an attempt to show that concepts and methods developed in that book can account with some rigor for the ways in which musical relationships are understood by, and shape the experience of, competent listeners:

> The relationships among events within musical compositions—even seemingly simple ones—are frequently surprisingly complex and subtle. The analyses explaining them are, accordingly, often complicated and involved. I have not sought to simplify the difficult, or to gloss over intricate interactions with plausible generalities and vague poetic appeals. Rather I have tried to make my analyses as precise and specific as my abilities and the subject allow. And while I take no particular pleasure in long and sometimes difficult discussion, I know of no other way of doing justice to the wonder of music and the miracle of human intelligence which makes and comprehends it.[99]

99. Meyer, *Explaining Music*, x.

3

Process and Morphology
in the Music of Mozart

1

In earlier studies I have suggested that once a patterned process is begun it tends to be continued to a point of relative stability.[1] As a result, patterned processes imply more or less specific modes of continuation and more or less probable points of closure or realization. In tonal music there are innumerable instances of such implicative processes: for example, triadic and changing-note melodies, bar forms and antecedent-consequent periods, harmonic sequences through the circle of fifths, fourth-species counterpoint relationships, anapest rhythmic groups, and so on.

The realization of an implicative process may be either proximate or remote. Even seemingly simple melodies usually generate a number of alternative processes.[2] Some of these alternatives will achieve relative stability before, or more often *at,* the point of closure. Realization is proximate. Other implicative processes will transcend closure: that is, they will be temporarily "suspended" and then resumed, reaching a point of relative stability after other alternative patterns have reached closure or after novel patterns (with their own implicative processes) have intervened. In such cases, realization is remote. Finally, there are cases in which realization does not occur at all.

I have also suggested that process must be distinguished from formal organization. These aspects of patterning are more or less independent of one another and may, at times, be noncongruent. For instance, the articulation of a formal structure—of a morphological length—may occur before a process has reached completion. This is typically the case with elisions. Or a process

Reprinted from the *Journal of Musicology* 1, no. 1 (1982): 67–94, by permission. Copyright © 1982 Imperial Printing Co., Inc.

I am grateful to Eugene Narmour, John Platoff, Leonard Ratner, and Eugene Wolf, who read this essay and made valuable comments, criticisms, and suggestions.

1. See Leonard B. Meyer, *Emotion and Meaning in Music* (Chicago, 1956), chap. 3, and *Explaining Music: Essays and Explorations* (Berkeley, Calif., 1973), pt. 2.

2. This point and others mentioned in the paragraph were in effect illustrated in the preceding essay.

may reach relative closure *before* an established morphological length is complete. "Echos" often serve to complete morphological lengths after processive closure has taken place.

In this essay I want to explore a hypothesis about a possible relationship between process and morphology with particular reference to the later music of Mozart. The hypothesis is this: in Mozart's later music there appear to be a significant number of cases in which the morphological length of an event (usually a transitional passage from first to second key area or from development to recapitulation) is coordinate with—and perhaps even defined by—the closural point that *would have been reached* had an implicative process, terminated earlier, been regularly continued. Stated differently: when a powerful process—for example, fourth-species (suspension) counterpoint, a circle-of-fifths progression, or a combination of these—is interrupted, modified, or replaced,[3] the morphological length of the passage between the termination of the process and either its subsequent resumption or the arrival at tonic stability (either the temporary tonic of the second key area or the main tonic, which marks the beginning of a recapitulation) is not infrequently identical with what it would have been had the original process been continued in a regular way.

The hypothesis being considered grew out of the analytic method of "normalization" developed in *Explaining Music*.[4] The method is simply that of discovering the processive relationship that underlies a musical pattern and then extrapolating and reconstructing what would have been its regular continuation to see what might have followed. Before turning to Mozart's music, let me illustrate this method (and the proposed hypothesis as well) with a few brief examples from the music of Bach and Handel.

In the B-Major Prelude (no. 23) from Book I of the *Well-Tempered Clavier (WTC)*,[5] a clear instance of fourth-species counterpoint (between soprano and bass), coupled with a circle-of-fifths progression, is begun in measure 3 (ex. 1, graph A). This "primary" process is complemented by a subsidiary, chromatic fourth-species progression (between the alto and the implied tenor; see graph B). Had the process continued in a regular way—as shown

3. These kinds of pattern breaks must be distinguished from one another. As we shall see, a process may be temporarily interrupted, or briefly modified (e.g., to avoid awkward tonal succession), and then resumed. Or a pattern-process may be replaced or superseded by a different process or series of processes, which may include a high-level elaboration of dominant harmony.

4. For references and examples, see the index of Meyer, *Explaining Music*.

5. All the examples from Bach's music, whether quoted or cited, are from Bk. I of the *Well-Tempered Clavier*.

Example 1 Bach, *WTC* I, Prelude no. 23

in the bracketed normalization, N[　]—it would have led to precisely the same cadential closure as that called for in the score. In this example the process is modified—perhaps to avoid the tritone (*), E to A♯; and it may be that the process can be resumed (as it is in m. 5) precisely because no alternative patterning is established.[6]

Sometimes, however, an established process is not merely modified but replaced by a significantly different mode of patterning or progression. In such cases processes are broken and superseded because of the need for what I have called "reversal."[7] Let me explain. Because powerful processes imply continuation, they cannot merely stop; they must be closed. For instance, had the fourth-species counterpoint plus circle-of-fifths process, begun in measures 19–22 of Bach's Prelude in G♯ Minor (ex. 2), been continued in a regular way (see analysis N[　]), the tonic would have been reached in measure 29— precisely where it does in fact come.[8] But closure would have been adventitious and unsatisfactory. To be convincing, closural articulation must be *composed:* that is, the kinetic energy of the ongoing process that leads to the cadence must be reversed and stabilized—usually through either dominant or tonic prolongation. In this prelude, the descending motion begun in measures 19– 22 (C♯–B–A♯–G♯, bass), and intensified in measures 23–24 (E–D♯–C♯–B–

6. For another comparable example, see Handel, Concerto Grosso in A Minor, op. 6, no. 4, second movement, mm. 76–81.

7. See Meyer, *Explaining Music,* p. 199 and passim.

8. Observe that in this case Bach does not avoid the tritone, E–A♯ (mm. 20–21)—perhaps because, unlike the case in ex. 1, the leap is to a consonance rather than to a dissonance.

Example 2 Bach, *WTC* I, Prelude no. 18

A–G♯), is reversed in measures 25–26 (F♯♯ *up* to B); and this reversal is followed by a cadential progression (ii^6–V$^6_4$$^{-5}_{-3}$) that leads to a tonic pedal.[9]

Besides making strong closure possible, changes in patterning perform a further function in passages such as this. For, had the process continued as "normalized" in the analysis, the circle of fifths would have begun to repeat just at the point where the change occurs. And such a continuation would have created considerable redundancy since the circle of fifths would have been repeated twice. In short, the need for variety is probably a sufficient cause for a change in process.[10]

Not infrequently contrapuntal processes are implicit rather than explicit. This is so in the Allemande from Handel's Suite no. 3 in D Minor for Harp-

9. The need for reversal may in part explain the process break in ex. 1 as well. However, since the cadence in ex. 1 occurs near the beginning of the piece rather than at its close, the reversal is minimal. It deflects the motion, and this enhances articulation; but the reversal does not destroy the sense of forward motion.

10. It is *not*, however, a necessary condition because processes can change for other reasons. Nor does the need for variety explain why the composer chose the particular kind of change he did. Since such explanations are essentially the province of the critical analysis of individual compositions, they will not be considered in this essay.

Example 3 Handel, Suite no. 3 for Harpsichord, Allemande

sichord (ex. 3). As shown in the analysis, the soprano F, on the third beat of measure 12, is implicitly continued through the first beats of measure 13 (it occurs on the second beat, but initially in the "wrong" octave), where it forms an implied seventh with the bass. This "dissonance" is resolved on the third beat of measure 13. If the harmonic (circle-of-fifths)-contrapuntal process is continued, as shown in the analysis, the suspension counterpoint reaches the same basic configuration as the music does at the beginning of measure 17—where the implicit suspension procedure is made explicit.

A central question for this essay is that of morphological length. Why, for instance, doesn't the G♯-Minor Prelude (ex. 2) end in measure 27 or 28? Or why isn't it extended for still another measure? No patent morphological module such as 4 + 4 + 4 seems to make closure in measure 29 especially compelling. What I am suggesting is that the length of the passage is at least partly a function of the closural point established by the process previously generated in measures 19–22.[11] And this, I will argue, is also the case in a number of passages from Mozart's music.

---

11. For another example, see Prelude no. 16 in G Minor. The fourth-species counterpoint, between soprano and alto, begins in m. 9 and is modified in m. 11. Had the process been regu-

Example 4 Modes of closure

Before turning to the music of Mozart, however, some remarks about methodology are in order. For the most part, the analyses under the music should speak for themselves. As in the examples already presented, the analyses are graphs of the essential musical process, and normalizations are marked by "N[   ]." Three points need to be made about the normalizations. (1) Once a process is broken and the graphed normalization diverges from what the composer actually wrote, I have simply continued the established process in a regular—indeed, mechanical—way, observing basic durational relationships as well as ones of pitch. In such extrapolations no tones have been added or omitted: that is, no critical judgments have been invoked to make the analyses conform to the hypothesis. (2) All processes have been treated as being basically diatonic, unless chromaticism is inescapably continuous. Thus, in a circle-of-fifths progression, the tritone is normally maintained in order for the process to stay within the established tonal realm. Chromatic progressions such as the one that occurs between the alto and the tenor in example 1 (graph B) are problematic. Entirely regular continuation leads to a whole-tone patterning (see ex. 4*d*, flatted notes in parentheses), while a diatonic continuation requires judgment about where to alter the process. Because its chromaticism is inescapably defined (and reinforced by a succession of applied dominants), one of the examples used in this essay has been normalized as a fully chromatic progression (see ex. 18 below). (3) I have allowed alternative versions of fourth-species counterpoint and circle-of-fifths progressions to serve as viable modes of closure and legitimate measures of morphological length. The possibilities, all latent in example 1 (but here transposed into the key of C), are given in example 4.

---

larly continued—but with a chromatic alteration to F♯ so that the cadential formula is similar to that in ex. 1:

$$\underline{\text{m. 18}} \qquad \underline{\text{m. 19}}$$
$$B^{\flat} — \underset{\smile}{A\,A} — G \mid G — F^{\sharp} — G$$
$$C — — — B^{\flat} — — \mid A — — — G$$

—then G would have been reached on the third quarter note of m. 19, as it is in the score.

For convenience the coincidence of process and morphology I am describing will be called *coordination,* the harmonic and contrapuntal relationships resulting in such coordination will be referred to as the *continuity-process,* and events within a constructed normalization will be termed *hypothetical.* To preclude misunderstanding, it should be recognized that coordination is not a necessary relationship but one that occurs only in some of Mozart's music. It seems to be a strategy that he employs occasionally [12]—though, as I will argue later, it occurs more often than can be explained by mere chance. It should also be emphasized that I have not looked for examples of coordination in all of Mozart's works, but only in his instrumental music; and, even within this repertory, the search was largely confined to transitions from first to second key areas and from developments to recapitulations in sonata-form movements. Though my investigation was neither systematic nor exhaustive—I looked at the symphonies, chamber music, piano sonatas and concertos, and some of the divertimentos and serenades—the sample is, I think, reasonably representative. However, since the sample is far from complete, the hypothesis being proposed cannot be said to have been satisfactorily confirmed.

2

The earliest of Mozart's works in which I have found coordination is the first movement of the Serenade in C Minor, K. 388. The work was written toward the end of 1782, during the period of his intimate contact with van Swieten's circle—about which more later.[13] The continuity-process, which begins in measure 115, is characterized by root motion through the circle of fifths—clearly spelled out in the bassoons (ex. 5).[14] The circle of fifths is combined with fourth-species counterpoint in the oboes. This continuity-process is broken in measure 122—just where it would have begun to

12. For a discussion of the nature of compositional strategies, see Meyer, *Style and Music: Theory, History, and Ideology* (Philadelphia, 1989), 20–23.

13. In the course of writing a "Commentary" (*Music Perception* 13, no. 3 [Spring 1996]: 481–82) on a number of papers about Mozart's Sonata for Piano, K. 282, I found an earlier (1774) instance of coordination. This calls into question the conjecture (proposed near the end of this essay) that Mozart's use of the strategy of coordination was connected with an increased familiarity with the music of Bach and Handel. Instead, he may have become acquainted with coordination through his earlier performance of Baroque music. In addition, coordination may perhaps have been a useful strategy in improvisation—of which Mozart was a master.

14. Only the voices essential to the definition of the process (first the oboes and bassoons, then the clarinets and horns as well) are given in the example. The G in the bass in m. 115 (in the analysis) is taken from the horn part.

Example 5 Mozart, Serenade in C Minor, K. 388, i

repeat. If the process is continued, then, as shown in the analysis (following N[   ]), the tonic triad occurs just as it does in the music. There is one slight modification: namely, the fourth-species pattern is not continued into measure 130. However, though fourth-species counterpoint intensifies the action, the main process consists of descending tenths every second measure beginning with measure 116.

It is worth noting that without the rest in measure 129 there would have been no coordination: that is, the recapitulation would have been coordinate with the hypothetical dominant. It is true, of course, that the rest also serves to complete the four-measure morphological length begun in measure 126. But this does not gainsay the fact that it also makes coordination possible. The problem is one that plagues the analysis of most temporal events—that is, that they are generally overdetermined. There are too many antecedents that can imply or can account for some consequent event.

Furthermore there are cases of coordination that cannot easily be explained on grounds of stylistically normal morphological lengths. For instance, the implied fourth-species process begun in measure 7 of the Fantasy

Example 6 Fantasy for Piano in D Minor, K. 397, mm. 6–11

$(V_4^{6(\natural)}/V \cdot V)$

$(IV_5^{6(\natural)} - V)$

for Piano in D Minor, K. 397, ends in the middle of measure 8 (ex. 6). Had the process been continued, as shown in the analysis (N[   ]), it would have reached the concluding low A in measure 11 on the same beat and in the same register as prescribed in the score. But what morphological lengths establish this as a point of closure? The fourth-species pattern moves by half measures, so that termination on beats 1 or 3 of any measure would have constituted possible points of closure. The phrase structure of the first six measures suggests four-measure (2 + 2) or six-measure lengths, in which case the low A comes in the midst of a morphological length.[15] Only if morphological lengths are counted in twos (on the lowest level) does the low A in measure 11 mark the beginning of a metric unit.

Nor can morphology alone account for the length of another passage from the D-Minor Fantasy (ex. 7).[16] The continuity-process begun in measure 18 consists of a chromatically descending melodic line that, combined with a circle-of-fifths motion in the bass, creates a veiled fourth-species counterpoint.[17] The process is suspended (not reversed or terminated) by the domi-

15. This may in part explain the fermata in m. 11; i.e., the fermata may not only facilitate the change of tempo (from Andante to Adagio) but indicate that the beginning of the Adagio should be congruent with what would have been m. 13 of the Andante, had it continued.

16. This example was called to my attention by Erica Ellenberger, a student in an analysis class at the University of Pennsylvania.

17. A slight temporal adjustment is made in the analysis. In Mozart's score, the chromatic soprano line and its harmonization occur on different eighth notes, but they are joined together in the analysis. Since it conforms to a familiar contrapuntal paradigm (see ex. 4*d*), this adjustment seems entirely legitimate.

Example 7 Fantasy for Piano in D Minor, K. 397, mm. 17–22

nant prolongation in measure 19. Then, on the last beat of measure 20, the chromatic descent is resumed and repeated in the bass. From the point of view of prevalent or normal morphological lengths there seems no special reason for the duration either of dominant harmony or of the repeated E's in measure 20.[18] But, as the analysis shows, if the chromaticism is exactly continued, the repeated chromatic descent occurs precisely as stipulated in the score. However, because Mozart's use of the G♯ in measure 18 (breaking the circle-of-fifths pattern) leaves the harmonic continuation in doubt, no normalization is given for the bass line.

Not all regular sequences involve fourth-species counterpoint or a progression through the circle of fifths. In the Piano Concerto in D Minor, K. 466, the continuity-process, which begins in measure 230 (ex. 8), modulates according to the following scheme:

⌊230–31⌋ ⌊232–33⌋ ⌊234–35⌋ ⌊236–37⌋ ⌊238–39⌋   ⌊240–41⌋ ⌊242 – – – – – – – 253⌋ ⌊254⌋
E♭ : I – – – V⁷/ii – – -ii
              f : i – – – V⁷/ii – – -ii
                         g : i – – – – – -V⁷/ii – – -[II^{♯3}]
                                         d : V (prolonged) – –i (recapitulation)

Once it is reached (as II^{♯3} of G minor), the dominant of D minor is prolonged for twelve measures (3 × 4). This morphological length is coordinate with the

---

18. Indeed, if one counts two-measure lengths from the beginning of the Adagio, then m. 18 comes as the beginning of a module, while m. 21, which is comparably patterned, comes as the end of a module.

Example 8 Piano Concerto in D Minor, K. 446, i

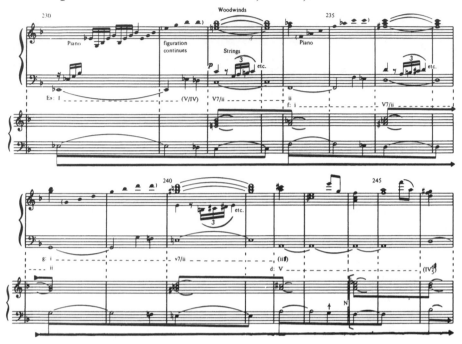

hypothetical continuation of the process. For, had the process been regular, D-minor harmony would have been reached at measure 254, which marks the beginning of the recapitulation.[19]

The dominant pedal at the end of the development section of the Piano Concerto in C Minor, K. 491, is preceded by a continuity-process that, though harmonically complex, is contrapuntally simple (ex. 9). The

---

19. Although it involves neither fourth-species counterpoint nor a circle-of-fifths progression, this process, too, is part of the large repertory of such patterns indigenous to eighteenth-century music. For a comparable example, see Leclair's Sonata 6 (Book 1), Allegro ma poco (mm. 19–22), quoted in F. T. Arnold, *The Art of Accompaniment from a Thorough Bass* (reprint, New York, 1965), 1:359. The patterning of Classic music is clearly augmented: what Leclair does in one measure lasts for four measures in Mozart's music.

It should be pointed out that the twelve-measure dominant prolongation (mm. 242–53) is the same length as the modulatory sequence that leads to it. This morphological parallelism may also contribute to our sense of the propriety of the timing of the recapitulation.

For reasons of economy, only the essential voices are given in ex. 8.

Example 8 *(continued)*

Example 9 Piano Concerto in C Minor, K. 491

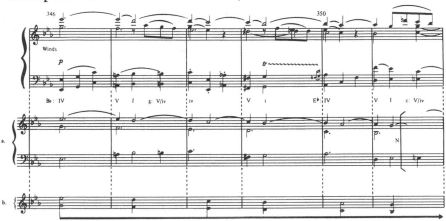

(continued on page 138)

Example 9 *(continued)*

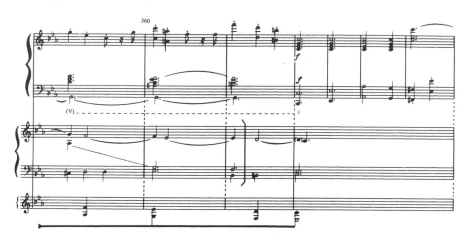

harmonic centers descend by thirds (B♭–g–E♭–c) and lead to a dominant prolongation beginning in measure 354. Though intensified by suspension counterpoint in the woodwinds, the essential melodic motion consists of descending parallel sixths, as shown in analytic graph b.[20] The normalization of the contrapuntal and harmonic processes leads to coordination at the beginning of the recapitulation (m. 362). What is strikingly clear in this example is that patterns may exhibit modes of organization on different hierarchic levels (ex. 10). On the foreground (bar) level, the organization is linear (E♭–D–C etc.); on the two-bar level, it is triadic (E♭–C–A♭ etc.); on the four-bar level, there is motion through a circle of fifths (E♭–A♭–D etc.); and, on the highest (eight-bar) level, the pattern is once again linear (E♭–D–C).[21]

The pattern analyzed in example 10 is complemented by an equally

20. In this example the wind parts, not the piano figuration, are given. In general, Mozart tends to use the woodwinds to represent contrapuntal processes in their most pristine form. As in the D-Minor Concerto, the length of the dominant prolongation (eight measures, 354–61) is the same as that of the preceding modulatory passage (mm. 346–53).

21. For another example of coordination in one of the concertos, see the first movement of the Piano Concerto in C Major, K. 503—from m. 276, where the continuity-process begins, through m. 290, where the recapitulation starts.

Example 10 Hierarchic levels of organization

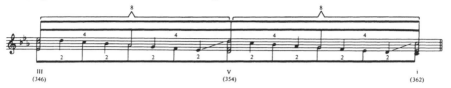

striking, long-range process—a circle-of-fifths progression begun in measure 330. The progression moves as follows:

harmony: $\lfloor V_5^6/c$ (m. 330)$\rfloor - \lfloor V_5^6/f$ (m. 334)$\rfloor - \lfloor V_5^6/b^\flat$(m. 338)$\rfloor - \lfloor V_5^6/e^\flat$(m. 342) $-\rfloor$

roots: G   C   F   B♭

Actual harmony: *mm. 346–61 = the progression given in ex. 9*

normalized
harmony: $\lfloor V_5^6/a^\flat$(m. 346)$\rfloor - \lfloor V_5^6/?$ (m. 350)$\rfloor - \lfloor V_5^6/g$ (m. 354)$\rfloor - \lfloor V_5^6/c$ (m. 358)$\rfloor \rfloor - \lfloor c$ minor (m. 362)$\rfloor$

roots: E♭   A♭   D   G   C

Notice that the close of the hypothetical progression (mm. 358ff.) is the same as the beginning of the circle-of-fifths process (m. 330). From this point of view, the whole passage can be regarded as a prolongation of the dominant of C minor. The coordination of this long-range harmonic progression with the contrapuntal process begun at measure 346 (ex. 9) would seem to make the arrival at the tonic in measure 362 especially compelling and memorable—the kind of experience so often characterized as seeming "inevitable."[22]

The relationship of process to morphological length may help explain a change that Mozart made in the final version of the first movement of the *Prague* Symphony, K. 504. As the sketches for the bridge passage connecting the first and second key areas in the exposition show (ex. 11, pt. 1),[23] Mozart added a measure (m. 70 in the finished score) by prolonging the cadential A (ex. 11, pt. 2). This addition might be explained on morphological grounds. From measure 63 on, the morphological units are three measures, and the added measure, functioning as both the close of a unit and the

22. This long-range process was called to my attention by John Platoff.
23. Mozart, *Neue Ausgabe sämtlicher Werke,* ser. 4, vol. 8 (Kassel, 1965), 123. I am grateful to Janet M. Levy for calling these sketches to my attention.

Example 11 Symphony no. 38 in D Major, *Prague*, K. 504, i

beginning of a new phrase, make it possible to interpret measures 69–71 as a three-measure group. But morphology is equivocal in this movement, and, as a result, it is not entirely clear how lengths should be counted. What is not equivocal, however, is the relationship of process to morphology. For, if the descent begun in measures 66–68 (linear in the soprano and by thirds in the bass) is continued, as shown in part 3 of example 11, the dominant occurs at the beginning of the new phrase—instead of in its midst, which would have been the case had the morphological length been shorter, as called for in the sketch.

The last movement of the *Prague* Symphony presents particularly inter-

Example 12 *Prague* Symphony, K. 504, iii

esting problems having to do with the relationship of process to morphology. From the very beginning of the movement (ex. 12), there is a question about how morphological lengths should be reckoned. Harmonically, the units begin with the first beat of the first measure, and the repetition of the pattern (a step higher) begins on the first beat of measure 9. Melodically, however, measure 1 consists of pickups to the structural A in measure 2, and the first phrase closes at the beginning of the fifth measure. In addition, the imitative entrance in the second violins and violas suggests that a harmonic unit, comparable to that begun in the first measure, accompanies the main melody. Nor does the extension that follows measure 5 clarify these ambiguities. For its essentially additive structure can support either of the morphological patterns thus far established. In effect, then, the first theme of the movement is characterized by overlapping, but equivalent, morphological lengths.

This has consequences in the development section (ex. 13). In it, appropriately, two distinguishable, though motivically similar, continuity-processes are generated. The first (labeled I in the analysis) begins in measure 152. It consists of an ascending motion in the bass, rising conjunctly every eight measures: C♯ (m. 152), D (m. 160), E (m. 168). The process breaks after measure 175 but is temporarily reconstituted with the cadence to G (m. 184), which is coordinate with the hypothetical continuation.[24] One measure later (m. 185) the second continuity-process (labelled II) begins. It consists of two parallel lines (a fifth apart) that also rise conjunctly every eight measures. This process ends at measure 204. If both processes are normalized and continued

24. This coordination seems more than fortuitous because it is complemented by harmonic bass motion from D.

(as shown in the analysis), the first (I) reaches tonic harmony at measure **216**, the *harmonic* beginning of the recapitulation, while the second (II) arrives at the melodic A of the first theme in measure **217** as the lower voice moves to the B that begins the fourth-species process once again—marking the *melodic* beginning of the recapitulation.

Example 13 *Prague* Symphony, K. 504, iii, development

Example 13 *(continued)*

Example 14 Piano Sonata in F Major, K. 533, i

Because the first key-area theme itself rises by step (from D to E) over an eight-measure span, process I of the development (which also rises conjunctly over eight measures) can be understood as continuing into the recapitulation. There is what I have called a "bifurcation of form and process."[25] That is, the process begun in the development section (m. 152) moves through and beyond the formal articulation that marks the beginning of the recapitulation.

The final movement of the *Prague* Symphony suggests that continuity-processes are, at times, so designed that the patterns they generate will be congruent with those at the beginning of the recapitulation. That is, I think, clearly the case in the first movement of the Piano Sonata in F. Major, K. 533 (ex. 14). Though presented as a series of imitative entrances at the fifth (A–D–G–C), the continuity-process begun in measure 125 is essentially

25. See Meyer, *Explaining Music,* 100–105, 265–68.

Example 14 *(continued)*

harmonic, as the root-motion analysis given in example 14 indicates. The process breaks in measure 135. In the dominant prolongation that follows, the motivic pattern and its attendant imitations disappear. Only the triplets remain. However, when the process is regularly continued, not only is there harmonic coordination at the point of recapitulation (mm. 145–46), but, as the analysis makes evident, the melodic structure of the continuity-process replicates that of the opening of the first theme group: both descend from an anacrustic fifth to the tonic with an intervening measure of elaboration between.[26]

Several instances of process-morphology coordination occur in Mozart's Symphony no. 39 in E♭ Major, K. 543. In the first movement, the continuity-process, which begins in measure 160, is an archetypal example of fourth-

26. In some instances the process continues not as the theme proper but as an accompaniment pattern. This is the case with the transition to the second key area in the Finale of the G-Minor Symphony, K. 550. The process, which begins at m. 56, is linear on the measure level, moving in parallel tenths (soprano: E♭, m. 56; D, m. 57; C, m. 58; etc.). The process is broken off in m. 64, just before the dominant preparation for the new key. Coordination occurs at m. 71, where the parallel tenths are continued as thirds between second violins and violas.

species counterpoint (ex. 15). The process is broken at measure 166 when the base moves chromatically through A♭ to G, as the dominant of the relative minor. This tonal area is prolonged for twelve measures (through m. 179), and a brief progression leads back to E♭ major, the tonic. Again, a measure of rest at once regularizes morphological length (beginning in m. 168: 4 + [2 + 2] + 4 + [rest + 3]) and makes coordination possible. For, if the fourth-species patterning begun in measures 160–65 is regularly continued, the tonic is reached just at the beginning of the recapitulation.

Example 15 Symphony no. 39 in E♭ Major, K. 543, i

Example 15 *(continued)*

Example 16 Symphony no. 39, iv, development

The next two examples are from the Finale of Symphony no. 39. The first (ex. 16) is from the beginning of the development section. It, too, suggests that rests may not only serve to fill out morphological lengths but allow time for latent continuity-processes to reach compositional goals. For, had the sequence begun with the upbeat to measure 105 been continued (tonally) through the rest (m. 107), it would have led to the presentation of the main melodic idea of the movement in A♭, just as it occurs beginning with the upbeat to measure 109.

The second example is that of the music leading from the second half of the development section to the recapitulation (ex. 17). The continuity-process, generated in measures 125–32, combines fourth-species counterpoint with harmonic motion through the circle of fifths (graphs 1 and 2). The two-bar level consists of a conjunct succession of first-inversion triads (mm. 127, 129, etc.). The contrapuntal/harmonic process closes with a cadence (mm. 151–53) like that given in example 4*a* and *b*. It is worth noting that the continuity-process of the first and last movements of the E♭ Symphony are similar in that both are characterized not only by descending processes but by an absence of any forceful dominant preparation.

Example 17 Symphony no. 39, iv, development-recapitulation

Example 17 (*continued*)

The continuity-process leading from development to recapitulation in the first movement of the *Jupiter* Symphony, K. 551, consists of a chromatic succession of applied dominants combined with implied fourth-species counterpoint (ex. 18). Because the generating process is *fully* and unequivocally chromatic, the normalization (mm. 177–87) is also constructed chromatically. As a result, for the first time in these examples, the hypothetical bass line (graph *b*) moves through all twelve tones of the chromatic scale—that is, from C in measure 177 to the G in measure 188, the penultimate measure leading to the recapitulation. Since the dominant preparation (mm. 181ff.) might easily have been two measures longer, making it conform with the preceding

Example 18 Symphony no. 41 in C Major, *Jupiter*, K. 551, i

(*continued on page 150*)

Example 18 *(continued)*

ten-measure lengths (mm. 161–70 and 171–80), the coordination of process and morphology at measures 188–89 seems more than coincidental.[27]

The next, and final, example—from the development section of the first movement of the String Quintet in D Major, K. 593 (ex. 19)—brings us full circle (as is only appropriate, considering the continuity-processes in most of the preceding examples). For the process of the development section of the quintet, though rhythmically and texturally more complex, is fundamentally

27. This is not to deny that the eight-measure length of the retransition prepares for the morphological length of the main theme. Actually Mozart creates a bit of ambiguity by reaching dominant harmony two measures before the change in figure, texture, dynamics, and instrumentation signals the "real" beginning of the retransition. Put another way, mm. 179 and 180 belong harmonically to the retransition but in all other ways to the preceding modulatory passage.

Example 19 String Quintet in D Major, K. 593, i, development

the same as that of the first movement of the Serenade in C Minor—the first of the Mozart examples.[28] But, in the quintet, it is almost impossible to account for the length of the passage in terms of either already-established lengths or stylistically "normal" ones. It begins with three four-measure units (mm. 123–26, 127–30, and 131–34); both the process and its concomitant

---

28. Obviously in ex. 19 motion occurs at the two-measure level, while in ex. 5 it takes place at the one-measure level. To save space, only pitches required for the delineation of process have

morphology break at measure 135. The following ten measures consist of a three-measure passage of imitation that moves to the dominant (m. 138), which is prolonged for seven measures $(2 + 2 + 1 + 1 + 1)$. Once again, the recapitulation could have begun a measure earlier—or a measure later—making the dominant preparation a more normal eight-measure unit. But neither of these possibilities would have resulted in the coordination of process and morphology found in Mozart's quintet.

3

The data and analyses presented in the preceding section suggest several large areas for further inquiry. The first of these is whether the hypothesis proposed at the outset is convincingly supported. Since the analytic method employed is straightforward—indeed, almost naive—it cannot be an issue. Rather the problem is theoretical: are the examples of process/morphology coordination more than fortuitous? There seem to be three possibilities: (1) coordination may be entirely a matter of chance, occurring with the same frequency in any and every repertory of compositions; (2) coordination may be a consequence of a significant connection, peculiar to the style of tonal music, between prevalent harmonic or contrapuntal processes, on the one hand, and typical morphological lengths, on the other; (3) coordination may be a compositional strategy characteristic of the idiom of some composers (in this case, Mozart) but not others, and it may be employed—like, say, canon and fugue—only in some compositions, not in all.[29]

1. Although I pretend to no competence in statistics, it seems highly unlikely, given the melodic, rhythmic, and harmonic resources and complexities of Western art music, that coordination is entirely accidental. The more so since coordination is dependent upon the generation of harmonic or contrapuntal processes that are style specific. In addition, this contention is supported by the fact that there seem to be very few instances of "extended" co-

---

been included in the example. The first line of analysis suggests that a high-level fourth-species counterpoint is latent. The D in m. 125 is made dissonant by the E (bass), m. 127, and this is resolved to C♯ in m. 129—and so on to m. 145.

29. A fourth possibility that needs to be considered is a fundamental methodological problem with the discovery of regularities such as those proposed in this essay and in other pattern-making theories—namely, that, according to Ramsey theory, "almost any pattern can be found in a system with sufficiently many parts—a fact that undoubtedly helped early stargazers see constellations and is the bane of network designers, who can be blindsided by unexpected connection patterns" (Barry Cipra, "A Visit to Asymptopia Yields Insight into Set Structures," *Science* 267 [17 February 1995]: 964).

ordination in the works of Haydn.[30] Put differently: if coordination occurred merely because of the statistical character of the sound materials employed, then it should be as common in Haydn's music as in Mozart's. But this does not appear to be the case.

2. These last remarks seem to eliminate the second possibility as well: namely, that coordination may be a consequence of stylistic probabilities. For, if coordination were simply a consequence of the constraints characteristic of the Classic style, it should be found as frequently in Haydn's music as in Mozart's. Hence the coordination found in Mozart's music would seem to have been explicitly devised.

This conclusion does not necessarily follow, however. There is another possibility—namely, that the syntax of tonal music does make coordination probable in a number of situations and that Mozart's compositional proclivities allow it to take place while Haydn's do not. There are, in fact, some grounds for suspecting that this is so. For, as many writers have pointed out, Haydn's phrase structure tends to be considerably less regular than Mozart's.[31] Thus, even if coordination were found to be highly probable, given the constraints governing the style of tonal music, it might be that Haydn's less regular phrase structure tends to prevent the coincidence of process and morphology.

3. Observe, however, that, if, on further study, this indeed proved to be the case, it would not gainsay the fact that coordination is a characteristic of some of Mozart's music. For allowing the probable to prevail is itself a compositional choice. Mozart, too, might have eschewed coordination.

These remarks raise still other questions, which, though they cannot be adequately dealt with here, must at least be considered. The first has to do with consciousness and intentionality. If coordination is confirmed as a characteristic of his mature style, was Mozart conscious of this relationship between process and morphology? Since, to the best of my knowledge, such matters are never mentioned in his correspondence or in comparable primary sources, I don't see how this question can be definitively settled. One can only suggest that Mozart *might* have been aware of such relationships because, according

---

30. My search for instances of coordination in Haydn's music was neither systematic nor exhaustive; but the repertory was, I think, reasonably representative. The search also suggested that instances of coordination are more common in the music of Bach than that of Handel.

31. See, e.g., Edward E. Lowinsky, "On Mozart's Rhythm," in *The Creative World of Mozart,* ed. Paul Henry Lang (New York, 1963). According to Lowinsky, "Periodicity, symmetry of phrase structure, regular recurrence of stress are so much a part of Mozart's musical thinking that it is superfluous to illustrate them" (p. 32). But Haydn's music is characterized as "impulsive; it moves in sudden spurts and stops, it loves surprise and shock and abrupt change" (p. 53).

to Erich Hertzmann, "Since contrapuntal writing did not come to him easily, he prepared it on separate sketch leaves before entering it in his score." [32]

About intentionality. Whatever a composer writes is evidence of intention.
The use of the most conventional formulas—for example, triadic melodic
patterns, authentic cadences, or Alberti bass figures—is the result of a choice
made by the composer from a number of alternative stylistic possibilities and
must, therefore, be considered intentional. Such intentions need not, of
course, be conscious and deliberate but may result from unconscious, ingrained habits of discrimination. Conscious intentionality seems to occur
where ingrained habits cannot solve compositional problems (as, say, with
Mozart's contrapuntal writing); and we, as critics, infer such intentionality
when the means the composer has employed are improbable given the constraints of the style. To the extent, then, that process/morphology coordination can be shown to be relatively improbable in the style of Classic music,
its occurrence in Mozart's oeuvre suggests that it may have been explicitly
intentional.[33]

The second question has to do with the relevance of coordination for musical experience. Is the competent listener even subliminally aware of the coincidence of process and morphology? Perhaps, for instance, coordination enhances the sense of long-range goal arrival, and this is experienced as a kind
of congenial congruity, a felicitous propriety. If this is so (and it certainly
needs careful study), then the hypothesis considered here would seem to have
significant implications for performance. For it suggests that, since they
would tend to obscure process/morphology coordination, ritards and other
sorts of "interpretive" articulations are inappropriate, disrupting musical relationships. The timing of the actual process resumption should, rather, co-
incide with that "predicted" by the generative patterning.

The third question—that of value—seems inescapable: Is coordination
per se desirable? That answer must, I believe, be no. Coordination may affect the character of compositions, making for smooth succession and un-
ruffled continuity, while its absence may emphasize the dramatic elements of
surprise, contrast, and tension. But the fact of coordination does not make a
composition better—only different.

These considerations suggest another large area of inquiry. Hypotheses are
accepted if they are convincing, but they are valued because they are illuminating. If the hypothesis proposed in this essay is tenable, it may prove fruit-

32. Erich Hertzmann, "Mozart's Creative Process," in *The Creative World of Mozart,* 29.
33. On the other hand, Mozart's musical sensibility was evidently so finely tuned that he may
simply have sensed the propriety of coordination in particular circumstances.

ful in a number of subdisciplines of musicology. In the field of criticism, the concept of coordination may, as suggested above, help explain aspects of the structure and character of individual compositions—for example, why morphological lengths are what they are, how structure is related to character, and so on. For instance, it may be significant that coordination occurs in the sparkling and buoyant finale of Mozart's Symphony no. 39 but not in the more intensely dramatic finale of his Fortieth Symphony.

In the area of style analysis, the hypothesis may help define differences between the idioms of composers. Thus the preceding discussion conjectured that coordination may be less common in Haydn's music than in Mozart's because Haydn's play is not with the relationship of process to morphology but with morphology itself—particularly as it relates to motivic continuity and return. The presence of coordination may, in addition, illuminate the compositional procedures of other composers of the common practice period who were preeminent contrapuntalists.[34] Brahms, for instance, seems a likely candidate. Indeed, an instance of coordination in Brahms's music—the close of the first theme of the first movement of his Fourth Symphony—was analyzed before the hypothesis being considered here was formulated.[35] Another composer whose oeuvre may well contain instances of coordination is Chopin—a superb contrapuntalist, though scarcely a devotee of polyphonic devices.

But the most important implications of the hypothesis being proposed may well be in the area of music theory. For the notion, mentioned earlier, that coordination might be a consequence of stylistic probability calls attention to a possibility of signal significance: namely, the possibility that there is a fundamental relationship between the syntax of tonality and the morphological lengths prevalent in the style. Such interdependence would in part explain why morphological lengths of two, four, and eight units are norms in the styles of tonal music.[36] Furthermore, it seems appropriate (and I trust not too self-serving) to point out that, if confirmed by further study, the present hypothesis lends considerable support to the implication-realization model of

34. It is important to distinguish counterpoint from polyphony. Counterpoint has essentially to do with the consonance/dissonance relationship between voices—i.e., with their *inter*dependence. Polyphony, on the other hand, has to do with the *in*dependence of melodic lines. Thus the passage from the *Well-Tempered Clavier* given in ex. 2 is both contrapuntal *and* polyphonic, while those from Mozart's D-Minor Fantasy (exx. 6 and 7) are contrapuntal but *not* polyphonic. Since the absence of criteria for determining consonance and dissonance precludes the possibility of counterpoint, serial music can only be polyphonic, not contrapuntal.

35. See Meyer, *Explaining Music,* 171–73.

36. This in no way denies that such lengths may also be related to human neural/motor behavior and bilateral symmetry. Syntax and psychophysiology may cooperate in favoring such morphological lengths.

musical patterning—a model that I, and others, have championed for a number of years.[37]

Historically, the proposed hypothesis may help account for aspects of Mozart's stylistic development. It was noted earlier that coordination is prevalent only in Mozart's mature works. Knowledgeable scholars seem to agree that "Mozart's full maturity may be counted from approximately 1782."[38] And, according to Alfred Einstein, "Bach is the important event in Mozart's life about 1782. . . . [T]he encounter with [Bach's] compositions resulted in a revolution and a crisis in his creative activity."[39] And Erich Hertzmann observes,

> In 1782 Mozart reached a crisis in his personal and artistic life. . . . This new independence and his life in a broader cultural climate opened up new artistic perspectives and brought his creative genius to fruition. After he became acquainted with the recent symphonies and quartets of Haydn, and with the works of Bach and Handel, in the circle of Baron van Swieten, he must have felt himself inadequate and in need of further studies. He copied for himself fugues and canons from the masters of the 17th and 18th centuries. . . . He studied the theorists from Fux to Kirnberger.[40]

There also seems to be agreement among scholars that the really significant consequence of Mozart's encounter with Baroque music—especially the music of Bach—was not primarily his subsequent use of polyphonic relationships (many of these he might have gleaned from the study of Haydn's works) but something more basic. But these scholars neither describe nor define the nature of such fundamental change. This study suggests that the essential change was not one of polyphonic practice but one of compositional conception: Mozart developed a habit or disposition of thinking contrapuntally— witness, for instance, its use in seemingly loosely constructed works such as the D-Minor Fantasy. To the extent, then, that coordination proves to be especially characteristic of Mozart's mature style, it, too, may be a consequence of his discovery of the music of J. S. Bach.

37. This view of musical process was first designated the *implication-realization model* by Eugene Narmour in *Beyond Schenkerism: The Need for Alternatives in Musical Analysis* (Chicago, 1977), chap. 10 and passim.

38. Hans T. David, "Mozartean Modulations," in *The Creative World of Mozart*, 65. Not infrequently the Serenade in C Minor (1782)—the first example of coordination presented in this essay—is mentioned as an important "landmark" in Mozart's stylistic development.

39. Alfred Einstein, *Mozart: His Character—His Work,* trans. Arthur Mendel and Nathan Broder (London, 1946), 149, 151.

40. Hertzmann, "Mozart's Creative Process," 25–26.

4

Melodic Processes and the Perception of Music

With Burton S. Rosner

I. The Perception and Classification of Two Archetypal Melodic Processes

It is a familiar fact that we tend to understand and remember experience in terms of categories and classes. And this is as true of aesthetic experience as of other realms of human activity. In literature, for instance, narrative plots—that is, goal-directed *processes* implying probable outcomes—seem to form readily recognizable types: "boy-meets-girl" stories, "who-done-it" mysteries, "revenge" dramas, and so on. Such narrative processes are often complemented by commonly replicated *formal* plans—for example, cyclic schemes, episodic successions, flashback structures, and the like. When they are considered to have transcended the confines of a particular cultural group or historical period, replicated kinds of processes and forms have frequently been referred to as *archetypes* (see, e.g., Frye 1957, 99–105 and passim)—a term we adopt here.[1]

Archetypes are important for a number of reasons. They establish fundamental frameworks in terms of which culturally competent audiences (not only members of the general public but also creators, performers, critics, and scholars) perceive, comprehend, and respond to works of art. For what audiences enjoy and appreciate are neither the successions of stimuli per se, nor general principles per se, but the relationship between them as actualized in a specific work of art. Just as we can delight in the play of a particular football game only if we understand the constraints governing the action down on the field (the rules, strategies, physical conditions, etc.), so we can enjoy and appreciate the playful ingenuity and expressive power of works of art only if we know—and such knowledge may be tacit, a matter of ingrained habits and

Reprinted from *The Psychology of Music,* edited by Diana Deutsch (Academic, 1982), 317–41, by permission. Copyright © 1982 Academic Press.

1. In later essays in this collection, the term *schema* rather than *archetype* is used to refer to a replicated pattern class.

Example 1 Excerpts from *(a)* Haydn, Symphony no. 100 in G Major
(Military), ii, mm. 1–2; *(b)* Haydn, String Quartet in B♭, op. 64, no. 3,
iii, mm. 40–42; and *(c)* Mozart, Symphony no. 40 in G Minor, K. 550,
iii, mm. 40–42. Notice a similar melodic process in all three.

∞ = "similar to"

dispositions—the constraints that governed the choices made by the artist
and, consequently, shaped the process and form of the particular work of
art. Thus, archetypes are, in a sense, embodiments of fundamental stylistic
constraints. As such, they connect understanding to other aspects of aesthetic
experience.

Our appreciation and evaluation of a work of art involves understanding not only what is actually presented but also what *might have been* presented given the constraints of the style. Put differently, a full appreciation
of the significance of an actual patterning includes an awareness of possible
alternatives that remain unrealized—what Eugene Narmour has called "implied structure" (Narmour 1977, 212). For the sake of brevity, consider an
example discussed at some length elsewhere (Meyer 1989, 26–30). The slow
movement of Haydn's *Military* Symphony (no. 100) opens with a two-
measure pattern that can without the slightest exaggeration be termed *archetypal* in the music of the eighteenth century (ex. 1, first part). But the pattern
belongs not to the class of *beginning* figures but to that of *closing* ones—as
in the second and third parts of example 1.[2] One consequence of this anomalous usage is that the movement might have ended with the very same figure
that it began with. (For other instances of movements that begin with a closing figure, see Meyer [1973, 212–17] and Levy [1981, 355–62].) And,
though Haydn did not choose this alternative, the competent listener's appreciation of the close of the movement includes some (perhaps unconscious)
awareness that this option was a very real possibility. That this was indeed a
possible alternative ending can, in this case, be convincingly documented. For
the second movement of the *Military* Symphony is based almost in its entirety
upon the slow movement of an earlier work by Haydn, his Concerto in G Ma-

2. See also essay 3, ex. 4.

jor for Two Hurdy Gurdies and Orchestra. And, in the Concerto, the movement closes with the same figure that it began with.

Because they are coherent, orderly, and simple, archetypes are easily learned and tend to be stable over time. For these reasons, they not only facilitate the appreciation and evaluation of particular works of art but also constitute an important means of cultural continuity. That is, they function as cognitive-mnemonic schemata—the replicated entities that Dawkins (1976) called "memes" because he considered them the cultural counterparts of the units of biological trait transmission. As such they may be an important basis for studying the histories of styles of art.

As suggested earlier, archetypes may play a significant role in shaping aesthetic experience and fostering cultural continuity in the absence of any conscious conceptualization about their existence, nature, or kinds. Rather, they may be and usually are internalized as habits of perception and cognition operating within a set of cultural constraints. One of us, who has known the opera for many years, only recently recognized that the plot of Mozart's *Magic Flute* belongs to the archetypal class of quest-trial stories of which Dante's *Divine Comedy,* Bunyan's *Pilgrim's Progress,* and Cervantes's *Don Quixote* are celebrated members. And, as will soon be apparent, very familiar melodies may be members of archetypal classes without our being conscious of the fact.

Music, too, tends to be understood and remembered in terms of types and classes, some of which can, as example 1 indicates, be thought of as archetypal. In the domain of musical form, this is abundantly clear. For, though not usually so characterized, many of the forms described and labeled in books about musical analysis can be considered archetypal: for instance, strophic patterns (AA'A" . . . A^n), exemplified in the theme and variation form; binary patterns (AB), the basis for many dance movements; bar forms (AA'B), the structural basis for countless melodies; ternary patterns (ABA), exemplified in *da capo* arias, many dance movements, and marches. Though formal organization is chiefly delineated by the syntactic processes of the primary parameters of music (melody, rhythm, and harmony), form is usually made particularly patent through the patterning of the secondary parameters (i.e., dynamics, tempi, register, instrumentation, sonority, and so on). The prevalence of such formal organizations has been amply documented both by theorists and historians of Western music and by ethnomusicologists.

The analysis and classification of the *processes* that complement such formal schemes have proved more problematic. As textbooks on form and analysis show, most of the achievements have been in the parameter of harmony. A number of the processes typical of Western tonal music have been identified: for example, the progression through the circle of fifths and characteristic cadences—authentic, plagal, and deceptive. On a more extended hierarchic level, an archetypal harmonic-contrapuntal patterning, the so-called *Ursatz*, has been posited in the theory of Heinrich Schenker (Schenker 1956; Yeston 1977). In the areas of rhythm and melody, there has been less success. Though there has been increasing interest in rhythm and meter in music and some typical groupings and patterns have been tentatively distinguished (Cooper and Meyer 1960), little agreement has been reached (Komar 1968; Yeston 1976).

The difficulties encountered in the analysis of melodic processes, the concern of this study, result from a combination of conceptual, methodological, and systemic problems. In the realm of human behavior, we tend to conceptualize and classify processes in terms of goals—and of the strategies devised for reaching them. Thus, reading a novel or seeing a play, we understand the succession of represented events in terms of the purposes of the protagonists: the union of boy and girl, despite her father's objections; the discovery of the criminal, despite his best efforts to avoid detection; the realization of revenge, despite obstacles of wealth or power. Because music is not well suited to, or essentially concerned with, the representation of specific human actions, successive events in a composition cannot readily be related to one another in terms of such goals. Partly for this reason, melodic processes have resisted theoretical formulation and analysis.

A second difficulty is that, while the formal plans, mentioned above, seem to be cross-cultural and atemporal, the syntactic processes generated by the primary parameters of melody, rhythm, and harmony are not. They are conventional: bound to a particular cultural context and limited to a specific historical epoch. The constraints governing melodic relationships and processes are not the same in Mozart's music as in Machaut's; nor are they the same in Western tonal music as in the music of Java. Put the other way around: it seems probable that we have a reasonably workable account of harmonic process precisely because what we have is *not* a fully general theory but one restricted to the practice of a particular culture and period—that of Western culture since the end of the Renaissance. If this observation has merit, then the search for "universal" principles may hinder the development of theories *(plural)* of melodic process.[3]

3. Here Meyer (not Rosner) capitulated to the prevalent vogue of cultural relativism. As the final essay of this "gathering" makes clear, I now believe that biopsychological universals (but *not* specifically musical ones) constrain the musical practice of all cultures. The search for

Example 2 Mozart, Oboe Quartet in F Major, K. 370, i, mm. 1–8. Graphs *a*, *b*, *c*, and *d* show analysis at increasingly higher levels of hierarchy. See text for explanation.

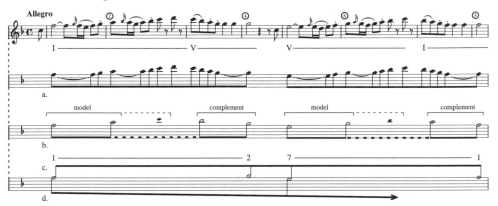

The third difficulty, and perhaps the most important, is systemic. It arises because melodies are frequently hierarchically structured. As a result, the kind of patterning exhibited by a particular melody tends to change from one hierarchic level to the next; and so, of course, does the class of archetype involved. Consider, for instance, the melody of the opening measures of Mozart's Oboe Quartet (ex. 2). As graph *a* of example 2 shows, the foreground (note-to-note) level is characterized by rising and falling linear (scale) patterns. On the next level (graph *b*), rising and falling thirds create pairs of complementary diads. An archetypal changing-note pattern (F–G–E–F) arises on the third hierarchic level (graph *c*). And on the highest level, that resulting from the relationship created by phrase beginnings, the patterning is again linear—the first notes of a descending F-major scale, which continues beyond the music given in this figure.

If the kind of patterning changes from one hierarchic level to another within the same melody, which of the possible patterns should be the basis for classification? For instance, should the melody given in example 2 be classed as linear on the basis of its foreground organization (graph *a*)? As two sets of complementary diads (graph *b*)? As a changing-note melody (graph *c*)? Or, on the highest level, as again linear (graph *d*)?

The view adopted here is that melodic patterns are classified by listeners,

----

such commonalities should be an important field of inquiry for both music theorists and ethnomusicologists.

as well as music theorists, in terms of the organization of the highest level on which significant closure is created by the parameters that shape musical relationships. Thus, example 2 would be classed as a changing-note melody because that is the organization of the highest structural level when pattern closure occurs in measure 8. Had the closure that defines the limits of the whole melody (which lasts for twenty measures) been the basis for typology, then the pattern would have been classed as linear (graph *d*). For analysis of the whole melody, see Meyer (1973, 192–95). In like manner, though the first half (AA′) of example 3 consists of disjunct, triadic motion and the second (B) involves conjunct linear descent, the patterning of the highest level of closure creates what will be called a gap-fill melody.

Ease or difficulty of classification of melodic processes may be related to another sort of melodic complexity—namely, the possibility that a single melody may contain two different strands of patterning on the *same* hierarchic level. For instance, the main pattern of the melody of the slow movement of Mozart's *Jupiter* Symphony is a changing-note figure (ex. 4, graph *a*). But

Example 3 Mozart, Symphony in F Major, K. 112, ii, mm. 1–4. Lower graph shows gap-fill process.

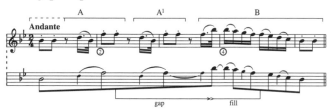

Example 4 Mozart, Symphony no. 41 in C Major, K. 551, ii, mm. 1–4. Lower graphs show analysis of alternative melodic structures. See text for explanation.

coordinate with this pattern is a subsidiary linear organization that is presented on weak beats (graph *c*). To classify this melody, the listener must distinguish the two strands and discern which is the main one. As graph *b* indicates, the next level of this strand transcends the melodic and harmonic closure reached in measure 4. It is linear and implies continuation to a structural A (not shown in ex. 4). Again, the basis for classification is the degree of closure. In measure 4 both the F (graph *a*) and the C (graph *c*) occur over stable, closed tonic harmony. But the F is more closed, both because it occurs on a stable, accented beat while the C comes on a mobile weak beat and because F is the stable tonic of the scale while C is the less stable fifth of the scale. As a result, the more closed changing-note pattern acts as the basis for melodic classification.

Of the primary parameters of music, melody has unquestionably been the most difficult to analyze and classify in terms of process. The paucity of practical and theoretical texts on the subject is evidence of this. So is the generally antitheoretical attitude expressed in the familiar maxim that, since melody is a matter of native gift and inspiration, melodic processes cannot be "reduced" to principles or "forced" into artificial classes and, consequently, melodic writing cannot be taught. Nevertheless, one of us (Meyer 1973) has attempted to show that, in the tonal music of Western culture, melodic processes can be separated into distinguishable classes on a particular hierarchic level—usually the level on which the pattern exhibits clear closure. Since two of these classes—gap-fill melodies and changing-note melodies—were investigated in an experiment described below, the characteristics of each class merit brief discussion.

A. Gap-Fill Melodies

Gap-fill melodies consist of two elements: (1) a disjunct interval or a succession of disjunct intervals moving in the same direction—the *gap* (or skip)—and (2) a succession of conjunct (stepwise) intervals that "fill" the gap by presenting all or most of the notes previously skipped over. The relationship is one in which the incompleteness created by a gap implies subsequent completeness through a fill; and, generally speaking, the larger the gap, the stronger the sense of incompleteness and the implication of fill.

The subject of the fugue from Geminiani's Concerto Grosso in E Minor, op. 3, no. 3, is an uncomplicated instance of a gap-fill melody (ex. 5). As the graph *(a)* beneath the example shows, the main gap consists of the octave from a low to a high E, and a subsidiary gap occurs from B up to E. This gap structure is immediately followed by conjunct motion—at first chromatic and then diatonic—that descends through the harmonic minor scale down to the tonic (E).

The same fundamental process, elaborated somewhat, forms the basis for the beginning of the chorus of the very familiar tune "Over the Rainbow," by Harold Arlen (ex. 6). Observe that, whereas Geminiani's fugue subject has essentially only one skip (gap), followed by a fill that is slightly embellished by passing chromaticism, the generating gap of "Over the Rainbow" is reinforced by "auxiliary" gaps in measures 3 and 5 and most of the tones of the fill are prolonged through melodic-rhythmic elaboration. These differences affect formal structure. For, instead of being a basically one-part form, as Geminiani's fugue subject (ex. 5) is, "Over the Rainbow" is a bar form (AA′B), as indicated over example 6. However, because the initial octave gap, the prime generating event, is immediately followed by the beginning of the

Example 5 Geminiani, Concerto Grosso in E Minor, op. 3, no. 3, mm. 1–4. Lower graph shows gap-fill process.

Example 6 "Over the Rainbow," by Harold Arlen and E. Y. Harburg. Copyright © 1938, 1939 (renewed 1966, 1967) Metro-Goldwyn-Mayer, Inc. Rights throughout the world controlled by Leo Feist, Inc. All rights reserved. Lower graph shows gap-fill processes. AA′B form indicated above. Chorus, mm. 1–8.

fill, one thinks of the gap as being much shorter than the fill. Although most gaps are upward skips, downward skips may also function as gaps (see Narmour [1977, 76–77] for an example). And, though upward skips are usually followed by descending fills and downward skips by rising fills, this is not necessarily the case: for instance, an ascending gap may be "filled" (completed) by a rising conjunct pattern. Moreover, the fill may be partly descending and partly ascending. For instance, in example 6 the third gap (m. 5) is partly filled by the subsidiary ascending line shown in graph *b*.

But the gap part of a gap-fill process may be prolonged, so that the components of the whole melodic entity are roughly equal in length. This is true of the opening measures of the slow movement of Mozart's Symphony in F Major, K. 112 (ex. 3). Thus, although the form (AA'B) is like that of example 6, the first half of Mozart's melody is concerned with creating the gap; the fill takes place only in the second half. It should also be noted that, as in many cases, the pitches that define the full extent of the gap (the octave from low to high B♭) are not directly connected but are the end points of a triad.

Gap-fill patterns may also occur in conjunction with the quasi-strophic form AA', called an antecedent-consequent period. The beginning of the Menuetto of Mozart's Flute Quartet in A Major, K. 298, illustrates this kind of process/form coupling (ex. 7). In the antecedent phrase, a brief, anacrustic gap moves rapidly through the tonic triad from a lower to an upper fifth. The following fill descends conjunctly from the high A. However, before it is completed, a half cadence (IV–V) creates partial closure on the second degree of the scale, E (m. 4). The consequent phrase begins like the antecedent, reiterating the gap and the beginning of the fill. But the end of the fill is modified so that a full cadence occurs on the tonic D (m. 8). Though the melody never descends to the lower A, the gap is understood as being satisfactorily filled

Example 7 Mozart, Flute Quartet in A Major, K. 298, ii, mm. 1–8. Lower graph shows gap-fill processes. Antecedent-consequent form indicated above.

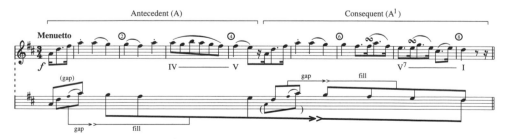

because the tonal/rhythmic closure at the end of the period (m. 8) is so decisive that whatever incompleteness might have been experienced is for the moment eclipsed.

B. Changing-Note Melodies

A changing-note melody is one in which the main structural tones of the pattern consist of the tonic (1), the seventh or leading tone of the scale (7), the second degree of the scale (2), and then the tonic again. As we have seen (ex. 2), the order of the middle pitches may be reversed, resulting in the succession 1–2, 7–1. A variant of the changing-note process may occur beginning on the third degree of the scale, producing the succession 3–2, 4–3 (or 3–4, 2–3): an example is discussed in essay 2, example 10. The pattern is always harmonized by a progression that moves from a tonic chord (I) to dominant harmony (V) and then from the dominant back to the tonic: that is, the progression is always I–V, V–I. Surrogates for these harmonies are possible: for example, vii for V or vi for I. The form complementing the changing-note pattern is quasi-strophic, AA'. Thus, the basic plan can be diagrammed as:

$$\frac{A}{I–V} : \frac{A'}{V–I}$$

It might be thought that the underlying regularity of a changing-note melody is really harmonic rather than melodic. However, since the same harmonic, and even formal, pattern may accompany other melodic processes—for instance, one that might be called a *sequential changing-note pattern* (see essay 5, ex. 1)—the parameters are at least partially independent.

Any or all of the structural tones in a changing-note pattern may be extended—through ornamentation, triadic prolongation, etc. Consider, for instance, the beginning of the last movement of Beethoven's String Quartet in F Major, op. 18, no. 1 (ex. 8). In the first measure the tonic F is prolonged first through a turn involving lower and upper neighbor notes and then through a linear descent. The leading tone E on the first beat of measure 2 is clearly structural despite the afterbeat G. In measure 3 a structural G, comparable in every way to the earlier F, is also prolonged and then moves down by octave transfer to the tonic F followed by an afterbeat (A).

The cultural "potency" of this archetype seems evident in the fact that it acts as the basis for "Hinky Dinky, Parlee-voo," a tune that was enormously popular during World War I (ex. 9a). The similarity between the melodic process of this commonplace ditty and that of the last movement of Beethoven's op. 18, no. 1, is evident enough. If the notation of its durational pattern is changed to conform to that of ex. 8, then, as ex. 9*b* shows, the metric schemes are similar as well.

Example 8 Beethoven, String Quartet, op. 18, no. 1, iv, mm. 1–4. Lower graph shows changing-note process and octave transfers. AA′ form indicated above.

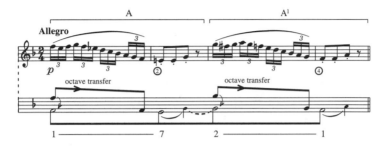

Example 9 (*a*) "Hinky Dinky, Parlee-voo," folk tune, mm. 1–8, with analysis of changing-note process underlying it. (*b*) Notation of meter of *a* divided to conform to the meter of ex. 8.

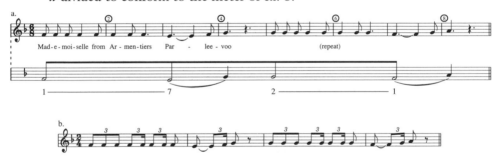

II. Experimental Findings

A. *Purpose*

The preceding analysis of melodic processes raises an obvious psychological question. Do the different types of processes identified by musical theory play any role in the perception of music? If they do, a subject untutored in formal musical analysis should at least be able to place melodies into the classes that the analysis specifies. This argument can be tested by a concept identification experiment in which different types of melodic processes define the different classes of stimuli. The processes should be represented at the highest hierarchical level for each stimulus. A subject should be able to learn to associate different responses with the different classes. The subject then should successfully generalize the responses to a new sample of melodies.

We carried out such a concept identification experiment.[4] In this experiment, subjects had to learn to place gap-fill melodies into one class and changing-note melodies into another. The subjects were to respond to gap-fill instances by saying "A" and to changing-note instances by saying "B," without any explicit education in melodic analysis and without any didactic training about these two types of melodic processes. Training was conducted by merely informing the subject after each response what the correct response should have been. We used recordings of fully instrumented passages from the musical literature for this experiment, rather than melodies of our own devising. This choice rested on two grounds. First, we wanted to keep style as homogeneous as possible. We found that we could select sufficient material from works of the Classical period (ca. 1750–1827). Second, we feared that we could all too easily make the concept identification task trivial by composing our own melodies. We also rejected the procedure of abstracting melodies from the musical literature and having them played on a single instrument, such as a clarinet. We wanted to see whether classification of different types of melodic processes could emerge despite the presence of the many other parameters that are characteristic of music. Therefore, we used short passages of four to fifteen measures' length chosen from works by Haydn, Mozart, Beethoven, and Schubert. Each passage reached significant closure and was an instance of either gap-fill or changing-note processes.

The results of this initial experiment suggested that subjects could indeed learn to place each melody into its appropriate class and could then generalize to new melodies. Inspection of the data, however, indicated that changing-note melodies generated fewer erroneous responses than did gap-fill ones. Subjects apparently carried out the task by first learning to respond correctly to the changing-note passages and then using the alternative response to all other passages. We could not conclude safely that the two types of melodic processes played more or less equal roles in the perception of music. Therefore, we redesigned the experiment as a two-part procedure. In one

4. The experiment grew out of a graduate seminar that we taught together in 1977. The students participated in the design of the experiment, the selection of passages, and running subjects. For their help, we thank James Copp, Erika Ellenberger, Christopher Foard, Robert Hopkins, Lief Laudamus, and Katherine Hirsch-Pasek. Scott Balthazar helped us collect further necessary data and organize the results.

part, subjects heard gap-fill melodies along with some that represented a variety of different melodic processes other than gap-fill or changing-note. The subjects had to respond by saying "Type A" to the former and "Not type A" to the latter. A generalization test followed training. In another part of the experiment, subjects learned to respond to changing-note melodies by saying "Type B" and to melodies representing various processes other than changing-note or gap-fill by saying "Not type B." Again, a generalization test followed training. No passage used in one part of the experiment ever appeared in the other.

B. Method

1. Selection of Passages

Fifty-nine passages were selected for this experiment from the works of Haydn, Mozart, Beethoven, and Schubert. They represented parts of symphonies, chamber music, concertos for solo instrument and orchestra, and sonatas for piano or for piano and violin. Tables 3 and 4 below provide lists of the passages selected for the gap-fill and changing-note parts of the experiment, respectively. The tables show composer, work, movement, and measures. On request, we will provide details about the particular recordings used.

2. Gap-Fill versus Non-Gap-Fill Passages (Part A)

Thirty passages were used in this part of the experiment. Eight gap-fill and eight non-gap-fill passages were used for training. Four of each type were of form AA′B, and the other four were antecedent-consequent forms. In an AA′B form, the passage contains an initial motif, a repetition or a variation of it, and then a longer concluding motif (see ex. 3). The antecedent-consequent form contains two related statements, the first of which does not resolve to the tonic, while the second does (e.g., ex. 7). There were two gap-fill passages of the form AA′B that ended on dominant harmony, and these were matched by a non-gap-fill passage of the same form that also ended on the dominant. In addition to the sixteen training stimuli, two more gap-fill passages were chosen for introductory examples at the start of training. One was of form AA′B, and the other was an antecedent-consequent passage. Since the non-gap-fill passages employed various melodic processes, no introductory examples of these selections were given. For the generalization test we chose six gap-fill and six non-gap-fill passages different from those used for training. Three gap-fill and three non-gap-fill passages had form AA'B. One of these ended on the dominant, and this was matched by a non-gap-fill passage that ended on the dominant. The other three gap-fill and the other three non-gap-fill passages were antecedent-consequent in form.

3. Changing-Note versus Non-Changing-Note Passages (Part B)

Twenty-nine passages were used in this part of the experiment. All had form AA' (see ex. 8). Eight changing-note and eight non-changing-note passages served as training stimuli, while an additional changing-note melody provided an introductory example at the start of training. A non-changing-note introductory example was not offered since passages in this category used a variety of melodic processes. The generalization test employed six changing-note and six non-changing-note passages different from those used in training.

4. Preparation of Tapes

Each passage was recorded on a master selection tape, from which it was rerecorded on separate segments of tape as many times as necessary. The segments then were spliced into the experimental tapes. There were a training tape and a generalization tape for each part (A and B) of the experiment.

For gap-fill training, the subject responded by saying "Type A" to all instances of gap-fill melodies and by saying "Not type A" to all non-gap-fill passages. The tape started with an announcer's voice stating, "This is an experiment in music perception. You will now hear an example of type A." The AA'B gap-fill introductory example then was played once. After a 10-second pause, the announcer's voice stated, "This is another example of type A," and the antecedent-consequent gap-fill introductory example was then played. The two introductory examples never reappeared in the rest of the experiment. The announcer then said, "Now start responding." After a 2-second delay, the first training passage was played. Ten seconds after its termination, the announcer identified it by saying, "That was type A," or, "That was not type A," as appropriate. The subject had to respond within the 10-second interval between the end of the passage and the announcer's identification of it. Five seconds after the identification, the announcer stated, "Next example," and another passage was begun 2 seconds later and followed 10 seconds after its conclusion by an identifying statement. The training tape continued, following this cycle of a warning of "Next example" 5 seconds after termination of the previous identification, a 2-second pause after the warning, a passage, a 10-second pause for the subject to respond, and then identification of the type of selection just heard.

A single training trial consisted of one playing of each the eight gap-fill passages and each of the eight non-gap-fill ones. The order of passages was randomized with the constraint that no more than three gap-fill or no more than three non-gap-fill selections could occur in sequence. One trial took about eight minutes. A different random order of the passages was used for different trials. The gap-fill training tape contained twelve trials, with no indication to the subject of where one trial ended and the next began. Our initial experiment had indicated that this would permit most subjects to reach a criterion of two successive trials with two errors or less on each.

The gap-fill generalization tape consisted of six gap-fill and six non-gap-fill passages in random order, with the constraint that no more than two of either type could occur in succession. The tape began with the message, "Now start responding." Two seconds later the first generalization passage began. It was repeated after a 2-second pause. Then a 10-second pause occurred, during which the subject was to respond. No information about correct identification was given. Instead, the announcer stated, "Next example," and, after a 2-second pause, two exposures to the next passage occurred. Ten seconds were then allowed for responding. The cycle of a warning, a 2-second pause, two playings of a passage, and a 10-second pause for responding continued throughout the gap-fill generalization tape. The entire tape ran for about 10 minutes.

The changing-note training tape was constructed exactly parallel to that for the gap-fill part of the experiment, with one minor exception. Since all passages were of form AA', only one example of a changing-note melody was played at the start of training. Subjects were supposed to respond with "Type B" to changing-note and with "Not type B" to non-changing-note passages. The introductory example on the training tape was preceded by the announcement, "This is an experiment in music perception. You will now hear an example of type B." Identifications after training passages were either, "That was type B," or, "That was not type B." The changing-note generalization tape followed exactly the pattern of the gap-fill generalization tape.

5. Subjects

Twenty subjects were recruited individually by one of the experimenters from students taking music courses at the University of Pennsylvania. They included undergraduate and graduate students. Among the former were majors in music or in other subjects. The graduate students were all studying composition. No subject had received any exposure to analysis of melodic processes, although some were versed in more traditional aspects of musical theory, such as harmony, counterpoint, and musical form. Each subject received six dollars at the end of two one-and-a-half-hour sessions.

6. Procedure

Each subject underwent gap-fill training and generalization (part A) in one session and changing-note training and generalization (part B) in the other. Half the subjects took part A first, and the other half took part B first. As they were recruited, subjects were assigned in alternation to one or the other initial condition. At the start of the first session, each subject filled out a questionnaire and a consent form. The questionnaire asked about academic status, previous training in musical performance, previous academic training in music, and current performance activities and listening habits.

The experimenter then read instructions to the subject and answered any questions. The instructions specified that subjects were to respond by saying "Type A" or "Not type A" for part A of the experiment (gap-fill) or "Type B" or "Not type B" for part B (changing-note). They also informed the subject that 10 seconds were allowed for responding after the end of a passage and that each failure to meet this requirement would result in losing ten cents. The experimenter then started the appropriate training tape, which was reproduced at a comfortable listening level over an Akai model 400DS Mark II tape deck. The subject and the experimenter each listened to the tape over stereophonic earphones. After each passage had been played, the subject responded verbally. The experimenter marked correct responses on a specially prepared data sheet. At the end of each trial, the experimenter added up the number of errors and decided whether the subject had met the criterion for training: two successive trials with no more than two errors each. If criterion had not been met, the next training trial proceeded. If it had been met, the experimenter stopped the training tape, rewound it, removed it from the tape deck, and put the generalization tape on the deck. If the subject ran through twelve training trials without meeting criterion, the experimenter moved on to the generalization test nevertheless. The subject therefore had a brief rest between hearing the training and the generalization tapes. The generalization tape was played, and responses were recorded just as for the training tape. At the end of each subject's second session, the experimenter explained the purpose of the study to the subject and asked the subject not to discuss the experiment with any other participant.

C. Results

1. Gap-Fill Selections (Part A)

During training, one subject failed to respond within the 10-second limit to a single selection. Table 1 summarizes the results of part A of the experiment. Owing to various exigencies, three subjects did not complete part A of the experiment. Fourteen of the remaining seventeen subjects met criterion in a median of 8.8 trials. They made a median of 37.0 errors in training and 4.7 errors out of a possible 12 in generalization. Three subjects went twelve trials without meeting criterion. They had a median of 58.0 errors during training, a median of only 5.0 errors out of a possible 32 on their final two training trials, and a median of 4.0 errors out of a possible 12 in generalization. All seventeen subjects together made a median of 4.5 errors during the generalization test. During generalization no subject ever failed to respond within the ten-second limit after the end of a passage.

We used the Kolmogorov-Smirnov test (Siegel 1956) to determine whether subjects responded better than chance in the generalization test. If the subjects were just guessing throughout generalization, their errors would

Table 1 Results of Concept Identification Experiment

	Gap-Fill Selections (A)	Changing-Note Selections (B)
Subjects meeting criterion	14	12
Median trials	8.8	9.3
Median errors	37.0	43.0
Median errors in generalization	4.7	4.6
Subjects going 12 trials	3	4
Without meeting criterion	0	0
Median errors	58.0	69.0
Median errors on last 2 trials	5.0	8.0
Median errors in generalization	4.0	4.3
Median errors in generalization for all subjects	4.5	4.4

Table 2 Analysis of Number of Generalization Errors

Errors	Binomial Cumulative Probabilities	Gap-Fill Cumulative Probabilities		Changing-Note Cumulative Probabilities	
		Subjects Meeting Criterion ($n = 14$)	Subjects Completing Experiment ($n = 17$)	Subjects Meeting Criterion ($n = 12$)	Subjects Completing Experiment ($n = 16$)
12	1.0000	1.0000	1.0000	1.0000	1.0000
11	.9998	1.0000	1.0000	1.0000	1.0000
10	.9968	1.0000	1.0000	1.0000	1.0000
9	.9807	.9286	.9412	1.0000	1.0000
8	.9270	.9286	.9412	1.0000	1.0000
7	.8061	.9286	.9412	.9167	.9375
6	.6128	.7857	.8235	.9167	.9375
5	.3872	.7143	.7059	.9167	.9375
4	.1938	.5000	.5294	.5000	.5625
3	.0730	.3571	.3529	.4167	.3125
2	.0192	.1428	.1765	.3333	.2500
1	.0032	.0714	.0588	.2500	.1875
0	.0002	.0714	.0588	.0833	.0625
D_{max}		.3271	.3356	.5295	.5503
$p <$		.10	.05	.01	.01

follow a binomial distribution. Table 2 shows the theoretical and the observed cumulative probabilities of error scores of at least a certain size. The observed cumulative probabilities are given for the fourteen subjects who met criterion and for all seventeen who completed the gap-fill part of the experiment. The last two lines of the table show the maximum deviation of the observed from the theoretical probabilities and the associated significance level from the Kolmogorov-Smirnov test. The seventeen subjects who completed part A of the experiment had fewer generalization errors than expected by chance; this difference was significant ($p = .05$). Therefore, these subjects acquired generalizable knowledge as a result of training. The fourteen subjects who reached criterion showed the same trend in their generalization error scores, but the difference fell just short of significance. The results indicate that subjects who did not reach criterion during training still learned to classify the passages for the most part correctly and could generalize their knowledge to a new sample of selections.

Inspection of the data indicated that passages differed in their difficulty during training and possibly during generalization. Table 3 lists the individual

Table 3 Errors on Gap-Fill Selections

Selection	Total Errors		
	Criterion Subjects ($n = 14$)	Noncriterion Subjects ($n = 3$)	All Subjects ($n = 17$)
Gap-fill training:			
Mozart: Piano Quintet in E♭, K. 452 (III), mm. 1–8	19	16	35
Mozart: Flute Quartet in A, K. 298 (II), mm. 1–8	9	8	17
Beethoven: Violin Concerto (III), mm. 1–8	24	4	28
Mozart: *Eine Kleine Nachtmusik,* K. 525 (IV), mm. 1–8	13	9	22
Schubert: String Quartet in E♭, op. 125, D. 87 (II), mm. 1–8	41	16	57
Mozart: Symphony no. 18 in F, K. 130 (III), mm. 1–8	8	5	13
Beethoven: String Quartet in C Minor, op. 18, no. 4 (I), mm. 42–49	31	22	53
Beethoven: Piano Sonata in A, op. 2, no. 2 (III), Trio, mm. 1–8	36	10	46
Friedman χ_r^2	31.63	8.13	31.51
$p \leq$	.001	. . .	.001
Non-gap-fill training:			
Mozart: String Quartet in E♭, K. 428 (IV), mm. 1–8	35	10	45
Mozart: String Quartet in D, K. 499 (II), Trio, mm. 1–8	52	4	56
Mozart: Symphony no. 41 in C, K. 551 (III), Trio, mm. 1–8	25	8	33
Beethoven: String Quartet in B♭, op. 130 (II), mm. 1–8	35	11	46
Haydn: String Quartet in E♭, op. 64, no. 6 (IV), mm. 1–4	35	14	49
Mozart: Piano Concerto in E♭, K. 482 (III), mm. 1–8	44	11	55
Haydn: String Quartet, op. 33, no. 6 (III), mm. 1–8	50	17	67
Haydn: String Quartet in G, op. 64, no. 4 (II), mm. 1–4	19	10	29
Friedman χ_r^2	4.53	6.46	5.03
$p \leq$	. . .	. . .	. . .

(continued on page 176)

Table 3 *(continued)*

Selection	Criterion Subjects ($n = 14$)	Noncriterion Subjects ($n = 3$)	All Subjects ($n = 17$)
		Total Errors	
A-NA Mdn[a]	−7.5	. . .	−6.5
T: $p \leq$	.01		.05
Gap-fill generalization:			
Haydn: Symphony no. 77 in B♭ (IV), mm. 72–80	6	0	6
Haydn: Symphony no. 79 (II), mm. 61–68	5	1	6
Mozart: Symphony no. 13 in F, K. 112 (II), mm. 1–5	2	1	3
Mozart: Symphony no. 24 in B♭, K. 182 (II), mm. 1–8	3	2	5
Mozart: Sonata for Piano and Violin in G, K. 301 (II), mm. 1–6	2	0	2
Beethoven: String Quartet in B♭, op. 18, no. 6 (IV), mm. 1–8	9	2	11
χ^2	. . .	. . .	9.0
$p \leq$			. . .
Non-gap-fill generalization:			
Mozart: String Quartet in B♭, K. 458 (III), mm. 1–8	8	0	8
Haydn: Symphony no. 104 in D (IV), mm. 3–10	6	1	7
Mozart: Symphony no. 35 in D, K. 385 (III), Trio, mm. 1–8	9	1	10
Haydn: Quartet, op. 33, no. 3, in C (IV), mm. 1–8	4	2	6
Mozart: Symphony in G, K. 45a (III), mm. 1–8	5	1	6
Haydn: String Quartet in G, op. 64, no. 4 (IV), mm. 1–4	4	1	5
χ^2	3.67	. . .	2.29
$p \leq$	. . .		. . .
GA-GNA Mdn[b]	.4	. . .	.5
T: $p \leq$	. . .		. . .

[a] The median difference in errors on gap-fill and non-gap-fill training passages, taken across subjects.

[b] The median difference in errors during generalization, taken across subjects.

selections used in part A of the experiment along with the errors made on them. Results are given separately for the subjects who met criterion during training and for those who did not, along with total errors for all subjects. The passages are separated into gap-fill and non-gap-fill sets, for both training and generalization. If all passages within a set were equally difficult, the same number of errors would be made on each. We performed Friedman two-way analyses of variance (Siegel 1956) on errors made during training in order to see whether passages differed in difficulty. The individual subjects were replicates, and the different passages were the conditions. Tests were done on the gap-fill passages for subjects who met criterion, for those who did not, and for all subjects combined. The results appear in table 3, which gives the value of χ_r^2 and their associated levels of significance. The results show that gap-fill training passages varied in difficulty. Three similar analyses on non-gap-fill training passages yielded no significant results, as table 3 shows. Finally, chi-square tests were made when possible on error data for individual selections during generalization. Tests were done on total errors per passage across all subjects for gap-fill and non-gap-fill passages and for total errors per non-gap-fill passage across subjects who met criterion. None of the results proved significant.

The data in table 3 also suggest that subjects made more errors on non-gap-fill than on gap-fill passages. To test this hypothesis, we used the Wilcoxon signed-ranks test for matched samples (Siegel 1956). The test was done on differences across subjects between total errors on gap-fill and total errors on non-gap-fill passages. Table 3 shows the results. Subjects who reached criterion and all subjects combined who finished part A of the experiment made significantly more errors on non-gap-fill than on gap-fill training passages. No similar difference in difficulty between gap-fill and non-gap-fill selections occurred during generalization.

In summary, subjects learned to put gap-fill and non-gap-fill melodies into different classes, without explicit academic training in musical analysis. They subsequently proved able to classify new instances of each type of melody in a generalization test. During training, gap-fill passages differed among themselves in difficulty, but non-gap-fill ones did not. The gap-fill training passages were easier to identify correctly than were the non-gap-fill ones. Generalization passages showed no variation in difficulty either within or between types of passages.

2. Changing-Note Selections (Part B)

Table 1 shows the results of part B of the experiment. During training, no subject ever failed to respond within the 10-second limit. Owing to various exigencies, four subjects did not finish this part of the experiment. Twelve subjects met criterion in a median of 9.3 trials. They made a median of 43 errors during training and a median of 4.6 errors during generalization. Another four subjects underwent 12 training trials without meeting criterion, generating a median of 69 errors. They made a median of 8 errors on the last two training trials and a median of 4.3 errors during generalization. All sixteen subjects made a median of 4.4 errors during the generalization test. No subject ever failed to respond within the 10-second limit during generalization.

Table 2 shows the cumulative probabilities that subjects made error scores of at least a certain size. Results are given separately for subjects who reached criterion and for all subjects who completed part B of the experiment. Kolmogorov-Smirnov tests showed that subjects who met criterion made significantly fewer errors than expected by chance, as did all subjects who completed part B. Subjects who met criterion and those who did not seemed to have acquired generalizable knowledge about changing-note melodies as a result of training.

Table 4 shows the individual passages used in part B and the errors made on them. Results are given separately for the subjects who met criterion, for those who did not, and for all subjects combined who completed part B. The passages are separated into changing-note and non-changing-note sets, for both training and generalization. Friedman tests indicate that both the changing-note and the non-changing-note passages varied among themselves in difficulty during training. The non-changing-note passages generated more errors than did the changing-note ones. Wilcoxon tests showed that this difference was statistically significant for subjects who met criterion and for all subjects combined. Chi-square tests were made when possible on generalization error scores and gave no indication that changing-note or non-changing-note passages varied in difficulty. Nor was there evidence from Wilcoxon tests that the changing-note passages differed in difficulty from non-changing-note ones.

3. Gap-Fill versus Changing-Note Selections

Of the twenty subjects who began the experiment, ten managed to meet criterion in both parts A and B. Data from the latter subjects permit

Table 4 Errors on Changing-Note Selections

| | Total Errors | | |
	Criterion Subjects ($n = 12$)	Noncriterion Subjects ($n = 4$)	All Subjects ($n = 16$)
Selection			
Changing-note training:			
Mozart: Piano Sonata in E♭, K. 282 (II), mm. 1–4	30	18	48
Mozart: Fantasy in D, K. 397, mm. 12–15	10	16	26
Mozart: Piano Quintet in E♭, K. 452 (III), mm. 17–20	33	19	52
Beethoven: Piano Sonata in C, op. 10, no. 1 (I), mm. 1–8	14	17	31
Mozart: Oboe Quartet in F, K. 370 (I), mm. 1–8	26	24	50
Beethoven: String Quartet in F, op. 18, no. 1 (IV), mm. 1–4	22	10	32
Mozart: Symphony no. 39 in E♭, K. 543 (III), Trio, mm. 1–8	24	10	34
Mozart: Piano Sonata, K. 311 (I), mm. 7–10	10	16	26
Friedman χ_r^2	26.60	2.52	21.75
$p \leq$	.001	. . .	.001
Non-changing-note training:			
Beethoven: Symphony no. 2 in D, op. 36 (III), mm. 85–92	27	13	40
Beethoven: Piano Sonata in G, op. 49, no. 2 (I), mm. 20–23	45	24	69
Mozart: Piano Quartet in G Minor, K. 478 (III), mm. 1–4	47	22	69
Mozart: String Quartet in A, K. 464 (I), mm. 1–8	49	25	74
Haydn: Symphony no. 94 in G (III), mm. 1–8	33	23	56
Beethoven: String Quartet, op. 18, no. 2 (III), mm. 1–8	29	16	45
Mozart: String Quartet in D Minor, K. 421 (IV), mm. 1–8	31	19	50
Haydn: String Quartet in D, op. 50, no. 6 (III), mm. 30–40	33	16	49
χ_r^2	13.83	5.92	16.97
$p \leq$	. . .	. . .	.02

(continued on page 180)

Table 4 *(continued)*

Selection	Criterion Subjects ($n = 12$)	Noncriterion Subjects ($n = 4$)	All Subjects ($n = 16$)
		Total Errors	
B-NB Mdn[a]	−10.	. . .	−10.8
T: p ≤	.01		.01
Changing-note generalization:			
Mozart: Piano Quartet in G Minor, K. 478 (I), mm. 1–8	6	0	6
Mozart: String Quintet in C, K. 515 (I), mm. 1–10	5	1	6
Mozart: String Trio in E♭, K. 563 (III), mm. 1–8	2	1	3
Haydn: String Quartet, op. 64, no. 5 (I), mm. 1–8	3	2	5
Haydn: Symphony no. 46 in B (II), mm. 1–4	2	0	2
Mozart: Symphony no. 41 in C, K. 551 (II), mm. 1–4	9	2	11
χ^2	. . .	. . .	. . .
p ≤			
Non-changing-note generalization:			
Mozart: Sextet in F, K. 522 (III), mm. 1–4	2	1	3
Beethoven: String Quartet, op. 18, no. 2 (II), mm. 1–6	3	0	3
Haydn: Symphony no. 101 in D (IV), mm. 1–8	4	0	4
Haydn: Quartet, op. 33, no. 2 (II), Trio, mm. 1–8	3	1	4
Mozart: String Quintet in E♭, K. 614 (I), mm. 1–8	9	2	11
Beethoven: Symphony no. 7 in A, op. 92 (III), mm. 149–63	5	2	7
χ^2	. . .	. . .	9.5
p ≤			. . .
B-NB Mdn[a]	.0		.4
p ≤	. . .		. . .

[a] The median difference for changing-note errors minus non-changing-note errors.

comparisons between the two parts of the experiment. During training, these subjects made a median of 6.0 more errors on gap-fill than on changing-note passages but took a median of 0.7 more trials to reach criterion on changing-note than on gap-fill passages. Wilcoxon tests showed that neither difference is significant. The ten subjects also made a median of 0.8 more errors in generalization on changing-note than on gap-fill selections; again, the difference is not significant. In brief, we have no evidence of any difference in difficulty between the gap-fill and the changing-note parts of the experiment.

D. *Discussion*

Our experimental results indicate that at least two classes of melodic processes obtained from theoretical analysis can act as a basis for perceptual differentiation between melodic types. The melodic types, therefore, meet the minimal requirement for attributing psychological significance to them. Explicit training in musical analysis is not necessary for the types to form the basis of perceptual distinctions. Our findings, although encouraging, are merely an initial step. Further studies are necessary in order to specify just what sort of psychological reality different types of melodic processes may be said to possess, to determine the levels at which this reality is represented, and to show the manner in which it operates. These tests will involve techniques such as direct judgments of similarity.

Training and generalization passages of every type in both parts A and B of the experiment differed among themselves in difficulty. One of the most important reasons for this variability is probably the hierarchic nature of the melodies themselves. As observed earlier, hierarchically complex melodies exhibit different kinds of patterning on different levels. And, the more hierarchic levels there are, the more likely that classification will be based upon the patterning of some level other than that of the highest level of closure. This may help explain why our subjects found the melody of the first movement of Mozart's Oboe Quartet (ex. 2) particularly difficult to classify. Not only are there at least four hierarchic levels, but the forceful linear motion of the highest level (ex. 2, graph *d*) may well mask the changing-note melody that patterns the highest closural level. The whole melody is analyzed as being linear in Meyer (1973, 192–95). The fourth movement of Beethoven's String Quartet in F Major (ex. 8) is also a changing-note melody. But it is hierarchically simple, and, despite octave transfers and potentially problematic afterbeats, our subjects found it relatively easy to classify. The preemptive force of a linear patterning that transcends the closure of a passage may also have made it difficult for subjects to recognize that the opening measures of

Schubert's String Quartet in E♭ create a gap-fill pattern (for an analysis of this passage, see Meyer [1973, 234–38]). But, in both these cases, errors were probably a result of other problems as well. In the Mozart example, for instance, the changing-note pattern was unusual: instead of moving 1–7–2–1 as in the other instances of this archetype, it moves 1–2–7–1. And, in the Schubert example, the gap is created by a downward skip rather than by the more usual upward one.

Inspection (as well as common sense) suggests more difficulty in learning to classify bilinear melodies, such as example 4, compared to those consisting of just a single melodic strand. The degree of internal redundancy also seems to affect ease of classification. For instance, both the Andante from Mozart's Symphony in F Major (ex. 3) and the last movement of Beethoven's String Quartet in B♭, op. 18, no. 6, are gap-fill melodies of the form AA′B. But the former, which is characterized by a high degree of internal redundancy (particularly, the first half involves repetition of a stable tonic triad), was generally classified correctly; the latter, which involves considerably less pitch and pattern repetition and is relatively unstable harmonically, proved much more difficult to classify. In this connection, it should be noted that, while changing-note melodies occur in only one form (AA′), gap-fill melodies occur either in antecedent-consequent form (AA′) or in so-called bar form (AA′B). The possibility of alternative forms may in part explain why subjects generally found it more difficult to classify gap-fill patterns than changing-note ones, although the difference was not statistically significant.

A review of passages in the light of differential error scores also suggests that secondary parameters—texture and tempo, dynamics and timbre—may significantly influence ease of classification. All else being equal, it seems probable that very rapid tempi and surprising changes in dynamics make melodies more difficult to classify. The organization of texture also seems to play a role in the ease with which the class of a melody is recognized. As one might expect, clear figure/ground division (as in a homophonic texture) facilitates the classification of melodies, while textural intricacy makes it more difficult. For instance, though the Adagio melody from Mozart's Fantasy for Piano in D Minor is quite complex (for a discussion, see Narmour [1977, 89–95]), our subjects seem to have learned its class quite readily. And perhaps they did so because the figure/ground relationship is very clear and the tempo is slow. It is possible, too, that familiarity facilitated classification in this case—and perhaps in some others as well. For Mozart's D-Minor Fantasy is often studied by beginning piano students, and it might have been known (and hence readily remembered) by some of our subjects.

Finally, in at least one case, the high number of errors can be attributed to the use of a passage that was not, properly speaking, a member of the class it was included to represent. The melody of the third movement of Mozart's Piano Quintet in E♭ is indeed a changing-note melody; but, instead of moving around the tonic (1–7–2–1), it moves around the third of the scale (3–4–2–3).

As the preceding discussion indicates, the ease or difficulty with which subjects classify a particular melody is a result of the intricate interaction among *all* the features and parameters that make the patterning what it is. It cannot be sufficiently emphasized that the passages that our subjects were asked to classify were not invented abstractions or contrived simplifications but real music as it was really performed. Not only melodic organization on all hierarchic levels, but rhythmic and harmonic structure, texture, tempo, and dynamics, at once shaped complex patterning and made the task of classification formidable. And, because for each passage the relative importance of the various factors is different, general rules explaining how the resulting idiosyncratic relationships help or hinder classification are difficult, perhaps impossible, to discover.

III. Implications

Melodic archetypes, such as those considered in this experiment, make possible an almost infinite variety of particular instantiations. Our analysis suggests that, unless the essential structural tones of a melodic process are kept intact, changing individual notes in a melody by one or several octaves at random should make recognition very difficult. Such octave shifts, for example, might transform a changing-note melody into something like an abortive gap-fill one. Deutsch (1972) found that octave displacements did interfere with recognition of a familiar tune. Dowling and Hollombe (1977) and Idson and Massaro (1978) have produced evidence that maintenance of contour can partly overcome the effects that Deutsch first reported. Having the undistorted tune available for comparison also facilitates recognition (see House 1977; and Deutsch 1978; Idson and Massaro also played undistorted tunes in their series). Therefore, maintenance of contour is only one factor that can oppose the effects of octave displacement. Other experimental work bears out the importance of contour in recognition of distorted melodies (Francès 1958; White 1960) and in perception of transpositions (Dowling and Fujitani 1971).

We suspect that one of the crucial considerations for recognition in the face of variation is the presence or absence of hierarchic structuring. If hierarchic organization is present, pattern recognition is possible even when there is significant alteration *as long as* the structural tones that shape the essential process maintain their functions. When these are changed, recognition should be increasingly difficult. And, if the melodies used in an experiment are without hierarchic structure, it should make less difference which tones are altered—recognition should be more or less equally affected.

The idea of different types of melodic processes also illuminates other experimental findings on recognition of melodies. White (1960) found that retrograde variations on a familiar melody were particularly destructive of recognition. Dowling (1971, 1972) has examined the effects of inversion, retrograde, and retrograde inversion on recognition of short atonal sequences in an immediate memory paradigm. A sequence was presented on each trial, followed immediately by a variation on it or by some different sequence. Subjects had to say whether the second sequence was a transformation of the first. Dowling found that retrograde inversion made recognition most difficult. Because they are syntactic and create a sense of goal-directed motion, tonal melodies should be more difficult to recognize in inversion, retrograde, and retrograde inversion than nontonal ones. The analysis of melodic process, however, suggests that the difficulty of recognizing a transformation will depend on the type of melody used. Changing-note melodies, for example, are more open to retrograde variation than are gap-fill ones. Different types of melodic processes will make one or another sort of transformation easier or harder to use while maintaining recognition. Generally, however, retrograde transformations are very likely to alter severely the process that underlies a particular melody and to render recognition harder. This fact gives some account of the findings of White and of Dowling.

Finally, some attention has been directed during the last ten years to effects of interleaving two melodies, binaurally or dichotically (Deutsch 1975; Dowling 1973; Butler 1979). Melodic interleaving is essential in the practice of polyphony. The analysis presented here suggests that some melodic types are probably better suited for polyphonic combination than others. For instance, because they quickly make clear the basic melodic process involved and employ motivically as well as functionally contrasting parts, gap-fill melodies—especially those with a patent initial skip and without complex hierarchic organization (see, e.g., ex. 3)—provide a particularly good basis for polyphonic combination, as even a casual glance at the fugue subjects in Bach's *Well-Tempered Clavier* makes evident. Because they are quite different in these respects, changing-note melodies are not especially well suited to polyphonic usage.

REFERENCES

Butler, D. A further study of melodic channeling. *Perception and Psychophysics* 25 (1979): 254–68.

Cooper, G. W., and L. B. Meyer. *The rhythmic structure of music.* Chicago, 1960.

Dawkins, R. *The selfish gene.* London, 1976.

Deutsch, D. Octave generalization and tune recognition. *Perception and Psychophysics* 11 (1972): 411–12.

Deutsch, D. Two-channel listening to musical scales. *Journal of the Acoustical Society of America* 57 (1975): 1156–60.

Deutsch, D. Octave generalization and melody identification. *Perception and Psychophysics* 23 (1978): 91–92.

Dowling, W. J. Recognition of inversions of melodies and melodic contours. *Perception and Psychophysics* 9 (1971): 348–49.

Dowling, W. J. Recognition of melodic transformations: Inversion, retrograde, and retrograde inversion. *Perception and Psychophysics* 12 (1972): 417–21.

Dowling, W. J. The perception of interleaved melodies. *Cognitive Psychology* 5 (1973): 322–37.

Dowling, W. J., and D. A. Fujitani. Contour, interval, and pitch recognition in memory for melodies. *Perception and Psychophysics* 9 (1971): 524–31.

Dowling, W. J., and A. W. Hollombe. The perception of melodies distorted by splitting into several octaves: Effects of increasing proximity and melodic contour. *Perception and Psychophysics* 21 (1977): 60–64.

Francès, R. *La perception de la musique.* Paris, 1958.

Frye, N. *Anatomy of criticism.* Princeton, N.J., 1957.

House, W. J. Octave generalization and the identification of distorted melodies. *Perception and Psychophysics* 21 (1977): 586–89.

Idson, W. L., and D. W. Massaro. A bidimensional model of pitch in the recognition of melodies. *Perception and Psychophysics* 24 (1978): 551–65.

Komar, A. *Theory of suspensions.* New York, 1968.

Levy, J. M. Gesture, form, and syntax in Haydn's music. In *Haydn studies,* ed. J. P. Larsen, H. Serwer, and J. Webster. New York, 1981.

Meyer, L. B. *Explaining music: Essays and explorations.* Berkeley, Calif.: 1973.

Meyer, L. B. *Style and Music.* Philadelphia, 1989; Chicago, 1996.

Narmour, E. *Beyond Schenkerism.* Chicago, 1977.

Schenker, H. *Der Freie Satz.* Vienna, 1956.

Siegel, S. *Nonparametric statistics for the behavioral sciences.* New York, 1956.

White, B. Recognition for distorted melodies. *American Journal of Psychology* 73 (1960): 100–107.

Yeston, M. *The stratification of musical rhythm.* New Haven, Conn., 1976.

Yeston, M., ed. *Reading in Schenker analysis.* New Haven, Conn., 1977.

III

Music, Culture, and History

5

Exploiting Limits: Creation, Archetypes, and Style Change

Creation

For the past three hundred years or so, the natural sciences have been conspicuously successful in formulating and testing theories that explain phenomena in the natural world. And they have had striking success in applying the knowledge gained through theorizing to other realms—for example, industrial, agricultural, and medical technology. As a result, the sciences have become the preferred paradigm not only for intellectual inquiry but also for accounts of creativity, originality, and cultural change in all areas of human endeavor.

This paradigm has emphasized that the most significant and valuable achievements in the sciences have resulted from the falsification of existing theories and the promulgation of new ones based on previously unformulated concepts or unimagined relationships. Because the scientists who wrought such revolutions have become exemplary cultural heroes, their names come readily to mind: Galileo and Kepler, Newton and Darwin, Mendel and Einstein. Whatever its validity for the sciences, this paradigm was transferred more or less intact to the arts. One result has been the assumption implicit in the title of this symposium—in the arts, as in the sciences, the creative act involves transcending limits.[1]

Of course, much depends on what is meant by the phrase *transcending limits*. But the prevalent view—which may serve as a reminder of the still-powerful presence of Romanticism in our culture—seems to be that expressed by Bronowski: "We expect artists as well as scientists to be forward-looking, to fly in the face of what is established, and to create not what is

Reprinted by permission of *Daedalus*, Journal of the American Academy of Arts and Sciences, from the issue entitled, "Intellect and Imagination—The Limits and Presuppositions of Intellectual Inquiry," Spring 1980, vol. 109, no. 2, pp. 177–205.

1. The title of the symposium sponsored by Emory University for which this paper was written contained the phrase *transcending limits*.

acceptable, but what will become acceptable."[2] This view, which is entirely compatible with common cultural scuttlebutt, implies that artistic change is the desirable and necessary consequence of experimentation (the scientific model is obvious) and that such experimentation results in revolutions in technical means and perhaps aesthetic ends as well. In short, what seems meant by *transcending limits* is the overturning of some prevalent style of art and the institution of a new one through a revolution comparable to those said by some to be characteristic of the sciences. The conception of creativity posited by this view seems to me to be partial and strained. When applied to the arts, it is misleading and mistaken in significant ways.[3]

It is misleading because it encourages historical distortion; the model makes it necessary that artists acknowledged to be "great" be radical innovators. For instance, Beethoven, perhaps *the* exemplary artist, has to be seen as combining the defiant heroism of Prometheus with the conceptual boldness of Galileo: a revolutionary toppling the rules and, in so doing, freeing music from the stifling confines of convention.[4] But sober study of his music indicates that, if his musical values are not confused with his seemingly equivocal political views, Beethoven overturned no fundamental syntactic rules. Rather, he was an incomparable strategist who *exploited* limits—the rules, forms, and conventions that he inherited from predecessors such as Haydn and Mozart, Handel and Bach—in richly inventive and strikingly original ways. In so doing, Beethoven extended the means of the Classic style. But extending is not transcending—it is not abrogating rules and overturning conventions.[5]

The association of the creative act with "transcending limits" tends to obscure a distinction of some moment, that between the historical importance of a work of art and its aesthetic significance or value. These are by no means the same. Because they initiated or strikingly exemplified a new rule or principle of organization, some works of art (or groups of works) are considered to have been of signal historical importance. Peri's *Orfeo* and the operas of the Florentine Camerata are such works. But few listeners, scholars, or critics would, I think, include these among the great works of Western music.

2. J. Bronowski, "The Creative Process," *Scientific American* 199, no. 3 (1958): 64.

3. Recently, Steven Weinberg has argued that the "revolution" paradigm is also misleading in accounting for the history of the sciences (see his "The Revolution That Didn't Happen," *New York Review of Books*, 8 October 1998).

4. In a comparable way, this model, coupled with a doubtful Hegelianism, leads Schönberg to transform Brahms into a "progressive" and encourages Webern to suggest that Bach anticipated the innovations of serialism (and was thus, despite customary belief, an innovator).

5. This in no way denies that innovations transcending existing limits have at times changed the history of the arts.

Mozart's *Marriage of Figaro,* on the other hand, must surely be counted one of the masterpieces of world music. But its modest innovations are confined to recombining and extending existing means.[6]

A moment's reflection—an informal mental survey of familiar classics—makes it evident that there is something suspect about associating creativity with transcending limits for few of the greatest artists have been promulgators of new principles. As Josephine Miles has observed, "It is surprising to note, perhaps, that the so-called great poets as we recognize them are not really the innovators; but if you stop to think about it, they shouldn't be. Rather they are the sustainers, the most deeply immersed in tradition, the most fully capable of making use of the current language available to them. When they do innovate, it is within a change begun by others, already taking place."[7] In music, the situation seems unequivocal. Though some composers have both invented new principles and devised new means for their realization, creating compositions of the highest aesthetic value—one thinks, perhaps, of the work of Monteverdi—many of those recognized as great masters have transcended no limits, promulgated no new principles. Rather, they have been inventive strategists, imaginative and resourceful in exploiting and extending existing limits. This pantheon includes masters such as Josquin and Lassus, Handel and Bach, Haydn and Mozart, Schubert and Chopin, Brahms and Verdi, and even, as I hope to show in this essay, such supposed revolutionaries as Hector Berlioz.

If these observations have merit, it would seem that two different sorts of creativity—and, by extension, originality—need to be distinguished. The first kind, most clearly exemplified in the work of renowned scientists, involves the discovery and formulation of new theories that make it possible to relate different phenomena to one another in coherent ways. The second kind of creativity, that manifested in the work of many of the greatest artists, involves exploiting and extending the possibilities potential in an existing set of principles in order to make a presentational pattern.[8]

6. The failure to distinguish between historical importance and aesthetic significance has influenced not only our culture's *view* of the history of the arts but the history of art itself because a considerable number of artists, as well as critics and historians, came to believe that the creative act, and, by extension, artistic originality, necessarily involved the invention and use of new syntactic means. As a result, the promulgation of new principles became a goal of art, until in an ultimate phase artists did not bother to make presentational works but simply presented the conceptual principles themselves.

7. Josephine Miles, "Values in Language; or, Where Have *Goodness, Truth* and *Beauty* Gone?" *Critical Inquiry* 3, no. 1 (1976): 11.

8. This discussion, as well as later ones, involves the distinction (made in the first essay of this "gathering") between general propositional concepts and particular presentational phenomena (such as works of art).

This suggests that the kinds of things created and, consequently, the modes of understanding and appreciation appropriate to each are different. Both kinds of creativity involve the use of particular phenomena and general principles, but they do so in quite opposite ways.

The kind of creativity that most often transcends limits makes use of particular phenomena observed in the natural world or in human cultures. However, instead of being of interest for their own sakes, such particulars—a falling star or a brilliant diamond, a chrysanthemum or a nesting bird, a supermarket or a Schumann symphony—are relegated to the role of data. They serve as means for the discovery, formulation, and testing of a theory. The theory, which is the goal and end result of the creative act, is a general proposition in terms of which diverse and divergent phenomena can be related to one another in coherent, understandable ways. And those theories are most highly prized (and, yes, most aesthetically satisfying) that encompass the widest range of phenomena within the simplest set of principles.

The second kind of creativity—that which exploits and extends limits, and the kind with which I will be concerned in the remainder of this essay—works quite the other way around. What is created is *not* a proposition about phenomena or about the relationships among them. *Hamlet* is not a tract about the behavior of indecisive princes or the uses of political power; nor is Picasso's *Guernica* primarily a propositional statement about the Spanish Civil War or the evils of fascism. What the second kind of creativity produces is not a generalization but a particular, not a propositional theory but a presentational phenomenon—a specific set of relationships designed to be directly understood and experienced by culturally competent audiences.

What the second sort of creative act gives us, then, is an idiosyncratic pattern, presented in time or space: in short, a work of art. As we listen to Major General Stanley sing his song,

> About binomial theorem I'm teeming with a lot o' news—
> With many cheerful facts about the square of the hypotenuse,

what we enjoy and appreciate are not the binomial or Pythagorean theorems or the perplexing principles of prosody that constrained and guided W. S. Gilbert's choice of words. What we respond to and delight in are the deft exploitation of cultural and linguistic habits, the playful coupling of a prosaic vocabulary with high-falutin concepts, and the rather preposterous extension of the conventions of rhyming.

General principles—laws, rules, and even conventions (e.g., rhymed couplets)—play an important role both in the creation of works of art and in our appreciation of them. For the artist, they constitute a set of constraints without which intelligent choice would be impossible; for the competent audience, they function as the rules of the game that form the basis for understanding and evaluating the particular presentational relationships that are the work of art: for instance, the specific verbal, visual, and gestural patterning that *is* the play *Hamlet,* as actualized in some interpretation.

The implied analogy to games may serve to illuminate something about the nature of appreciation. In works of art, as well as in games, what we enjoy and respond to is not our knowledge of governing principles or rules but the peculiar relationships discerned in a specific composition or the idiosyncratic play of a particular game. And just as our delight in the play of a particular game of football depends in crucial ways on our understanding of the constraints governing the game—the established rules, prevalent strategies, physical circumstances, and so on—so our enjoyment and evaluation of art depends on our knowledge (which may be tacit) of the constraints that governed the choices made by the artist and, hence, the relationships presented in the work of art.[9]

The analogy to games cannot, however, be sustained, and the point at which it breaks down is revealing. In games, the constraints (the rules, prevalent strategies, and so on) are explicitly known and conceptualized by all concerned—coaches, players, onlookers: "Three strikes, and you're out!" "A bishop may move diagonally in either direction." In the arts, on the other hand, some of the most fundamental constraints governing aesthetic relationships may be *un*known or not be explicitly conceptualized, even by those most accomplished and imaginative in their use, that is, creative artists. They know the constraints of a style not in the sense of being able to conceptualize them or state them as propositions but in the sense of knowing how to use them effectively. As with knowledge of a language, what is involved is the acquisition of a skill, the internalization of the constraints as unconscious modes of perception, cognition, and response. The same is true of most performers, critics, and audiences. They, too, know the constraints of a style—the laws, rules, and strategies that limited the composer's choices—in this tacit way.

What composers, performers, critics, and listeners—and, yes, musicologists—*do* know consciously and explicitly are particular realizations (often

---

9. Knowledge of prevailing constraints is indispensable because understanding, enjoyment, and evaluation depend not simply upon perceiving what *actually* happens in a game or is presented in a work of art but also upon the observer's ability to sense what *might have happened* or been presented. The significance of the road taken, to use Frost's metaphor, invariably includes an awareness of other possibilities that were not, but might have been, taken.

grouped into types or classes) of more general stylistic principles. And, from such realizations, music theorists attempt to infer the general principles that constrained, but did not determine, the choices made by composers. As constraints have changed over time, so have the patterns that are the basis for style classifications. We readily recognize that certain melodies or harmonic progressions are characteristic of the Classic style while others are typical of the Romantic, that this Crucifixion painting is Renaissance, another is Baroque.

There are cases, however, in which fundamental similarities of form or process transcend traditional stylistic boundaries. Some kinds of patterning seem, if not universal, at least *archetypal* within one of the major cultural traditions, such as that of Western Europe.[10] And the most patently archetypal patternings are, one suspects, those that couple compellingly coherent processive relationships with patently ordered formal plans.[11] An archetypal pattern may serve as the basis for countless individual realizations, each of which is the result of some newly devised strategy. And, however modest and unprepossessing the novelty may be, it is nonetheless evidence of a creative act that exploited, but did not transcend, limits. Examples of archetypes come readily to mind: quest/trial plots from Homer to Joyce; gap-fill melodies from Gregorian chant to "Somewhere over the Rainbow."

Archetypes are important because they establish fundamental frameworks in terms of which culturally competent audiences (creators and performers, critics and scholars, as well as members of the general public) perceive, comprehend, and respond to the playful ingenuity and expressive power of the idiosyncratic patterns presented in works of art. They are important for other reasons as well.

Because they are coherent, orderly, and simple, archetypes are memorable and tend to be stable over time. Since they are general types, the number of archetypes is limited. For these reasons, they are an important basis for stylistic learning. They are what children learn when they tediously reiterate nurs-

---

10. In what follows it may occasionally seem that archetypes have been given a kind of Platonic reality or have been reified in some way. Thus it should be emphasized that, in my view, archetypes are cognitive constructs abstracted from particular patternings that are grouped together because of their similar syntactic shapes and/or formal plans. That is, archetypes are classlike patterns that are specially compelling because they result from the consonant conjoining of prevalent stylistic constraints with the neuro/cognitive proclivities of the human mind.

11. As implied in this description, coherence of process can and should be distinguished from formal ordering. There are both archetypal processes (such as a circle-of-fifths progression in tonal harmony) and archetypal forms (such as strophic, ritornello, and binary kinds). An archetypal *pattern,* as I intend the term, combines such a process with such a form.

ery rhymes, intone tiresome chants, and make visual images that only fond parents delight in, psychiatrists regard as interesting, and Wordsworthian Romantics find profound.

Archetypes, therefore, are an important basis for cultural continuity. They are the cognitive-mnemonic schemas that Richard Dawkins called "memes" because he thought of them as the cultural counterparts of the units of biological trait transmission.[12] Like genes, they tend to persist—but in culture rather than nature. And, because they persist, archetypes may help illuminate the nature of the changes that have occurred in the history of an art such as music. That is, using an archetype as a constant may enable us to perceive, and perhaps eventually to explain, the nature of the succession of different realizations that constitute the history of music.

It is this possibility that I plan to explore in what follows. Obviously, in an essay such as this, I can do no more than discuss a few realizations of a single archetype, considering how, and perhaps why, the realizations changed over time. The relationship between the general scheme of the archetype and particular realizations of it will first be illustrated with instances from the oeuvre of Mozart. Then I will present an example of the way in which Beethoven realizes the archetype and suggest the significance of some of his modifications. Finally, I will consider how Berlioz realizes the same fundamental schema and attempt to relate the peculiarities of his actualization to what I take to be some of the significant facets of Romanticism in music.

The Archetype

Before particular realizations of the archetype are considered, the bare bones of the schema must be described and discussed for, to appreciate the similarities and differences among particular realizations, the salient features of the schema must be recognized and remembered. The basic pattern of the archetype is given in example 1. The schema is divided into two parts, marked A and B in line *a* of the example. The parts are distinguished by differences in melodic pattern and by the harmonic and rhythmic closure that occurs when mobile dominant harmony (V) resolves to stable tonic harmony (I) at the end of part A. In particular realizations, moreover, contrasts

---

12. In *The Selfish Gene* (New York: Oxford University Press, 1976), 206ff., Richard Dawkins suggests that "full-blown" tunes such as "Auld Lang Syne" are "memes." In my view, the archetypes of which the tune is composed are the units of cultural transmission.

Example 1

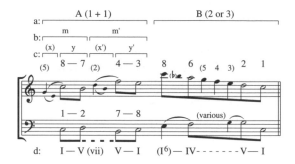

in texture (e.g., accompaniment figure) and dynamics often serve to emphasize the distinction between parts.

In the instances that I have come across, this scheme may be the basis for the patterning of a whole theme or parts of it. In the latter case, the archetype may structure both parts of a larger melody, as in an antecedent-consequent period (A–A′); or the archetype may, as we shall see, structure only one part (usually the first) of a higher-level binary form (A–B).

Part A itself consists of two melodic/rhythmic entities, designed *m* and *m′* on line *b*. These are always similar in melodic contour and in rhythmic pattern.[13] As a result of this similarity, the morphology of the first part of the archetype is always in the proportion (1 + 1). The length of the second part is more variable; but, as a rule, it is either equal to or half again as long as the first part. The whole pattern, then, is generally in the proportion (1 + 1) + 2 or (1 + 1) + 3.

The patterns *m* and *m′* may themselves be subdivided into motives *x* and *y* and motives *x′* and *y′*, but, as the parentheses (on line *c*) indicate, motive *x* is not invariably present. When it is, it usually centers around the fifth degree of the scale (5); at times, the third of the scale (3) is also part of the patterning of *x*; when *x′* is present, it usually centers on the second degree of the scale (2) and perhaps touches the seventh (7) as well.[14] Thus, though its presence may be characteristic, motive *x* does not define the first part of the archetype.

What define the archetype are the melodic and harmonic relationships between *y* and *y′*. As indicated in example 1, *y* consists of a melodic motion from

13. They are differentiated from each other by the very fact of melodic-rhythmic repetition, however varied, and by the presence of some sort of rhythmic, melodic, or harmonic articulation, however modest, separating *m* from *m′*.

14. What is important here is emphasis, not order. Even though the third is heard first, as in ex. 5 below, the fifth may predominate from a structural point of view.

the tonic (1 or 8) to the seventh degree of the scale, accompanied by a harmonic progression from the tonic triad (I) to a chord built on the dominant (V) or some substitute for it (vii); y' consists of a melodic motion from the fourth degree of the scale (4) to the third (3), harmonized by a progression from the dominant (or a substitute) back to the tonic.[15] Though what is crucial is its harmonic function, the melodic contour of the bass is usually the opposite of that of the melody: that is, when the melody descends, the bass ascends, and vice versa. The most common bass pattern is that shown in the example: namely, 1–2:7–8.[16]

Part B of the archetype is considerably more variable in form and process than part A. Melodically, it usually begins with the upper octave of the tonic, marked "8v" in example 1. This note, which will be called the *upper tonic*, is often harmonized by the first inversion of the tonic triad (I^6). The first important structural pitch, however, is usually the sixth degree of the scale, accompanied by subdominant harmony (IV or ii^6). Melodically, what most often follows is stepwise descending motion through the fifth, fourth, and third of the scale—with various possible harmonizations—to the second degree, harmonized by a dominant triad. This is resolved to the first degree of the scale harmonized by the tonic triad.

Conjunct descending motion is not, however, the only possible melodic patterning. To understand why this is so, we must consider the kinds of processes generated by motives y and y'. One of these is what I have called a *gap-fill* process.[17] When a skip occurs in a melodic pattern, we are aware, though perhaps unconsciously so, that some of the steps of the scale have been "left out." The sense of incompleteness created by such a gap implies a subsequent fill—a stepwise melodic motion that creates a sense of completeness by

---

15. Or a substitute chord, e.g., vi or $I^{7\flat} = V^7/IV$.

16. This makes it evident that the archetype being discussed in this essay is a special case of a larger class—the class of changing-note melodies, whose first part is typically organized as follows:

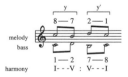

17. See my *Emotion and Meaning in Music* (Chicago: University of Chicago Press, 1956), 128–35, and *Explaining Music: Essays and Explorations* (Berkeley: University of California Press, 1975), 145–57. Also see essay 4, above.

Example 2

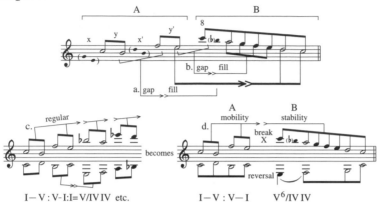

I − V : V - I:I= V/IV IV etc.   I − V : V − I   V⁶/IV IV

presenting the pitches previously skipped over.[18] And, though ascending gaps are most often followed by descending fills, all or part of a fill may, as we shall see, consist of rising motion.

For the sake of later discussion, it is important to analyze the processes characteristic of the archetype in a bit more detail. Because y and y' are intervallically identical (each descends a half step) and are usually alike in metric placement, duration, and so on, we relate them to *each other* despite the fact that a different motive, x', may have come between them. Thus the skip from the end of motive y to the beginning of y' is understood as a gap implying conjunct fill.[19] As graph a of example 2 shows, the fill begins when the fourth degree of the scale moves to the third at the close of motive y'. Further motion, through the second degree to the tonic, is, of course, implied. But such continuation is delayed until the end of the archetypal scheme. It is delayed because a second process, generated by the relationship between y and y', creates a further gap. This process is "sequential." The sequence consists of motive y and its repetition a perfect fourth higher (y'). This regularity implies continuation. And, had the sequence been continued exactly, it would have been as shown in graph c of example 2. The harmony, too, would have moved sequentially, as shown beneath graph c, to the subdominant—and perhaps beyond.

18. Usually the gap and fill parts of such a melody move in opposite directions: if the gap is created by a rising motion, the fill falls, and vice versa. But this is not invariably the case. Occasionally, as we shall see, a rising gap may be followed by a fill, at least part of which also rises. What is essential is the relation of gap to fill rather than the direction of the motion.

19. The implication is specially forceful in this case because the interval of the skip—the diminished fifth from the leading tone (7) to the fourth (4)—itself requires, and strongly implies, resolution to the third of the scale (3).

However, though the subdominant is characteristically the first structural harmony of part B (see graph *d*), the sequence is broken. For, instead of skipping in exact sequence to B♭, *y'* is followed by a skip to the upper tonic. What remains of the sequential process is the structurally important motion to the sixth degree of the scale, harmonized by the subdominant.

The skip from the third of the scale to the upper tonic creates a second gap. But, as graph *b* indicates, the fill really begins with the sixth of the scale and descends to the third. Only then is the process generated by the first gap (graph *a*) completed by a fill that reaches the tonic.

From a syntactic point of view, the second part of the archetype complements the first. In part B, that is, the implications generated in part A are realized through the filling of melodic gaps, the curbing of harmonic expansion, and a general emphasis on stability. This "reversal" from the relative tension and uncertainty of ongoing mobility, present in part A of the scheme, to the relative relaxation and certainty of arrival and provisional closure, characteristic of part B, constitutes what I shall call the syntactic climax of the archetypal structure.[20]

*

Let us consider three instances of the archetype as they occur in the oeuvre of Mozart. The first instance (ex. 3) is the beginning of the first movement of the Piano Sonata in G Major (K. 283). The theme exhibits almost all the features said to be characteristic of the archetype. Its two parts are clearly differentiated by motivic pattern, direction of melodic motion, accompaniment figure, and dynamics. The structural lengths are (2 + 2) + 6. Though motives *x* and *x'* are unusually well defined and discrete, lack of harmonic motion within them makes their subsidiary nature clear. The sequential gap-fill motion from *y* to *y'* is patent, as is the arrival at the upper tonic—though the high G is harmonized by a root-position triad rather than one in first inversion. As indicated in the analytic graphs, the bass motion and harmonic progression are typical.[21]

20. The term *reversal* is, of course, borrowed from Aristotle's *Poetics* and is, I think, used in an appropriately analogous way to refer to the process in which one moves from the tension and uncertainty of relative ignorance to the stability and resolution of relative knowledge. For a discussion of this process in music, see *Emotion and Meaning in Music*, 93ff., and *Explaining Music*, 119ff. and passim.

21. The only other point that needs to be mentioned has to do with analytic technique. The high C in m. 8 has been analyzed as a structural tone in the descending fill because the octave transfers D to D (at the beginning of the measure) and C to C (ending after the first beat of m. 9) are unequivocal, given the patent hemiola meter.

Example 3

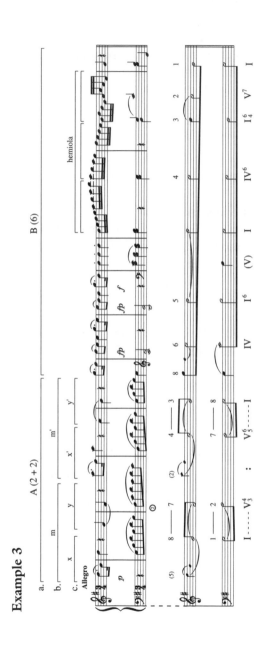

Example 4

The second instance, example 4, is from the opening theme of the last movement of Symphony no. 29 in A Major (K. 201). The archetypal scheme structures both parts of an antecedent-consequent period—but only the consequent period will be considered here. In this instance, motive *x* consists of a single pitch, the fifth of the scale, that functions as an upbeat to motive *y*. As a result, *x* virtually loses its identity as a motive. Motive *x'*, which is differentiated only rhythmically, is essentially absorbed into motive *y'*. Although subject to octave transfers, motive *y* and *y'* move unequivocally through the typical pattern (8–7, 4–3) accompanied by the usual harmonic progression and changing-note figure in the bass. Particularly in the consequent phrase, the conjunct descending fill as well as the contrast in rhythm, dynamics, and register differentiate the second part of the archetype from the first.[22]

Example 5 is the first C major section from the second movement of the Piano Sonata in C Major (K. 309). In this instance, x and x' are at least as patently shaped as y and y'. As in the archetypal model, the fifth is the most prominent tone in x, while the second of the scale is so in x'. Despite their relative brevity, there is no doubt that the cadential progression implicit in y and y' articulates the form and generates the process that structures this melody. Though the bass moves to the fifth in measure 35, the leading tone is present, and the harmonic progression is characteristic.

Part B begins with the customary progression from I^6 to the subdominant (ii^6). But, instead of descending, the upper tonic is reiterated, while rising motion in a lower line begins the fill. As the analysis shows, the upper tonic ultimately descends as both lines converge on the sixth of the scale, the A in measure 39. Such emphasis is entirely appropriate, not only because A is typically a focal point in the archetypal scheme, but also because it begins the last in a series of conventional patternings suggesting closure[23] a fact that will be important when the instance from Berlioz's music is considered.

22. It should perhaps be noted that the fill is quite complete—except that the second degree of the scale is only weakly present. This is compensated for at the close of the second key area of the recapitulation (mm. 146–55), where a descent from the sixth degree of the scale to the tonic, guided by fourth-species counterpoint, strongly emphasizes the second degree through deceptive cadences.

23. For instance, the end of the opening motive of this melody (part a, below) is similar in significant ways to that which first closes the Rondeau theme of Mozart's Piano Sonata in D, K. 311 (part b, below); and the falling seventh at the beginning of m. 37 (part c, below) occurs quite often at closes, such as that near the end of the exposition section of the first movement of Mozart's Piano Sonata in B♭, K. 570 (part d, below).

The cadential character of this realization of the archetype may be related to what appears to be a kind of formal ambiguity. When we first hear this melody, it is taken to be the main tune of the second key area of the movement. But, when it returns in elaborated form after the main

Example 5

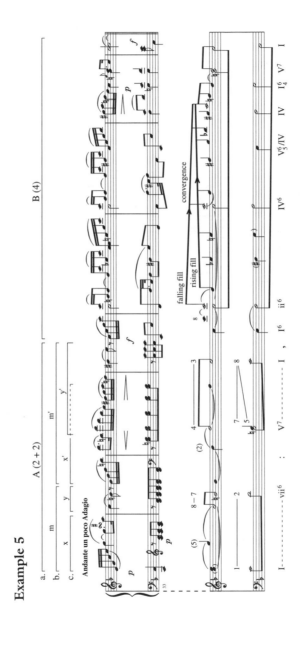

Example 6

(Example 3)

(Example 4)

(Example 5)

Analyses abstracted from Mozart's realizations of the archetype are given in example 6.[24] For convenient comparison, all analyses are given in the key of C. The family resemblance is inescapable, though the realizations differ markedly in aural patterning—in foreground melody and rhythm, harmony and texture, meter and tempo. Faced with such underlying commonality, one cannot fail to ask what limits Mozart is here transcending. The answer, of

---

theme has been presented in the tonic (F major), it is not in the tonic, as it would be were this the second key area of a sonata without development; it is in the dominant, as when first presented. In other words, the theme really functions as a dominant prolongation. And it is perhaps to compensate for this disparity between form and function that the melody consists of a succession of cadential formulas.

24. To facilitate comparison, the graphs given in the original examples have at times been slightly modified: the lowest level of structural tones has been omitted, and registers have been made more or less uniform.

course, is none. Rather, it is his genius to exploit his, and our, familiarity with the constraints (the limits) of the Classic style.

Style Change

All the preceding instances were composed during the 1770s. Now I shall discuss two instances of the archetype taken from works written more than forty years later. The first, one of the last works of the Classic style, was written by Beethoven in 1826; the second, one of the exemplary works of the Romantic style, was written by Berlioz in 1830.

The work from Beethoven's oeuvre (ex. 7) is the theme of the fourth movement of the String Quartet in C♯ Minor, op. 131. The theme is in two periods (labeled P^1 and P^2 in the example); each of the periods is repeated in somewhat varied form.[25] The first period (P^1), an antecedentlike phrase, presents a version of the archetype. And part A is an almost pristine distillation of the pattern—with no trace of an x motive and no hint of harmonic elaboration.[26] Part B of the archetype begins typically with the upper tonic over first-inversion tonic harmony. The melody then descends linearly, developing considerable mobility as the result of a harmonic sequence that, following emphasis on subdominant harmony, closes on the dominant (mm. 8 and 16).

Instead of a "proper" consequent phrase, however, what follows is a new sequence that, while maintaining the rhythmic figure established in P^1, moves from the second degree of the scale (B) back to the upper tonic.[27] (It is as though the fill of the second part of the archetype was not entirely satisfactory. In "compensation," the ascending line of the second period emphasizes the second and fifth of the scale, important tones touched only lightly [m. 7] in the descending fill of the first period.) In contrast to the first period, the

25. The overall structure of the theme, then, is P^1–P^1: P^2–P^2. Since the differences between the versions of P^1 and P^2 are irrelevant for present purposes, only one version of each is given in the example: for P^1, mm. 1–8; for P^2, mm. 25–32.

26. What is mostly responsible for the special savor of the theme is the unusual rhythmic patterning and the instrumental hocket that supports it. As line *d* of the example shows, the rhythmic group is one in which the mobile anacrusis is three times as long as the stable accent that follows it; i.e.,

27. Notice that hints of the archetype are present in the foreground patterning of the bass (analysis line *e*).

Example 7

rising sequence of the second makes reaching the upper tonic seem a more significant achievement. This is so for several reasons. First, rising lines generally engender a greater sense of effort than do falling ones. And this sense tends to be specially strong when the rising line is not only sequential but what might be called "Sisyphean"—that is, when the motive, which is the basis for the sequence, itself rises (implying continued upward motion), only to fall back.[28] And the force of such upward goal-directed motion is heightened by the growth and decay of dynamics within measures 25 and 27. At measure 29, the sequence ends as the rising line moves directly to the high A. Again, dynamics—the crescendo in measures 29–30—help heighten the sense of ascending motion, while the expansion of registral sonority (in the middle voices) and the appoggiatura, G♯, strongly stress the arrival of the A. Once this goal is achieved, dynamics die away, register and sonority return to normal, and the melodic line descends toward closure on the tonic.

This description calls attention to a distinction of importance, that between syntactic climax and statistical climax. A *syntactic climax* is a result of what was earlier called *reversal:* that is, a change in which forms and processes shaped by the primary parameters of melody, rhythm, and harmony move from a state characterized by relative mobility, ambiguity, uniformity, or irregularity to one of relative stability, coherent process, and clear form. A *statistical climax,* or "apotheosis," on the other hand, consists of a gradual increase in the intensity of the more physical attributes of sound, the arrival at a tensional "high point," followed by a usually rapid decline in activity—a falling away to quiet and closure. Because the intensity of the secondary parameters that shape such processes can be measured and quantified—for example, the increase or decrease in dynamics (intensity), pitch (as frequency), rate of note succession, timbre, and tempo—they have been called *statistical.* One further point: though an intensification of secondary parameters—higher pitches, louder dynamics, and so on—often accompanies syntactic climax, such heightened activity is not a necessary condition for—but a concomitant, a symptom, of—such climax.[29] In a statistical

---

28. In this case, e.g., the B to C♯ (m. 25) implies, but does not continue directly to, D. Similarly, the linear motion B–C♯–D (m. 26) implies continuation to an accented E, but the melody falls back to C♯ on the first beat of m. 27, moving to an accented E only on the first beat of m. 28. A well-known instance of a Sisyphean sequence is the melody that begins the "Liebestod" from Wagner's *Tristan.*

29. In theory, at least, a syntactic climax can occur at a low, soft, less active part of a structure *if* that is where ongoing processes are reversed and stabilized. See, e.g., the first prelude in Bach's *Well-Tempered Clavier,* mm. 20–24.

climax, however, the high point of activity *is* the central tensional event—
which either subsides to closure or "resolves" into a forthright affirmative
musical assertion.

Returning now to Beethoven's theme, both periods are shaped by syntax,
but, in the second (P^2), the syntactic climax in measures 29–30 is led up to
and complemented by features characteristic of statistical climax: the gradual
increase in intensity that results from the sequential rise, the crescendo, and
the enlargement of registral sonority, all followed by a quick decline in intensity. This interpretation is supported by another difference between the first
and the second periods of the theme. Instead of occurring halfway through,
as in the first period, the high point now occurs in the sixth measure—three-
fourths of the way through. For reasons that I will present later, such placement nearer to the end of a process is characteristic of the high point of a
statistical apotheosis.[30]

The final actualization of the archetype that I will consider is the main
melody, the famous *idée fixe,* from the first movement of Berlioz's *Symphonie
fantastique* (ex. 8). The work was written only four years after Beethoven's
C♯-Minor Quartet, but Berlioz was Beethoven's junior by more than thirty
years, and thus the difference in style is very striking.[31]

Despite significant differences, however, salient features of the archetype

30. In this connection, see George E. Muns, "The Climax in Music" (Ph.D. diss., University of North Carolina at Chapel Hill, 1955). I am grateful to my former student, Dr. John Ches-
nut, for calling Muns's essay to my attention and, more important, for suggesting, through his
own work on the shape of intensity curves in music, the distinction between what I am calling
statistical and *syntactic climax.*

31. In my view, it is *not* surprising that Beethoven's usage is more like Mozart's than like
Berlioz's—even though the last of Mozart's works considered here preceded the C♯-Minor
Quartet by forty years while Beethoven's precedes Berlioz's work by only four years. What most
affects compositional choices is the internalization of prevalent musical constraints, and such
learning almost always takes place before a composer is twenty. In this respect, Beethoven and
Mozart, who were born fourteen years apart, were near contemporaries; while Beethoven and
Berlioz, who were born thirty-three years apart, were not. Beethoven's ingrained Classicism
seems evident in the high-level organization that unites the first and second periods for it is an
archetypal changing-note pattern, similar to that which structures the bass of pt. A of P^1. This
pattern is

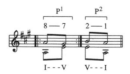

Example 8

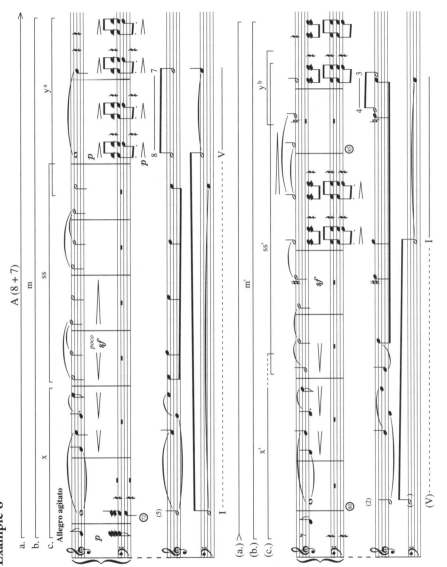

(continued on page 210)

Example 8 *(continued)*

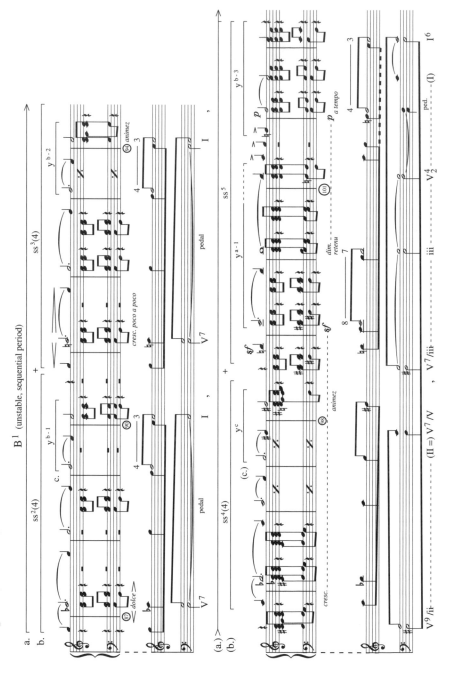

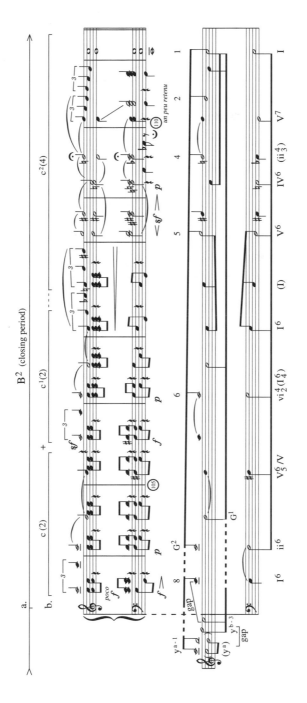

are unquestionably present. In what follows, I will first show that Berlioz's melody is, in fact, a member of the class I have been describing. Then I will consider how and why Berlioz has modified the archetypal scheme and attempt to relate such changes to what I take to be some of the leading currents of Romanticism in music.

That Berlioz's melody is a member of the archetypal class I have described seems indisputable—though not necessarily obvious. As the analysis given in example 8 shows, the first part of the melody is divided into two long phrases that are comparable to those designated as *m* and *m'* in the archetypal scheme. Each phrase begins with a triadic pattern that prolongs a single harmony: these are the *x* motives. As in the instances already considered, motive *x* centers on the fifth of the scale (G), motive *x'* on the second degree (D). Typically, the first phrase *(m)* closes with a motive (here labeled y^a) that descends a half step from the tonic (C) to the leading tone (B); and the second phrase *(m')* also closes with a descending half step (labeled y^b) that moves from the fourth of the scale (F) to the third (E). As in previous instances, the underlying harmonic plan is I–V:V–1.[32]

Berlioz's melody is certainly in agreement with my earlier observation that the second part of the archetype allows for greater variability than the first. Instead of beginning with the usual skip to the upper tonic, thus continuing the sequential gap process begun in part A, the second part of the *idée fixe* (labeled B^1) first reaches the upper tonic (the C in m. 99) through a new linear sequence based on a motive (labeled *ss*) that was initially presented between motives *x* and y^a. In a sense, this first upper tonic occurs as part of the wrong sequence. Moreover, it is a mobile dissonance—an appoggiatura that calls for resolution. But, in the archetypal scheme, and in all the instances of it presented, the upper tonic was relatively stable; usually, it was part of the tonic triad.

A satisfactory upper tonic does occur at the beginning of the last part of the melody (B^2). Harmonized, as it often is, by the first inversion of the tonic chord, the stable high C (m. 103) moves in familiar fashion to the sixth of the scale (m. 105). As in the second part of the instances already discussed, the remainder of B^2 descends to closure on the lower tonic. As shown in graphs

32. Because it is at times doubtful which of Berlioz's bass tones should be considered structural—e.g., in m. 78, is the G or the D the main structural tone?—I have treated the first eighth note of Berlioz's succession of pairs as being structural, except where a patently ordered pattern preempts aural attention (as in mm. 95–101).

G^1 and G^2, gaps generated earlier—from y^a to y^b and from y^{b-3} to the high C (m. 103)—are filled by gradual descending motion. At the same time, the fill also accommodates a succession of closing figures.

Though I do not doubt that the archetypal patterning is central to the form and process of Berlioz's melody, the need to argue the case at all suggests that salient features of the archetype have been obscured. The question is not only *why* the lineaments of the scheme have been veiled but also *how* the particular changes made are related to the presumed need for disguise.

In my view, Berlioz's exploitation and extension of the archetype can be interpreted as an exemplary and revealing response to two of the beliefs central to Romanticism. The first is the belief that conventions, whether in human behavior or in the realm of art, are not merely deplorable but also somehow decadent and immoral. Habitually denigrated and disparaged as being impersonal formulas, calculated contrivances, or lifeless clichés, conventions were at the very least considered to be symptomatic of the detested fetters that, according to Rousseau, enchain mankind.

A number of different beliefs and attitudes characteristic of Romanticism can be related to one another through their common incompatibility with the conventional as it was understood at the time. The following are examples of attitudes toward the conventional that have a connection with the arts:

1. The personal expression of the artist as individual, assigned a position of prime importance in the aesthetics of Romanticism, could not easily be reconciled with the apparent impersonality and commonality of prevalent convention. Also, the artist's role as "revolutionary liberator," still with us here today, called on him to overturn rules and conventions—to transcend limits.

2. Inspiration, regarded with almost religious awe by devout Romantics, seemed diametrically opposed to convention. Far from being learned and culturally shared, as conventions were, inspiration was supposed to flow spontaneously from the artist's inmost being, as natural and unpremeditated art.

3. The perspicacity imputed to innocent infants (trailing their glorious clouds behind them) and the virtue patronizingly attributed to the uncorrupted honesty of presumably uncultivated primitives—these, too, testify to the low esteem in which culturally learned conventions were generally held.

4. The magical power of such Romantic heroes as Siegfried and Parsifal is intimately connected with their cultural innocence—with the fact that they had not been defiled by the conventions of civilization.

As Charles Rosen and Henry Zerner point out, one of the deepest ambitions of Romantic artists was "the achievement of 'immediacy,' of forms of expression directly understandable without convention and without previous knowledge of tradition." [33]

Thus arises what I take to be a problem of signal importance for the history of music in the nineteenth century. From an ideological, conceptual point of view, the conventional, the formulaic, the archetypal is anathema—something strenuously to be shunned. But, from a practical point of view, those who compose tonal music cannot do without conventions of grammar and syntax and the archetypal schemas that make relational richness possible. [34] While this dilemma was not satisfactorily resolved during the nineteenth century, a workable arrangement was reached. [35] Conventions, formulas, and archetypes were permitted in this arrangement, but they were

---

33. Charles Rosen and Henry Zerner, "The Permanent Revolution," *New York Review of Books* 26, no. 18 (22 November 1979): 27. Antipathy toward the conventional may also help explain the well-known, yet curious, penchant of Romanticism for the deformed and decrepit, the diseased, and even the plain ugly. The point of such unsavory, even disgusting images seems to be that their truth is guaranteed; i.e., since no one would deliberately distort or disgust, representations of the repulsive must be "honest." Artifice cannot have masked their truth. (Or, to put the matter in terms of the Romantic belief in the virtues of the natural: what is deformed, diseased, and so on must be natural and, therefore, "good.") The next step carries us to paradox. If Truth and Beauty are one, the equation is clear: ugliness, which is natural and guileless, guarantees truth; truth is beauty; therefore ugliness and beauty are, if not indistinguishable, at least not opposites.

34. This problem is, I suspect, less pressing in literature and the visual arts because novel subject matter can divert attention away from conventions of form and process. In architecture, and to some extent in the representational arts as well, the problem was ameliorated by adopting the conventions of a more remote past or of other cultures. Evidently, conventions seemed less oppressive when thus chosen. Music, too, followed this course, escaping the compulsive constraints of the immediate past by turning to folk music.

35. The dilemma has been solved in the twentieth century—at least for those composers who have abandoned tonality. But this has created an even more formidable problem, that of devising viable constraints to replace those of tonality, for, without constraints of some sort, choice is impossible. Thus, if the history of music in the nineteenth century can be understood as a continuing effort to reconcile the claims of the ideology of Romanticism with the practical need for conventional constraints, the history of music in the twentieth century can be seen, at least in part, as a succession of attempts to devise constraints that are at once nonconventional ("natural"? "logical"?) and artistically fruitful.

to be veiled or disguised in some way. In music, one of the discoveries of Romanticism was how to hide your archetype and have it too!

A second belief central to Romanticism is a corollary of the deprecation of convention. It affirms the excellence and value of what is natural—of spontaneous action, unreflecting feeling, untutored genius, and informal, unarranged landscapes. This enthusiasm, at times reverence, for the natural can be related to an important characteristic of nineteenth-century music: that is, the increasingly important role played by secondary parameters in the shaping of musical process and the articulation of musical form.

To understand this relationship it is necessary to recognize that the secondary parameters are, perhaps paradoxically, a more "natural" means for shaping musical processes and articulating musical forms than are the primary ones. For instance, the ritard and diminuendo, the thinning of texture, and the descending succession of pitches in measures 100–103 of Berlioz's melody all seem to foster and presage closure—even without the help of the articulation created by melody, harmony, and rhythm. This is because the physical patterning of the sound continuum—of pitch frequency, concord and discord, dynamic intensity, rate of impulse, instrumental timbre, and so on—shapes states of tension and repose in an almost unmediated, direct way. However, the subtle equivocal closure created (in the same measures) by the relationships among melody, harmony, and rhythm can be comprehended and experienced only by those who have internalized the constraints—have learned the conventions—of the style of tonal music.[36] Partly because they seemed more "natural," and hence compatible with the prevailing ideology, secondary parameters became more and more important during the course of the nineteenth century. Complementing the increased importance of the secondary parameters in shaping music was a decline in the importance of large-scale tonal relationships created by the primary parameters.

A corollary of this change in emphasis was an increase in the importance of statistical climax, or apotheosis, relative to syntactic climax in the shaping of musical structure—until the former comes to overshadow the latter. Such sta-

---

36. It is important not to make the common mistake of supposing that because something is conventional it is necessarily arbitrary. To be experientially viable the constraints of a musical style must be consonant with the broad lawlike constraints of the physical, biological, and psychological realms. But different sets of conventional constraints may satisfy such requirements.

tistical high points generally occur quite late in a form: roughly two-thirds rather than halfway through, as is commonly the case with syntactic climax. The reasons for this appear to be more or less as follows.

A syntactic climax need not, and usually does not, lead directly to closure. The reversal that articulates the climax is from a situation characterized by tonal ambiguity, unpredictability of uniform processes and weakened shapes, and uncertain formal organization to one of secure tonal/harmonic orientation, strongly shaped patterns, and clear, formal organization. But tonal/harmonic processes may be coherent without being closed; patterns may be patently shaped, though some implications remain to be realized; and formal organization may be clear without formal structure being complete.[37] Because syntactic climax need not be directly followed by closure, it can occur as early as halfway through formal entity—as it does, for instance, in Mozart's realizations of the archetype.

The high point in any statistical climax, however, usually occurs fairly late in the pattern. Otherwise the falling-off toward closure, unsustained by syntax, will be too long, and boredom will ensue. The only way to "prolong" an apotheosis process is to begin a new buildup as the earlier one is subsiding. From this building up again and again arises the cumulative wave-form pattern quite common in the music of the nineteenth century. In fact, it was a miniature version of such a wave-form pattern that was earlier called a Sisyphean sequence. And this brings us back to Berlioz's melody.

One of the obvious differences between Berlioz's melody and the instances considered earlier is that it is four times longer. Thus motive *m*, which was two measures long in all the earlier instances, lasts for eight measures in Berlioz's theme.[38] This increase in magnitude, itself a characteristic of much Romantic music (particularly that for orchestra), acts both directly and indirectly to obscure the archetypal pattern. It obscures directly because the change in size increases the *absolute* temporal distance between the pattern-

37. To take a brief but clear case: in the first prelude of Bach's *Well-Tempered Clavier,* a descending sequential process (mm. 5–20), guided by implied fourth-species counterpoint, is broken and reversed when a skip of a fifth (C down to F) in the bass is followed by chromatic rising motion that moves to the dominant (G) in m. 24. At this point the syntactic situation is clear; but closure is delayed for eleven measures through the prolongation first of dominant and then of tonic harmony. The statistical processes generated by secondary parameters cannot, however, delay closure in this way.

38. These are a specially clear instance of what Edward T. Cone has called *hypermeasures* (see his *Musical Form and Performance* [New York: Norton, 1968], 79ff.).

generating motives, y^a and y^b, making it more difficult for the listener to connect them. Indirectly, and more important, the change in size involves a change in structure, both within and between the parts of the archetype. The nature of the relationship of size to structure in music is at once of central importance for the history of music and still highly problematic. I can only suggest that D'Arcy Thompson's observations about the interdependency of size and structure in the natural world hold, with appropriate modifications, in the worlds of human culture.[39] And, just as one cannot simply increase the size of, say, a mosquito tenfold and still keep its functions and activities constant, so one cannot merely augment a musical pattern fourfold and yet maintain its functional relationships.

From this point of view, seeing how Berlioz modified the archetype by amplifying (and thereby disguising) it may serve to illustrate some of the compositional problems of nineteenth-century music. Phrases *m* and *m'* of part A of the archetypal model are enlarged through both augmentation and addition. The model's motives *x* and *y* are augmented: each is two measures, instead of one measure, long. What is added is a new motive not previously encountered in instances of the archetype, labeled *ss*, for Sisyphean sequence. In internal construction it rises only to fall, and from phrase to phrase it is the basis for an ascending sequence. Motives *ss* and ss^1 tend to obscure the relationship between y^a and y^b (so fundamental for an understanding of the archetypal pattern) for three reasons. First, they add another item to be remembered. Second, it is unclear precisely where *ss* and ss^1 end and y^a and y^b begin. Finally, the relationship between y^a and y^b is weakened by the lack of parallel rhythmic patterning and by the shortening of y^b by one measure.

Harmonic usage also serves to disguise the archetype. Because dominant harmony (V) ends the first phrase *(m)* and occurs as part of motive *x'*, it is understood to underlie the beginning of the second phrase *(m')*.[40] There is a resolution to tonic harmony in measure 84, but the context is wrong, as is

39. D'Arcy W. Thompson, *On Growth and Form,* abr. ed., ed. J. T. Bonner (Cambridge: Cambridge University Press, 1966), chap. 2. If one of the most important constraints governing the relationship of size to structure in the natural world is gravity, perhaps the comparable constraint governing relationships in human cultures is the principles of cognition—especially, I suspect, those of human memory. On the relationship between size and form, see also essay 8, pp. 285f.

40. Edward T. Cone's discussion of this passage is illuminating (see his edition: *Berlioz, Fantastic Symphony* [New York: Norton, 1971], 254–56).

the timing (see symbols under analytic graphs).[41] Had the sense of dominant harmony persisted, the archetypal patterning

$$\frac{y^a}{\text{I–V}} : \frac{y^b}{\text{V–I}}$$

would have been more patent. But Berlioz subverted what might have been an unambiguous authentic cadence (V–I), probably because he sought to avoid even the slightest hint of the formulaic and the routine.

His distaste for the formulaic and the conventional—including authentic cadences—is evident throughout his writings, as these excerpts from his memoirs[42] indicate: "the appealing quantity of *platitudes* for which the piano is daily responsible; the *lure of conventional* sonorities" (p. 41); "hence those convenient vocal *formulas* . . . that eternal *device* of the final [authentic] cadence" (p. 212); "the deadliest enemies of genius are those lost souls who worship at the *temple of Routine*" (p. 218); "those *perfect cadences, recurring every minute,* account by themselves for some two-thirds of the score. . . . [Cimarosa's] *Secret Marriage* is an opera fit only for fairs and carnivals" (p. 317; emphasis added). This antipathy toward the conventional may help explain why the force of other authentic cadences in this theme is enervated by tonic pedals (mm. 88–90, 93–94, 102–3), dissipated by silence (m. 89), and weakened by voice leading (mm. 102–3). In fact, there is only *one* unambiguous, conventional authentic cadence in the forty measures of Berlioz's *idée fixe,* the one at the very end.

The next part (B[1]) of Berlioz's melody is related to, yet independent of, the archetypal pattern. It is related to the pattern motivically. As if to compensate for the weak closure of y^b (and perhaps its shortened length as well), phrases ss^2 and ss^3 (each a normal four measures long) end with reiterations of motive y^b; in the second of these (mm. 93–94), no rest in the accompaniment weakens the connection between dominant and tonic.[43] More impor-

41. The context is wrong because the V/V suggested by the melody in m. 83 should lead to a I$^6_4$ chord in m. 84; instead, the tonic chord is in root position. The timing is wrong because the occurrence of tonic harmony at this point seriously weakens whatever sense of authentic cadence might have been experienced at mm. 85–86. In my view, Cone overstates the case when he asserts that the dominant is understood in m. 85 (ibid., 256). If it is so, it is largely in retrospect—after the closure in m. 86.

42. *Memoirs of Hector Berlioz,* trans. and ed. David Cairns (New York: Knopf, 1969); in each case, the page reference is given in parentheses after the quotation.

43. However, as noted earlier, the conventional character of the cadence is veiled by the tonic pedal. It should perhaps be mentioned that the stronger closure created by this proximate con-

Example 9

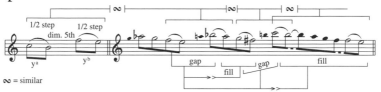

tant, the essential intervallic structure of the first part of the archetype seems to guide the sequential progression. As example 9 shows, the motion from one level of the sequence to the next involves the same intervallic pattern—that is, down a semitone, up a diminished fifth, and down a semitone—as is characteristic of the progression from y^a to y^b.[44]

Two considerations suggest, however, that, though the second part (B^1) capitalizes on relationships borrowed from the archetype, it is essentially independent of the archetype. First, the similarity between the closes of parts A (mm. 85–86) and B^1 (mm. 102–3) makes it clear that virtually nothing has happened. In terms of the processes generated by the archetypal pattern in the first period, we are literally, as well as figuratively, back at chord I. Second, as was noted in the discussion of part A, motive *ss* extends, and thereby obscures, archetypal relationships, but it does not alter them. And, since part B^1 is based almost entirely on motive *ss*, it seems that it can, for purposes of analysis, be considered independent of the archetypal process. That this suggestion is not entirely implausible can be shown by an analytic experiment. If all traces of motive *ss* are removed from Berlioz's melody, and if measures 102 and 103 are substituted for measure 86 (which is not unreasonable since they are equivalent), then the "melody" would be as shown in example 10. And this pattern is not unlike that of, say, the second movement of Mozart's Piano Sonata in C Major (K. 309) (ex. 5).

This analysis calls attention to something of some significance. As suggested earlier, a growth in size has resulted in a change in structure. Instead of two parts, processively connected through the relation of gap-to-fill, there are now three parts. Part A generates processes: in addition to the gap sequence

---

nection, plus the striking change of harmony in the second half of m. 94, produces a (4 + 4) pattern in mm. 87–98.

44. Just as this pattern gave rise to a gap-fill process in the model, archetypal y–y', so it does here. And the resulting diminished-fifth gaps (E–B♭ and F♯–C) are both followed by stepwise fills.

Example 10

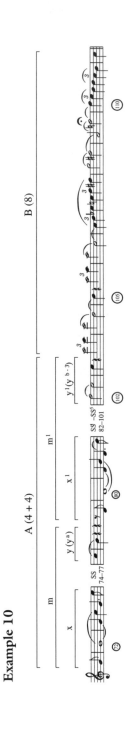

Example 11

typical of the archetype, it begins the sequence that is continued in the second part (B^1), as example 11 shows. In the second part (B^1) these processes are developed, reaching a culminating high point and then falling away toward closure. The third part (B^2) creates satisfactory closure through, among other things, the realization of previously generated implicative processes (see ex. 8).

Though the sequential part (B^1) of the melody is not, properly speaking, an element in the archetypal scheme, it by no means follows that it is unimportant. It is obviously the longest and most continuous part of the melody. More significantly, it is the most intense and characteristically Romantic. Not only is the goal-directed striving of the Sisyphean pattern expressive of Romantic yearning, but many of the hallmarks of statistical apotheosis are patently present: the slowly rising sequence, the gradual crescendo and accelerando *(animez),* the increased activity in the accompaniment (from two eighth notes per measure to four), the sense of achieved arrival resulting from the relative stability of concordant resolution (to the E-minor triad in m. 100), the placement of the high point about three-fourths of the way through the melody, the falling away from the high point through the diminuendo and the descending melodic line, and the broadening of the final phrase that results from the retention of the B (mm. 100–101) and the ritard that accompanies it.[45]

The broadening of the final phrase of B^1 is significant because of its proximate effects and its remote relationships. Within B^1, the broadening at once

45. In terms of function, pt. B^1 is to the whole of Berlioz's theme as motive *ss* is to the first phrase *(m)* and motive ss^1 is to the second phrase *(m')*. I am grateful to Janet M. Levy, not only for calling this relationship to my attention, but for her scrupulous criticism of this essay.

It is amusing, and not irrelevant, to observe that if the "experiment" of ex. 10 were reversed—if motives *x* and *y* were deleted and only the succession of *ss* motives were presented—one would have something approximating pure apotheosis: i.e., the quintessence of Romantic melody.

stabilizes and emphasizes the achievement of apotheosis. The stretching of the phrase length from four to five measures also serves to maintain expressive tension even as the relaxation of the dying away to closure is taking place.[46] The measure "added" to this phrase is, I suspect, also related to the shortened length of the second phrase of part A *(m')*. For, despite his avowed distaste for the regular and the routine, and Fetis's carping notwithstanding,[47] Berlioz evidently possessed a powerful sense of periodicity. This added measure not only contributes to the effectiveness of the last phrase of B^1 but also restores the balance disturbed by the measure removed from the end of the first period. As a result, the whole can be understood as a variation of the morphology more typical of the archetypal scheme: that is, $(8 + 8) + 24$. And the relationship, posited earlier, between y^b and y^{b-3} is made clear.

The scope and intensity of the second part are symptomatic of a significant shift in stylistic emphasis, from the syntactic to the statistical. Perhaps the nature of this shift can best be illustrated by considering the role of the upper tonic, as it has occurred in these examples. To put the matter much too briefly: in the instances from Mozart's oeuvre, the upper tonic, which occurs only once in each realization, serves as the root of a stable tonic triad and functions as part of the syntactic climax of the pattern. In the Beethoven (ex. 7), the upper tonic occurs twice: first, as part of the syntactic climax of an antecedentlike version of the archetype and, second, as both the stable high point and the syntactic climax in the second part of the theme. Though features of apotheosis—the Sisyphean sequence, crescendo, and so on—are undeniably present, the fundamental processes are unequivocally syntactic.

Berlioz's melody also contains two upper tonics (ex. 8). The first (m. 99) is the unstable high point of a cumulative, forceful statistical process. The second upper tonic (at the beginning of the final part, m. 103) represents what remains of the syntactic climax characteristic of the archetype. Not only has the preceding apotheosis overshadowed the syntactic function of the high C (m. 103), but the upward gap of a sixth (from E to C), which led to the reversal in the model and earlier instances, has here been masked by voice lead-

46. "Stretching" is an important expressive means in Romantic music. It can be a matter of interval as well as of duration. A very clear example occurs in "Träumerie" from Schumann's *Kinderszenen,* when what had been a perfect fourth (C–F, m. 2) in the first phrase is "stretched" to a major sixth (C–A, m. 6) in the equivalent point in the second phrase. See *Style and Music: Theory, History, and Ideology* (Philadelphia: University of Pennsylvania Press, 1989), 260–68.
47. Compare Cone, ed., *Berlioz, Fantastic Symphony,* 219.

ing. That is, the high C (m. 103) is perceived as following from the B over dominant harmony (m. 101) at least as much as from the E (of y^{b-3}), and the E tends to be heard as leading to the D in measure 104.

To summarize: in Beethoven's theme, syntactic climax dominates apotheosis; in Berlioz's melody, statistical apotheosis dominates syntactic climax. As noted earlier, throughout the Romantic period the importance of the secondary parameters in shaping musical process and form increases relative to that of the primary parameters. Thus, in a late Romantic piece such as the first movement of Mahler's Fifth Symphony, it is often difficult to find a single decisive syntactic climax to which lesser ones are related. Rather, there seems to be a succession of more or less equal, and local, syntactic turning points. But it is not difficult to discover the main statistical climax of the movement for just before no. 29 in the Peters edition, at a point of patent apotheosis, Mahler wrote *Höhepunkt* in the score![48]

Closure, which is the chief business of the final part, is established and enhanced in several ways:

1. The realization of implications generated by the archetypal pattern in the first part (A) fosters closure: for example, the arrival of the upper tonic (m. 103) and the subsequent filling of gaps.

2. Although initially undermined by irregular resolution, the patent motion from subdominant to dominant harmony (mm. 105–6, 109–10) strongly implies the decisive cadence that closes the melody.

3. Harmonic closure is complemented by rhythmic closure. The largely mobile phrase rhythms of part A (8 + 7) and part B¹ (4 + 4) and (4 + 5) are replaced by a closed, end-accented anapest grouping:

$$2 \; + \; 2 \; + \; 4$$

4. But the most remarkable characteristic of this part is that, melodically, it consists of a succession of largely formulaic ending patterns. To recognize the conventionality of Berlioz's motives, it is necessary only to compare them casually with closing patterns from works by Mozart, which have, for the sake

---

48. In this connection see Zohar Eitan, *Highpoints: A Study of Melodic Peaks* (Philadelphia: University of Pennsylvania Press, 1997).

Nor is Mahler the end of Romanticism: many of its characteristic traits are with us today. I do not mean merely in the music of composers but in music that is often thought to be very "advanced." For what, after all, is the explicitly statistical music of a composer such as Xenakis (or that of countless electronic composers) but Mahler without any syntax whatsoever?

of convenience, been transposed into the key of C in example 12. The first of
the Mozart examples (A) is from the closing section of the slow movement of
the String Quartet in D Major (K. 575); the second (B) is from the first movement of the Piano Sonata in C Minor (K. 457).

Example 12

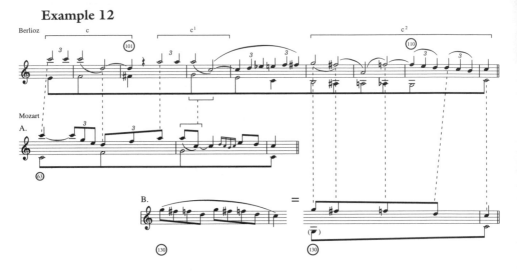

Given Berlioz's asserted antipathy to the formulaic and his avoidance earlier in this melody of the conventional, how is this overt use of almost stock
patterning to be explained? The answer is that, for Berlioz, the significant,
expressive, and creative part of the *idée fixe* is over and that, for this reason,
the closing period can—almost like a coda—employ conventional materials
without disguise and without disdain. If this conjecture has merit, Berlioz's
own compositional practice is, so to speak, behavioral evidence of his Romantic stance. For him, the heart of the melody lies not in syntactic relationships such as those of gap to fill, but in the crescendo of activity characteristic of statistical climax—that is, in the excitement of culminating
apotheosis.

*

It is now time for my own coda. I have sought to show that creativity in the arts need not involve transcending limits. The idea that a goal of the
arts, and a characteristic of their history, is to overturn the rules of a prevalent
style and institute new ones—as in scientific revolutions—rests on a confusion. The confusion is between the histories of conceptual theories and the

histories of the phenomena that the theories are devised to explain. The histories of theories have evidently tended to involve revolutions that overturned prevailing paradigms. But the histories of the phenomena that such theories are designed to explain have not, for the most part, done so. What is comparable to the history of an art such as music is not the history of conceptual theories but the history of some phenomenon, such as the forms of life. And, just as natural history has been one of combining and recombining according to fundamental principles, so the history of music has, for the most part, involved the strategic manipulation of established rules. What François Jacob has said of biological evolution holds, I think, with minor reservations, for the history of music: "Evolution does not produce novelties from scratch. It works on what already exists, either transforming a system to give it new functions or combining several systems to produce a more elaborate one. . . . It is always a matter of using the same elements, of adjusting them, of altering here and there, of arranging various combinations to produce new objects of increasing complexity. *It is always a matter of tinkering*"[49] (italics added). Though the idea of moving toward greater complexity seems suspect in the arts, regarding the history of music as having been largely a matter of "tinkering" is a salutary antidote to notions of history as dialectical necessity or as progress through revolution. And, since archetypes are what composers often tinker with, understanding how they work may help us understand and explain the history of music.[50]

49. François Jacob, "Evolution and Tinkering," *Science* 196, no. 4295 (1979): 1165.
50. Though I had not planned to discuss another realization of the archetype, an odd coincidence leads me to do so. A few weeks before this essay was sent to *Daedalus*, my wife remarked, quite casually, that a Baroque realization of the archetype would probably be more continuous than any of the ones I had discussed in this essay. I was able to think of a Baroque instance right off because, as chance would have it, I had analyzed such an instance in *Explaining Music*—though without being aware of its archetypal patterning. The essential structure of the subject of the Fugue in F Minor from Book II of Bach's *Well-Tempered Clavier* is a slightly modified version of part A of the archetype (y' descends a whole step instead of a half step), and the characteristic sequence *is* indeed continued (a possibility noted in ex. 2, graph *c*) when the answer enters with the same archetypal pattern.

6

Nature, Nurture, and Convention: The Cadential Six-Four Progression

1. Introduction: About Origins

There is evidently a deep and abiding human need to know about origins. Our most important myths have to do with the beginnings of things: of the universe, of life, of humankind, and of culture. And, as Stephen Jay Gould has observed, "we extend the same psychic need to our accomplishments and institutions—and we have origin myths and stories for the beginning of hunting, of language, of art, of kindness, of war, of boxing, bowties, and brassieres."[1] The ubiquity and intensity of this concern is not merely a matter of curiosity about our own beginnings. Rather, we want to know about origins because our understanding of what something is is intimately connected with our beliefs about its initiation. Perhaps even more important, the compulsion to know about origins is profound because successful choice, which is necessary for survival, depends on the ability to envisage the consequences of alternative courses of action[2] and, since ancient Greek times, the main model for envisaging and predicting has been at once causal and teleological. Because causal chains are incompatible with infinite regressions—there must, that is, be a *first* cause in such a chain—knowledge about beginnings becomes imperative.

Not only is successful choice necessary for survival, but it is crucial for control and power. During the centuries that followed the Middle Ages, the basis for control and power gradually shifted from inherited privilege to acquired personal possession. Novel invention—originality—became a basis for possession and possession the chief source of power. In the nineteenth

Reprinted from *Convention in Eighteenth- and Nineteenth-Century Music: Essays in Honor of Leonard G. Ratner*, edited by W. J. Allanbrook, J. M. Levy, and W. P. Mahrt (Pendragon, 1992), 473–514, by permission of Pendragon Press.

1. Stephen Jay Gould, "The Creation Myths of Cooperstown," *Natural History* 98 (November 1989): 16.

2. In this connection, see essay 8, pp. 294ff.

century, as originality became a prime cultural value, the search for origins increased, manifesting itself in an intense concern with history—individual, national, and biological. Indeed, the concern with beginnings was so compelling that one of the most famous books of the nineteenth century was mistitled. Darwin's *On the Origin of Species* is not essentially about origins. The theory of evolution is not about the beginnings of kinds and form but about their persistence and replication and about their demise and disappearance.

Musicologists, too, have been preoccupied with origins—for instance, with the beginnings of tonality, the first use of pizzicato, the genesis of tempered tuning, and, above all, with the invention of novel compositional means. We have been thus preoccupied because to identify novelty is ipso facto to know the first instance of some relationship or practice. And to know a first instance (the origin of something) is to establish the beginning of a putatively causal chain—linked together by beliefs about inherent historical change, dialectical processes, or the bonding of successive influences. The valuing of artistic originality became a virtual obsession during the nineteenth and twentieth centuries. For the prevalent ideology of Romanticism involved the adoration of geniuses (who were, by definition, innovators), faith in historical progress (which resulted from innovation), and the prizing of private property (possessing one's own invention—like the White Knight).

But our concern with origins is misguided. It is misguided because it is impossible to know everything that ever happened. Consequently, it is not possible to be sure that any particular instance was the *first* instance.[3] Second, and centrally for the history of music, what is crucial is not the origin of musical means but their replication within the oeuvre of a composer or a compositional community. As I have observed elsewhere:

> In any reasonably rich culture, novelty abounds. Indeed, it is omnipresent because every act and every artifact that is not an exact replica of an existing one is in some way different and, in that respect, novel. Put in another way, all composers—even those who write the most routine and pedestrian music—are continually devising new relationships. Most of these are historically inconsequential realizations of existing constraints. . . . Because cultures are replete with possibilities, it is not primarily the advent of novelty

---

3. It is important to notice that the first instance of something may not be the influential instance. See the discussion of "exemplary works" in my *Style and Music: Theory, History, and Ideology* (Philadelphia: University of Pennsylvania Press, 1989), 151.

that needs to be explained, but its use and, even more importantly, its sub-sequent *replication*.[4]

If explaining replication is an important concern of music history generally, it is an inescapable one—a sine qua non—in the case of convention. For a convention is, by definition, a relationship that is replicated. Notice, however, that, although every convention involves replication, not all replications can be considered conventions. Nature is abundant with replications that would not count as conventions—for instance, the life cycles of animals or the ways in which atoms combine to form molecules. Indeed, no replication that is solely the result of "natural forces" would be thought of as conventional. Convention invariably involves learning.

Not all learning, however, results in convention. For example, some species of birds learn (are imprinted with) a specific variant of a more general, innate pitch-time pattern. But, because the pattern has become fixed so that subsequent replications allow for no alternatives, such songs would not be considered the result of convention. Necessity, that is, precludes convention. As W. V. Quine observes: "Very roughly, the keynote of convention is a certain indifference; the syllable 'big' could have meant 'small' for all we care, and the red light could have meant 'go,' and black ties could have been counted less formal than fancy ones. Such is the initial intuition; but the appropriate sense of indifference, or of 'could have meant,' needs a lot of refining."[5]

One refinement seems obvious. Namely, in cultural life indifference is seldom absolute; it does not involve arbitrary interchangeability. The words *big* and *small* may be interchangeable (at least in theory), but the length of these words is probably not fortuitous. There is, I suspect, a cognitive proclivity that relates the length of words to the frequency of their use in ordinary discourse; the more frequent the occurrence of a word, the more likely that it will be short.[6]

In any realm of human activity, the degree of "indifference" or inter-changeability of convention is variable. In music, for instance, closure can be a result of the syntactic stipulation of the primary parameters (melody, har-

4. Ibid., 135.
5. W. V. Quine in his foreword to David K. Lewis, *Convention: A Philosophic Study* (Cambridge, Mass.: Harvard University Press, 1969), xii.
6. Since writing this, I discovered that I had "rediscovered" Zipf's law (1949). In this connection, also see essay 8, p. 285.

mony, rhythm) and/or of the gradual abatement of the secondary parameters (descending pitches, lower dynamics, slowing activity, less complex or dense textures).[7] But the indifference levels of these closural means are not the same.

The indifference level of the secondary parameters that create what Leonard Ratner has called the "dynamic curve" is very low.[8] Because the gradual intensification and abatement of the dynamic curve involves the arousal and action of motor, sensory, and physiological processes characteristic of a host of human activities, it is difficult to imagine what alternative means would achieve the same result—that is, what the dynamic curve could be exchanged for. In short, because the means that create abatement have, in Quine's terms, a low indifference level, abatement is not an unambiguous instance of a musical convention. And this is true even though patterns of abatement were frequently replicated in the music of Romanticism. Put differently: although the dynamic curve was a common (one might even say "conventional") choice, the musical relationships employed were not essentially conventional.

The closure created by a hierarchy of pitch relationships, however, has a considerable degree of indifference. Tonal systems, in other words, are unquestionably conventions. Witness the variability of closural progressions in Western art music from Machaut to, say, Prokofiev—not to mention the profusion of closing patterns in the musics of other cultures. And the same seems to be true, though to a lesser degree, of rhythmic relationships. Such interchangeability, however, is far from absolute; it is limited by the constraints of human cognition.

How cognitive constraints establish the necessary conditions for replication, thereby making it possible for a particular pattern to become a convention, will be one part of my concern in this essay. The other part concerns sufficiency: that is, the cultural conditions that induce the compositional community to replicate particular patterns so that they actually become conventions. In other words, though nature must be agreeable, because patterns incompatible with the constraints of human cognition are not likely to be frequently replicated, nature is not enough. If a relationship is to be commonly

7. The role of secondary parameters in creating closure is discussed in Robert G. Hopkins, *Closure in Mahler's Music: The Role of Secondary Parameters* (Philadelphia: University of Pennsylvania Press, 1990), chaps. 2–3.

8. Leonard G. Ratner, *Music: The Listener's Art,* 2d ed. (New York: McGraw-Hill, 1966), 315.

used—become a stylistic convention—it must also be consonant with other constraints of the style and be nurtured by the values, ideological as well as aesthetic, of the broader culture in which it exists.

In what follows, I hope to support this viewpoint by showing how both nature and nurture have shaped the history of what is often referred to as the cadential $^6_4$ progression: that is, the progression that goes pre-dominant (IV or ii)–I$^6_4$ (on some level of metric accent)–V–usually I (or vi or other deceptive progression).[9]

2. Nature: Cognitive Constraints

To understand the role of nature—of human cognitive constraints— in the history of the cadential $^6_4$ progression, it is convenient to begin with some observations about tonal cadences in general.

In common-practice tonality a tonal center is specified by a progression from pre-dominant harmony (IV or ii) to dominant harmony (V).[10] The pre-dominant to dominant progression need not be followed by the implied tonic in order for the tonal center to be clear. This much seems generally agreed upon.[11] It has also been observed that the tritone ($\hat{4}$–$\hat{7}$) implies a tonal center;[12] and recently Richmond Browne has argued that the power of the tritone to specify a tonal center is a result of its uniqueness in the repertory of diatonic intervals.[13]

9. "Usually" because the cadential $^6_4$ progression may end on a half cadence. Perhaps I should note here that many theorists believe that what I am calling a six-four chord should be construed as a double appoggiatura over dominant harmony (see, e.g., Edward Aldwell and Carl Schachter, *Harmony and Voice Leading* [New York: Harcourt Brace Jovanovich, 1978], 1:126–27). I grant the plausibility of such an interpretation but find it more convenient, and for my purposes more illuminating, to cling to the more traditional (conventional?) interpretation and symbology. For a discussion of other interpretations of the cadential $^6_4$ progression, see David Beach, "The Cadential Six-Four as Support for Scale Degree Three of the Fundamental Line," *Journal of Music Theory* 34 (1990): 81–99; and, for an account of the occurrences of the six-four chord, see Glen Haydon, *The Evolution of the Six-Four Chord* (Berkeley: University of California Press, 1933).

10. For convenience, chords will be symbolized in the text as though the mode of the key were major (e.g., I, ii, etc.). The reader can readily make the necessary adjustments if the mode is minor.

11. By historians as well as theorists. See, e.g., David G. Hughes, *A History of European Music* (New York: McGraw-Hill, 1974), 238.

12. See Leonard G. Ratner, *Harmony: Structure and Style* (New York: McGraw-Hill, 1962), 37–41.

13. Richmond Browne, "Tonal Implications of the Diatonic Set," *In Theory Only* 5, nos. 6–7 (1981): 3–21. See also David Butler and Helen Brown, "Tonal Structure versus Function: Studies in the Recognition of Harmonic Motion," *Music Perception* 2, no. 1 (1984): 6–24.

Example 1

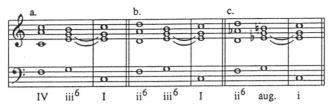

Implicit in this argument is that the ability of uniqueness to specify function is a result of the natural constraints of human cognition. And it would seem to follow from this that the progression from pre-dominant to dominant (to tonic) became the main means for specifying a tonal center because the pre-dominant contains the fourth degree of the scale and the dominant contains the seventh degree. However, although the tritone may be a necessary condition for tonal specification, it cannot be a sufficient condition. This is evident in the fact that a progression from either IV or ii to the triad built on the mediant (iii) also involves a chord containing $\hat{4}$ followed by one containing $\hat{7}$. Leonard Ratner is one of the few who has remarked on this, observing that, "although III contains the leading tone, it uses it as part of a completely stable interval, the perfect fifth. Therefore, it lacks the sense of movement within the key which is necessary to create the dominant function of a satisfactory cadence."[14]

I would suggest that the presence of iii in a cadential schema would be problematic for other reasons as well. The several harmonies that specify a tonal center constitute a cohesive, unitary schema—one that becomes a crucial convention in Western music from the seventeenth century into the twentieth. An important constraint in the formation and stability of the schema involves the relationship of the pre-dominant to the dominant to an implied tonic. One reason why the triad on the mediant is unsatisfactory as part of a cadential progression is that the perception and cognition of patterns (and hence the formation of schemata) are dependent on clear differentiation between successive stimuli. More specifically, forceful harmonic progression depends in part on the amount of pitch change between successive triads. Although there is maximum change from either IV or ii to iii (no shared pitches), there is only minimal change from iii to I (only one pitch changes, as shown in ex. 1*a* and *b*). This lack of marked motion may help explain why

14. Ratner, *Harmony*, 42.

iii did not become part of a cadential schema. An even more important reason may be that the triad on the mediant is essentially precluded in the minor mode. The problem is that, if both the leading tone ($\hat{7}$) and the mode-defining lowered $\hat{3}$ are present, the resulting triad is augmented (ex. 1*c*)—a simultaneity that is forbidden for grammatical reasons (though it may occur as a passing chord that results from voice leading). This prohibition is also a consequence of natural, cognitive constraints. Complete uniformity, such as that of the augmented triad (or of the whole-tone scale to which the triad is related), cannot serve as the basis of syntactic relationships and cannot, therefore, create cadential closure.

Natural constraints such as those that shaped aspects of tonal syntax also affected the history of the six-four chord and the progression of which it formed a part. Six-four chords occur fairly frequently in late Renaissance music. Though the chord arises out of the constraints of voice leading, it does not seem to function as an important dissonance.[15] As in William Byrd's *Ego sum panis vivus* (ex. 2),[16] the six-four chord almost always leads to the more discordant five-four sonority and only after that to resolution on the five-three chord. It would appear that the explicit discord of a second (in this case, F against G) or a seventh was deemed necessary to drive the contrapuntal process to convincing cadential closure.

One reason why early instances of the six-four chord lack driving force is that, because of the constraints of counterpoint, the tones of the triad are seldom sounded simultaneously. Again nature plays a part; but so does nurture. The discordant force of any interval or chord is a function not only of interval but also of attack. Thus there is a patent difference in sonic quality between the six-four chord at the close of Byrd's *Ego sum panis vivus* (ex. 3), where the tones of the triad are not attacked simultaneously, and that of the cadence near the close of the third movement of Mozart's Piano Concerto in C Major, K. 467 (ex. 4, m. 402), where they are. In addition, the six-four chord tends to lack force when, as is often the case in late Renaissance music

---

15. *Concord* and *discord* need to be distinguished from *consonance* and *dissonance*. The former terms have to do with psychoacoustic tension—the sonic quality of the vertical sound combination, regardless of the rules (if any) for their succession; the latter have to do with the tensions engendered by syntactic constraints as well as sonic quality. In this connection, see also essay 8, p. 288.

16. For reasons considered later (in the section on methodology), the musical examples used in this study are taken from vols. 1 and 2 of *The Norton Scores: An Anthology for Listening,* ed. Roger Kamien (New York: Norton, 1970). The texts have been omitted from exx. 2 and 3.

Example 2 Byrd, *Ego sum panis vivus*

Example 3 Byrd, *Ego sum panis vivus*

Example 4 Mozart, Piano Concerto in C Major, K. 467, iii

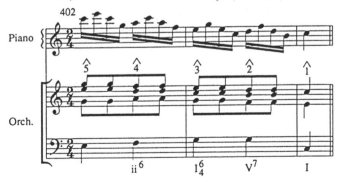

(see ex. 3), it occurs in a weak metric position. Nurture was involved in the shift from the constraints of linear counterpoint to those of vertical harmony. As the triad gradually became thought of as a compositional entity in its own right, simultaneities tended to increase, and metric positioning became both important and apparent.

Mention of sonic quality suggests another possible reason why, during the Renaissance, the perfect fourth came to seem less stable and to be treated more as a discord. These changes occurred both for reasons having to do with the constraints of counterpoint, especially the conventions of cadential closure, and for reasons having to do with increased acoustic tension. The "natural" constraints of acoustic tension are what concern us here.

The increase in acoustic tension was, I suspect, partly a result of the expansion of registral range (the distance between the bass, $\hat{5}$, and tonic, $\hat{1}$, in one of the upper voices) that took place during the Renaissance. Such registral separation, fostered by the growing prevalence of instrumental music, contributed to the greater instability of the perfect fourth. That is, when the perfect fourth is in closed position, discord is minimal because it is only between partials—the third partial of the lower pitch and the second partial of the upper one (ex. 5*a*); and discords between higher partials are even weaker. When the fourth is extended by one or two octaves, however, discord is stronger because it is produced by the clash between a fundamental and the fairly strong third partial (ex. 5*b*). More generally, as long as registral spacing was relatively closed, composers tended to choose explicit discords such as seconds and sevenths in order to give direction and drive to contrapuntal processes.

The final cadence of *Ego sum panis vivus* (see ex. 3) is typical of late Renaissance music. In this case, the six-four chord functions as an upper neighbor to the five-three chord (beat 1). Such neighbor-note six-four chords, which serve to slow down motion and delay closure, continue to be used well into the nineteenth century. The prevalence of this patterning calls attention

Example 5

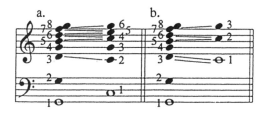

Example 6 Mozart, Symphony no. 40 in G Minor, K. 550, i, mm. 134–38

to an analytic point worth mentioning: namely, seemingly similar patterns may have somewhat different meanings. The final cadence of Byrd's piece, for instance, might be likened to the reiterated $\frac{5-6}{3-4}$ neighbor-note pattern in Mozart's Symphony no. 40 in G Minor, K. 550 (ex. 6). But Mozart's neighbor-note motion animates a dominant pedal and both signals and emphasizes the half cadence that precedes the retransition. Byrd's neighbor-note motion, on the other hand, arises out of the constraints of counterpoint, occurring as part of a cadential pattern in which the tenor descends conjunctly to the tonic (here from G down to B♭).

Such conjunct descent, characteristic of Renaissance music, constitutes a compositional constraint whose importance is in no way diminished by the fact that it was a convention, as should be evident from a few brief observations. When the fifth of the scale is in the bass, which (as in ex. 3) is often the case, the $\hat{3}$ (here D) is frequently accompanied by the $\hat{1}$ (here B♭), or sometimes the $\hat{5}$, in the highest voice.[17] One consequence of the tenor's descent to the tonic is that the highest voice cannot move $\hat{3}$–$\hat{2}$–$\hat{1}$ at cadences. More relevant for present purposes, the occurrence in early Baroque music (and subsequently) of the $\hat{3}$–$\hat{2}$–$\hat{1}$ cadential motion in the melody is a result of a profound stylistic change in which the syntax of tonal harmony becomes a dominant parameter, guiding compositional choice and taking precedence over the claims of counterpoint.[18]

17. This is so because the only other pitch that could form a triad would be $\hat{7}$, and not only would $\hat{7}$ result in a syntactically unusual iii⁶ chord (F–D–A in ex. 3), but the ensuing motion to the tonic would be quite weak.

18. See *Style and Music*, 17–19.

Example 7

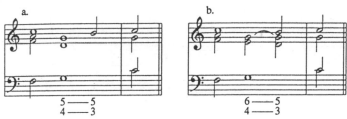

The change from the constraints of Renaissance music to those of the Baroque is described by Grout and Palisca, who observe that during the early Baroque "counterpoint continued to be the basis of composition. But a new kind of counterpoint did gradually take over in the seventeenth century. . . . It was still a blending of different melodic lines; now the lines all had to fit into the regulative framework of a series of simultaneities or chords. . . . This was the beginning of harmonically governed counterpoint *whose individual lines were subordinate to a succession of chords."* [19] Such a succession of chords could govern counterpoint because harmony had changed from being a parameter dependent on the constraints of voice leading to one governed by its own panoply of potent syntactic constraints.

I am unable to explain the origin of this change. Some of the natural constraints already considered probably played a part. It should be recognized, too, that a seemingly slight modification may have major ramifications. For instance, to transform the contrapuntal $^5_4$–$^5_3$ succession (ex. *7a*) into the harmonic $^6_4$–$^5_3$ progression (ex. *7b*) only a single note needs to be changed—in this case, the D, a fifth above the bass, to an E, a sixth above the bass.

As mentioned above, one of the consequences of the syntactification of harmony was that conjunct melodic descent to the tonic could easily be moved from a lower voice to the soprano, as in example 4. Such melodic descents are characteristic of important cadences in tonal music. And this is relevant because a high percentage of such cadences are accompanied by the cadential $^6_4$ progression.

19. Donald J. Grout and Claude V. Palisca, *A History of Western Music,* 4th ed. (New York: Norton, 1988), 354 (emphasis added). Much the same point is made by Hughes (*History of European Music,* 252). If these accounts have merit, then the Schenkerian assumption of the primacy of voice leading in common-practice tonal music is called into question.

The conjunction of melodic descent in the soprano with the cadential $^6_4$ progression is not fortuitous. It results from the problem of harmonizing $\hat{3}$ (in a $\hat{3}-\hat{2}-\hat{1}$ descent) or $\hat{1}$ (in a $\hat{1}-\hat{7}-\hat{1}$ pattern) while maintaining the relationship between the subdominant ($\hat{4}$) and the dominant ($\hat{7}$) that specifies a tonal center.[20] For, if either $\hat{3}$ or $\hat{1}$ is harmonized by the tonic triad (or the submediant) in root position, the resulting stability tends to weaken the syntactic connection upon which a sense of progression depends.[21] Thus the cadential six-four chord not only provides a grammatically correct harmonization of $\hat{3}$ (or $\hat{1}$) but is, at the same time, acoustically (naturally) discordant enough to deprive the tonic triad of syntactic stability.[22]

The most important point in this brief "analytic history," however, is that, once harmony became a fully syntactic parameter, explicit discord, upon which contrapuntal action depends, could be dispensed with. Implicative progression and convincing closure could be created solely through the power of harmonic syntax. This had momentous consequences because cadential structuring now resulted from the interaction of natural cognitive proclivities and the learned conventions of tonal harmony.

The preceding discussion has been chiefly concerned with how *natural* constraints—the constraints of human perception and cognition—affected the choices made by composers. It was argued that these constraints, together with changes in musical style, help explain why the cadential $^6_4$ progression became a compositional resource. But they cannot explain why the progression was actually used by the compositional community. Nor

---

20. In the Baroque and Classic works found in vol. 1 of the *Norton Scores,* there are as many $\hat{3}-\hat{2}-\hat{1}$ cadential $^6_4$ progressions as all other kinds, and, if $\hat{1}-\hat{7}-\hat{1}$ (or $\hat{1}-\hat{2}-\hat{1}$) patterns are included, then in two-thirds of all instances of the cadential progression the six-four chord harmonizes $\hat{3}$ or $\hat{1}$ in the soprano.

I take the conjoining of the cadential $^6_4$ progression with $\hat{3}-\hat{2}-\hat{1}$ motion in the highest voice as indicative of the advent of fully developed tonal syntax. In the *Norton Scores* the first instance of such conjoining occurs in Corelli's Sonata da chiesa, op. 3, no. 7. This is compatible with David Hughes's observation that Corelli was one of the first composers "in whose works tonality is consistently used as the basic organizing principle" (*A History of European Music,* 281).

21. Other possibilities are also problematic: the first inversion of the tonic triad is avoided because it involves doubling the third; the first inversion of the submediant is improbable because the concordance between the outer voices ($\hat{1}$ in the bass and $\hat{3}$ in the soprano) creates an impression of unwanted stability; and mediant harmony (iii) is syntactically very unlikely. The $\hat{1}$ can, of course, be harmonized by IV, but then no cadential $^6_4$ progression is present.

22. In addition, as if to "make assurance double sure," the six-four chord is often followed by V[7] so that the relationship between $\hat{4}$ and $\hat{7}$ is simultaneous, explicit, and unequivocal.

can they explain why the progression was chosen with increasing frequency during the eighteenth and early nineteenth centuries—or why it fell into disuse during the second half of the nineteenth century. Tracing the frequency of the occurrence of the cadential $^6_4$ progression over time entails deciding which instances to count from the enormous number present in the repertory. For this reason, the methodology that I have employed in selecting data and quantifying different instantiations of the progression needs to be made explicit.

3. Methodology

In order to limit the size of the sample from which instances of the cadential $^6_4$ progression were selected, I used volumes 1 and 2 of *The Norton Scores: An Anthology for Listening.*[23] I chose this collection not only in order to limit the size of the sample but because it seemed plausible to suppose that the works included in the anthology were selected because they were considered to be stylistically representative. After my statistical work was well along, I happened to glance at the preface only to discover, to my dismay, that salesmanship had triumphed over scholarship. For, according to the preface, "the works . . . have been chosen from among those most frequently studied in introductory music courses."[24] And so I can only hope that the works used in introductory music courses are not merely canonic and easily taught (given the tenets of current music theory and the genetic assumptions of much music history) but reasonably representative of the styles they were included to exemplify.

This section of my study explains the method I used to quantify the occurrence of the cadential $^6_4$ progression in the compositions contained in the *Norton Scores*. Because the six-four chord occurs in a variety of versions and contexts, it is necessary to specify what is to count as an instance of the cadential $^6_4$ progression and how the numerical values upon which quantification depends are determined. For example, should neighbor-note six-four chords, such as those in example 6, be considered instances? If so, what numerical value should be assigned? How should a progression that ends with a half ca-

23. See n. 15 above. Though represented in the *Norton Scores,* composers before Josquin and after Schönberg were not included in the sample used in this study.
24. *Norton Scores,* 1 : vii.

dence be counted? And so on. The following set of rules was used for making such determinations:

1. A pattern is considered an instance of the cadential progression and is assigned a numerical value of ten (10) if all the following conditions obtain:
   - *a)* all three tones of the tonic triad are sounded;
   - *b)* the six-four chord occurs on either a primary or a secondary metric accent;
   - *c)* at least two pitches of the chord sound simultaneously;
   - *d)* the six-four chord is preceded by a pre-dominant harmony;
   - *e)* the six-four chord is followed by dominant harmony;
   - *f)* the progression ends with dominant harmony (i.e., in a half cadence) or the dominant moves to any chord that is grammatically correct given the constraints of tonal harmony.
2. The following kinds of relationships and contexts either do not constitute instances of the cadential $^6_4$ progression or are instances whose assigned numerical value is reduced:
   - *a)* if the six-four chord occurs on a beat that is not a primary or secondary metric accent, the numerical value of the instance is reduced by half;
   - *b)* if the six-four chord is not preceded by pre-dominant harmony, its value is halved;
   - *c)* if a "diversionary" chord intervenes between $^6_4$ and $^5_3$, the value of the progression is halved;
   - *d)* if a progression is *immediately* repeated, only one instance is counted;
   - *e)* if a cadential progression is "indigenous" to a strophic form such as a passacaglia or theme and variations, the total value of all instances is divided by four;
   - *f)* either the fourth or the sixth of the six-four chord ($\hat{1}$ or $\hat{3}$) may be a suspension sounded before the fifth of the scale sounds in the bass; in such cases the value of the instance is halved, except when the tied note occurs in another voice on the same beat as the bass note;
   - *g)* a neighbor-note pattern is not counted as an instance of the cadential $^6_4$ progression unless it begins with the six-four chord.

(Thus ex. 6 would not be counted as an instance.) If the neighbor-note pattern does begin with a six-four chord, the chord is counted only as a single instance no matter how many times it is sounded;

  h) if the progression moves from $V(\frac{5}{3})$ to ii, iii, or IV, its value is halved.

3. To calculate the prevalence of the cadential $\frac{6}{4}$ progression in the works contained in the *Norton Scores,* the following procedure was used:

  a) the numerical value of each instance of the progression was determined according to the rules set forth in 1 and 2 above;

  b) in counting instances, repeat signs (‖: :‖) were ignored;

  c) the recitatives included in the *Norton Scores* were not considered part of the sample;

  d) the values of all the instances in a given unit (e.g., piece, movement, or other complete part) were added together, and this sum was divided by the number of measures in the unit. The results, given in tables A1 and A2 of the appendix, constitute the percentage of cadential $\frac{6}{4}$ progressions in each unit;

  e) the values of all instances of the $\frac{6}{4}$ progression in the work of each composer included in the sample were added together, and the sum was divided by the total number of measures in the works of the composer. The results, given in tables A1 and A2 of the appendix, represent the percentage of cadential $\frac{6}{4}$ progressions in the works of the composers in the sample;

  f) the sample was also divided according to traditional style periods (Renaissance, Baroque, Classic, and Romantic). The values for each period, given in table A3 of the appendix, were derived by averaging the percentage of cadential $\frac{6}{4}$ progressions for all the composers included in the period;

  g) the percentage of cadential $\frac{6}{4}$ progressions in the works of the composers represented in the sample was plotted against the dates of the composers' births. (The birthdate of the composers was used as the basis for chronology not only because works by a single composer were often written years apart but because there are reasons for believing that the early years of learning and creative activity are the ones in which a composer's basic stylistic stance—his or her ingrained habits of mind, cultural values, and aesthetic preferences—is formed.) This relationship is presented in figure 1.

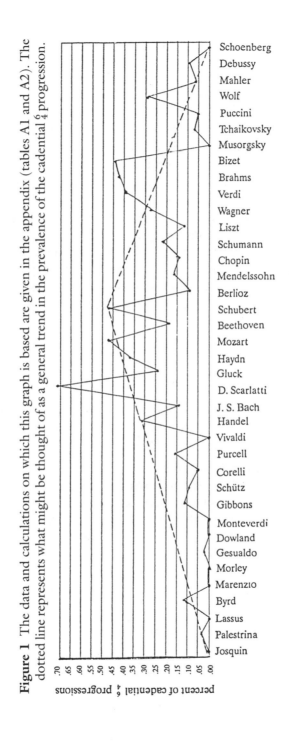

Figure 1 The data and calculations on which this graph is based are given in the appendix (tables A1 and A2). The dotted line represents what might be thought of as a general trend in the prevalence of the cadential $^6_4$ progression.

The graph in figure 1 represents the relative frequency with which the cadential $^6_4$ progression occurs in the compositions (from Josquin to Schön-berg) collected in the *Norton Scores*. The question is obvious: once the constraints of tonal harmony were established, why did the rate of replication change over time as it did—increasing from the seventeenth to the early nineteenth century and then declining to nothingness in the twentieth century? Why, put differently, did composers living at the same time make similar choices? The answer proposed here and substantiated in the next section of this essay is that compositional choices are significantly constrained both by the values/goals established by the ideology of a culture and by the characteristics/needs of a particular audience. In sum, although *nature*— that is, the constraints of human cognition—establishes the conditions that make it possible for the cadential $^6_4$ progression to imply and define a tonal center, the frequency with which the progression was replicated (chosen by composers) depended in large measure on cultural constraints, that is, on *nurture*.

4. Nurture: Cultural Constraints and Compositional Choices
Baroque Selections

By the middle of the seventeenth century, however, new resources of harmony, color, and form are solidified—a common language with a firm vocabulary, grammar, and syntax.[25]

Though the advent of fully syntactic harmony made the cadential $^6_4$ progression an available stylistic possibility, the progression was not very common during the seventeenth and early eighteenth centuries. This is evident if one compares the frequency of the progression in the Baroque sample (Monteverdi through J. S. Bach) in the *Norton Scores*, which is 0.115, with that in the Classic period (Domenico Scarlatti through Beethoven), which is 0.401.[26] In the Baroque sample, the progression generally occurs near or at the end of a movement or a piece. In slow movements, however, the pro-

25. Grout and Palisca, *A History of Western Music*, 349. Also see p. 236 above.

26. See appendix table A3. The method used to calculate the frequency figures (percentages) given here and elsewhere in this study is described in sec. 3, point 3, p. 240.

Scarlatti is included in the Classic sample because, though he was born in the same year as Bach and Handel, most historians classify him as a Classic composer. Because Beethoven's music

gression may also articulate internal closure. For instance, in the music of Handel given in the *Norton Scores,* the overall percentage of cadential $^6_4$ progressions is 0.331.[27] But in ensemble pieces, especially fast contrapuntal ones, the frequency of the progression is only 0.212, while in solo pieces (e.g., arias) the percentage is 0.466. This is also true of the music of J. S. Bach: there are no cadential $^6_4$ progressions in the fast movements of the Second Brandenburg Concerto, while the frequency of the progression in the second (slow) movement is relatively high, 0.615. The cadential $^6_4$ progression occurs quite often in slow movements because the articulation that it produces is consonant with their generally homophonic texture and aria-like sectionality. Conversely, the momentum generated by rapid motion is incompatible with the discontinuities created by decisive cadences.

Composers of the Baroque period did not choose to use the cadential $^6_4$ progression with great frequency because the decisive structural divisions created by the progression were not consonant with the aesthetic goals and values of the musical/cultural community. Of these goals, probably the most important—certainly the most discussed, both then and now—was the representation of clearly delineated affective states. In the words of Charles Batteux: "The fundamental character of the subject will determine the expression, and whether it is to be grandiose or simple, gentle or strong. If joy is the theme, every musical turn of phrase, every dance step must take on a smiling colour; and although the songs and airs may vary as they follow and take over from one another, the underlying idea that is common to them all will in no way be altered."[28]

Unity of affect finds musical expression in continuous movement, motivic persistence, and avoidance of contrast.[29] The most characteristic Baroque genres (e.g., canon, fugue, and passacaglia) foster such movement, and so do typical techniques such as the so-called walking bass, beginning-accented rhythms, and contrapuntal overlapping. Conversely, decisive closures, such as those created by abrupt contrast and by the cadential $^6_4$ progression, are in-

---

is characterized by Romantic as well as Classic traits, the figures for the frequency of his use of the cadential $^6_4$ progression have been included in the calculations of both periods.

27. See appendix table A1.

28. Charles Batteux, *Les Beaux-arts réduit à un même principe* (1746), excerpted in Peter le Huray and James Day, *Music and Aesthetics in the Eighteenth and Early-Nineteenth Centuries* (Cambridge: Cambridge University Press, 1981), 50–51.

29. The claims of a text may, of course, make contrast appropriate.

frequently replicated because they weaken continuity of motion, affect, and expression.

The Baroque use of genres and techniques that foster continuousness may also be related to the valuing of rhetoric—a rhetoric that seeks to persuade through insistent, if varied, reiteration. That is, because contrast (whether of function or affect) leads to structural articulation, Baroque "argument" seldom involves dialectic difference. Rather, the argument is, in a broader than musical sense, monothematic. Indeed, it sometimes seems as though affect and rhetoric have become one—as though affect calls not for empathy but for a kind of social acquiescence or compliance. Perhaps this is why Handel's oratorios fail as stage works, why the characters seem to be addressing the audience rather than one another. And this may be why when Mozart and Verdi want to persuade us about quasi-philosophical matters—at the ends of *Don Giovanni* and *Falstaff*—they choose to use Baroque genres. For after the dramatic action is over what is wanted is not conflict and contrast but consensus.

Classic Selections

By about 1730 in Italy, and somewhat later elsewhere, Baroque style had lost its vitality. The "Age of Reason" had arrived and its goals were not the lofty rhetorical ones of the seventeenth century, but rather the rationalistic aims of clarity, order, naturalness, elegance.[30]

The valuing of clarity, order, and perhaps naturalness and elegance is manifest in many of the characteristics of Classic music—for instance, in the prevalence of periodicity, proportion, and symmetry.[31] These traits are dependent on the existence of well-defined musical patterns—patterns whose integrity is to a considerable extent the result of cadential closure and whose identity is often enhanced by melodic contrast.[32] The patterns thus defined are related to one another in patently structured hierarchies. And crucial for the specification of hierarchic level is a hierarchy of differing degrees of cadential

30. Hughes, *A History of European Music*, 315. An interesting consequence of this difference in goals and styles is that, when Hughes presents a summary of the traits of Baroque music under the rubric "Forms" (p. 277), what he actually lists are genres such as opera, oratorio, and instrumental music but, when he summarizes the traits of Classic music under the same rubric, he presents the formal schemata of sonata form and rondo as well as the order of multimovement compositions.

31. In this connection, see Leonard G. Ratner, *Classic Music: Expression, Form, and Style* (New York: Schirmer, 1980), chap. 3.

32. Ibid., 219.

Example 8 Mozart, Piano Concerto in C Major, K. 467, i

closure. In Leonard Ratner's words: "Cadences . . . are controlling and shaping factors in the motion of the period toward its conclusion; each has a lesser or greater effect of periodicity according to its impression of finality." [33]

The cadential $^6_4$ progression was an important resource for the definition of hierarchic organization in Classic music. [34] It became a sign of definitive closure from the phrase level to the highest level of structure. Of course the level of closure was shaped by parameters other than harmony. For instance, the $^{6-5}_{4-3}$ component of the progression could be extended as a neighbor-note motion (see ex. 8), and the durational emphasis resulting from this strategy made it evident that high-level closure was at hand. [35]

33. Ibid., 34.

34. In this connection, see my *Explaining Music: Essays and Explorations* (Berkeley: University of California Press, 1973), 89.

35. Mozart evidently felt that, after such an extensive delay (seven measures), the listener needed an additional signal that closure was actually at hand and, for this reason, increased the degree of acoustic discord in mm. 381–83. Such acoustic intensification had a venerable past, as exx. 2 and 3 show.

The importance of the sign function of the cadential $^6_4$ progression can scarcely be exaggerated. As the composition of the concert audience gradually changed, from the last part of the eighteenth century into the nineteenth, its sophistication in matters of tonal syntax decreased. And the striking sonic quality of the six-four chord makes it an especially salient sign of cadential closure. As Leonard Ratner has pointed out, "When the [six-four chord] sounds, we receive a clear and strong impression that a cadence will be made. This chord is the signal for an authentic cadence."[36]

Sonic individuality is enhanced when consecutive triads are in different modes. This may in part explain the increased use, during the late eighteenth and early nineteenth centuries, of ii^6 when the mode is major and of the Neapolitan sixth (N^6) when the mode is minor.[37] Furthermore, because in each of the resulting progressions (ii^6–I$^6_4$ and N^6–i$^6_4$) all tones change from the first triad to the second, there is a strong sense of harmonic motion, and such marked harmonic motion contributes to the ability of the cadential $^6_4$ progression to act as a sign of closure.[38] The importance of clear signaling may also help explain why, in high Classic and early Romantic music, cadential $^6_4$ progressions seem to come in clusters—that is, several in succession.[39]

The preceding paragraphs argue that the prevalence of the cadential $^6_4$ progression can be related both to ideology—to the fact that the clarity, proportion, and symmetry valued by the culture depended on the existence of a well-defined hierarchy of closural means—and to changes in the composition and sophistication of the audience. Finally, what Donald Tovey characterized as the "dramatic" nature of Classic music is enhanced by the cadential $^6_4$ progression. For central to the "drama" is the arousal of expectation and its resolution through satisfactory closure. And the expectation on which dramatic

36. Ratner, *Harmony,* 110. The very salience of the six-four sound ultimately led to its disuse (see below, p. 248).

37. The triad built on the supertonic usually occurs in first inversion—and for an interesting reason having to do with the psychology of listening. Were harmonic motion by root position, the uniformity of the progression, ii–V–I, would imply pattern continuation (to IV and perhaps beyond). As a result, the impression of closure would be considerably weakened.

38. When ii$^6_5$ moves to I$^6_4$, there is, of course, a common tone; but increased acoustic discord "compensates" for any possible weakening of motion.

39. Often the early members of such a series are either incomplete (e.g., a half cadence) or weakened in some way (e.g., by lack of a pre-dominant or by suspensions), as described in the reduction rules, *2a–h,* on pp. 239f.

effect depends is most forceful when a goal is at once plainly signaled and significantly delayed—which is what the cadential $^6_4$ progression does with clarity and strength.

Romantic Selections

> When Beethoven died, in 1827, music already found itself in the midst of an intellectual movement that decided the art of the whole nineteenth century and to some extent that of our days: the romantic movement.[40]

The fundamental changes that occurred in the ideology of Western culture during the latter part of the eighteenth century had a profound influence on the choices made by composers of the nineteenth century, though, as the graph in figure 1 indicates, the prevalence of the cadential $^6_4$ progression was not immediately affected. In discussing the ideology of Romanticism and its influence on the fortunes of the cadential $^6_4$ progression, it is difficult to discern a clear "causal" chain. The various strands of ideology are so intertwined—one is tempted to say *tangled*—that one might begin with any one of a number of cultural beliefs and attitudes. I will begin with the repudiation of convention.

Of all the beliefs basic to Romanticism none was more important than the valuing of what was natural and necessary, as opposed to what was considered artificial and arbitrary. It is only a slight exaggeration to suggest that the French Revolution, probably the most important political/social event in the history of modern thought, was partly a consequence of this valuing. In music, the valuing of the "natural" profoundly affected the choices made by composers. The negative side of this valuing involved the repudiation of whatever was deemed artificial and arbitrary—that is, whatever seemed *conventional*. A single quotation, albeit one from perhaps the central figure of musical Romanticism, will have to stand for a plethora of other possibilities. According to Wagner, "the most perfect form of art . . . is that wherein all vestiges of conventionality are completely removed from the drama as well as from the music."[41]

---

40. Alfred Einstein, *A Short History of Music* (New York: Vintage, 1954), 149.
41. Quoted in Jack M. Stein, *Richard Wagner and the Synthesis of the Arts* (Westport, Conn.: Greenwood, 1973), 167.

Perhaps in response to changes in the character (the class structure) of the audience, the prevalence of authentic cadences, especially those signaling the closure of a symphonic movement or the act of an opera, increased markedly during the early nineteenth century—so much so that Berlioz bitterly complained about "that external device of the final cadence" and "those perfect cadences, recurring every minute."[42] The ubiquity of the authentic cadence, of which the cadential $^6_4$ progression was a special case, made it seem the epitome of conventionality. The rejection of the artificial and conventional was reinforced by two other important values of Romanticism: originality and individuality. Neither was consonant with the replication of a patterning that was deemed formulaic and impersonal. The very sonic salience that made the cadential $^6_4$ progression such a forceful signal made it seem routine and commonplace—a bit blatant. This is one reason why, as the years passed, the cadential $^6_4$ progression was less and less frequently chosen by composers.

Other ideological values were also involved. Romanticism placed a premium on gradual change, continuous processes, and open forms.[43] These values are obviously incompatible with the forceful closure created by the cadential $^6_4$ progression. For this reason, composers tended to choose alternative cadential possibilities—for instance, plagal cadences and ones in which an augmented sixth chord moves not to a six-four chord but, functioning as a kind of dominant, directly to the tonic in root position. The same values also led to the incremental and sequential motivic processes so characteristic of nineteenth-century music. Everything tended to become thematic. For instance, what had been an ornamental turn in the Baroque and Classic periods became part of a motivic process in *Tristan und Isolde*.[44] And this also seems to have happened with the cadential $^6_4$ progression. In the "Dance of the Reed Pipes" from Tchaikovsky's *The Nutcracker* a cadential $^6_4$ progression occurs six times. It does so, however, not as part of a high-level

42. *Memoirs of Hector Berlioz,* trans. and ed. David Cairns (New York: Knopf, 1969), 212, 317. This antipathy, together with the ongoing character of the music, may in part explain the very low percentage (0.090) of cadential $^6_4$ progressions in the Berlioz movement given in the *Norton Scores* (see app. table A2).

43. The valuing of gradual change and continuous process was intensified by the firm cultural belief that change—e.g., evolution, whether biological or social—was per se essentially beneficent.

44. This change is illustrated in my *Style and Music,* 317–18.

Example 9 Tchaikovsky, "Dance of the Reed Pipes," *The Nutcracker*

closural pattern but as a harmonization of the main thematic idea of the movement (ex. 9).[45]

Openness, which is an obvious corollary of gradual change and continuous process, is also related to the prevalence of weak and often ambiguous tonal relationships. Composers chose relationships such as these not only because they allowed scope for originality and individuality but because the dependence of tonal syntax on learning made strongly syntactic processes seem conventional and hence suspect. Wanting more "natural" ways of shaping musical experience, composers increasingly relied on the secondary parameters of music—on dynamics, tempo, register, acoustic tension, attack rates, and texture. Because they need not depend on syntactic sophistication, relationships created by the patterning of secondary parameters could be appreciated even by the tyros in the growing audience.[46]

What is pertinent to the argument of this essay is that the forms created by the secondary parameters have their own ways of ending. The last part of the dynamic curve[47] consists of a slow, incremental dying away—an abatement in which closure results from progressively softer dynamics,

45. Two points merit mention in connection with this example. First, the closural force of the progression is weak both because there is no pre-dominant and because tempo and duration make it seem perfunctory—as does its position early in the melody. Second, not only does the harmony instantiate, yet at the same time depreciate, a familiar pattern, but the melody does so as well. It "trivializes" the changing-note schema $\hat{1}$–$\hat{7}$/$\hat{2}$–$\hat{1}$, which forms the basic structure of countless Classic and early Romantic melodies.

46. These matters are considered more fully in *Style and Music*, 14–16, 303–11, and passim.

47. See n. 7 above.

Example 10 Mahler, Symphony no. 4 in G Major, iv

diminished rates of activity, slower tempi, descending pitches, decreasing discord, and less elaborate textures.[48] Consonant with the values of Romanticism, such abatements are gradual, continuous, and open.[49] They have no
need for—indeed would be incompatible with—the decisive closure created
by a typical cadential $^6_4$ progression.

The cadential $^6_4$ progression was, of course, not entirely abandoned. It continued to be used in popular music and in the music of somewhat conventional composers. And it was occasionally chosen by composers of a more ad-
venturous kind. But in such cases the progression usually served some special
purpose. For instance, there is an unequivocal cadential $^6_4$ progression in the
final movement of Mahler's Fourth Symphony (ex. 10). It occurs, as it
"should," just before the coda. One feels, however, that it was chosen not primarily because of its syntactic function (it is the only such progression in the
movement) but because its very clear conventionality serves as a way for
Mahler to comment on the text, which reads: "are excellent court musicians"
("sind treffliche Hofmusikanten").

*

In the course of this study I have traced the fortunes of the cadential
$^6_4$ progression. But tracing its rise and demise was subsidiary to more general
points. The first is that style history is concerned with the use and replication

---

48. The term *abatement* is taken from Hopkins, *Closure and Mahler's Music,* 5–9 and
passim.

49. When, e.g., do decrescendos or ritardandos literally close? The answer is never. They can
die away into nothingness—into silence—but they cannot close.

of musical relationships rather than with their origins. The second point is that use and replication can be explained only in the light of hypotheses, hypotheses based either on lawlike psychological constraints or on more limited cultural constraints such as ideological beliefs and socioeconomic conditions. In short, to construct a history—to explain (rather than merely describe and chronicle) the choices made by composers—it is necessary to acknowledge the claims of both nature and nurture.

Appendix Table A1

Composer (Birthdate) and Work(s)	Number of Cadential $^6_4$ Progressions	Rules for Reduction (see pp. 239–40)	Total Value of Cadential $^6_4$ Progressions	Total No. of Measures	Percentage of Cadential $^6_4$ Progressions
Josquin des Prés (ca. 1440):					
4. *Ave Maria*[a]	0			21	.000
Palestrina (ca. 1525):					
5. Kyrie from the *Pope Marcellus Mass*[b]	1	2f, 2h	$(10 \times .5 \times .5) = 2.5$	77	.032
Lassus (1532):					
6. *Tristis est anima mea*[c]	0			63	.000
Byrd (1543):					
7. *Ego sum panis vivus*[d]	1	2f	$(10 \times .5) = 5$	36	.138
Marenzio (1553):					
8. *S'io parto, i' moro*	0			60	.000
Morley (1557):					
9. *Sing We and Chant It*	0			23	.000
Gesualdo (1560):					
10. *Moro lasso*	1	2b, 2f	$(10 \times .5 \times .5) = 2.5$	69	.036
Dowland (1562):					
11. *My Thoughts Are Wing'd with Hope*	0			24	.000
Monteverdi (1567):					
12. *Tu se' morta* from *L'Orfeo*	0			38	.000
13. *Zefiro torna*	0			157	.000
Gibbons (1583):					
14. *The Silver Swan*	1	2a, 2b	$(10 \times .5 \times .5) = 2.5$	21	.119

Schütz (1585):				
15. *Saul, Saul*	1	2f	$(10 \times .5) = 5$	68	.073
Corelli (1653):				
16. Sonata da chiesa, op. 3, no. 7:[c]				
First movement	1	2f	$(10 \times .5) = 5$	20	.250
Second, third, and fourth movements	0			100	.000
Corelli totals	1		5	120	.042
Purcell (1659):				
17. Dido's lament from *Dido and Aeneas*[f]	5	2e, 2f	$[(20 \times .5) + 30] \times .25 = 10$	64	.156
Vivaldi (1678):				
18. Concerto Grosso in D Minor, op. 3, no. 11, movements 1–3	0[g]			197	.000
Handel (1685):				
19. "Piangerò" from *Giulio Cesare*	0			69	.000
20. Excerpts from *Messiah*:[h]				
Overture	2	2a, 2f	$(10 \times .5 \times .5) + 10 = 12.5$	97	.129
Comfort Ye	2		20	37	.540
Ev'ry Valley	3		30	84	.357
For unto Us a Child Is Born	0		0	99	.000
He Was Despised	7		70	67	1.045
Hallelujah	5		50	98	.510
Handel totals			182.5	551	.331
J. S. Bach (1685):				
21. Organ Fugue in G Minor ("Little")	0			68	.000

(continued on page 254)

Appendix Table A1 (*continued*)

Composer (Birthdate) and Work(s)	Number of Cadential $^6_4$ Progressions	Rules for Reduction	Total Value of Cadential $^6_4$ Progressions	Total No. of Measures	Percentage of Cadential $^6_4$ Progressions
22. Organ Passacaglia and Fugue in C Minor:					
Passacaglia	9	2e	$(9 \times 10) \times .25 = 22.5$	168	.134[i]
Fugue	2		20	124	.161
23. Brandenburg Concerto no. 2 in F Major:					
First and third movements	0			257	.000
Second movement	4		40	65	.615[j]
24. Prelude and Fugue in C Minor (*WTC* I):					
Prelude	1		10	35	.285
Fugue	1		10	31	.322
25. Suite no. 3 in D Major:					
Air	1		10	18	.555
Gigue	2		20	72	.417
26. Cantata no. 140, *Wachet auf:*					
"Wachet auf"	3	2b	30	189	.159
"Wann kommst du, mein Heil?"	0		0	81	.000
"Zion hört die Wächter singen"	6		$(6 \times 10) \times .5 = 30$	73	.410
"Mein Freund ist mein"	6		60	73	.822
"Gloria sei dir gesungen" (chorale)	0			36	.000

	n		points	total	proportion
27. Crucifixus from Mass in B Minor	5	2e	$(5 \times 10) \times .25 = 12.5$	53	.236
Bach totals	40		265	1,343	.197
Domenico Scarlatti (1685):					
28. Sonata in C Minor	2		20	28	.714[k]
Gluck (1714):					
29. Scenes from *Orphée et Euridice*	7	2e	70	281	.249[l]
and "J'ai perdue mon Euridice"	7		$(7 \times 10) \times .5 = 35$	70	.500
Gluck totals	14		105	351	.299
Haydn (1732)					
30. Symphony no. 94 in G Major:					
Second movement	1		10	156	.064
Fourth movement	12		120	268	.448
31. String Quartet in C Major, op. 76, no. 3:					
First movement	7		70	121	.578
Second movement	10	2e	$(10 \times 10) \times .25 = 25$	104	.240
Third movement	5		50	100	.500
Fourth movement	8	2a	$(2 \times 10 \times .5) + 60 = 70$	188	.372
Haydn totals	43		345	937	.368
Mozart (1756)					
32. Piano Concerto in C Major, K. 467:					
First movement	21		210	417	.504
Second movement	3		30	104	.288
Third movement	16		160	447	.357

(continued on page 256)

Appendix Table A1 (*continued*)

Composer (Birthdate) and Work(s)	Number of Cadential $^6_4$ Progressions	Rules for Reduction	Total Value of Cadential $^6_4$ Progressions	Total No. of Measures	Percentage of Cadential $^6_4$ Progressions
33. Eine kleine Nachtmusik:					
First movement	8		80	137	.584
Second movement	8		80	73	1.095
Third movement	0		0	36	.000
Fourth movement	9		90	163	.552
34. Three excerpts from Don Giovanni:					
Act 1, no. 1, introduction	14	2b	$(2 \times 10 \times .5) + 120 = 130$	208	.625
Catalog aria	5	2b	$(2 \times 10 \times .5) + 30 = 40$	172	.233
"Là ci darem la mano"	6		60	82	.731
35. Symphony no. 40 in G Minor, K. 550:					
First movement	12		120	299	.401
Second movement	10	2b	$(2 \times 10 \times .5) + 80 = 90$	123	.732
Third movement	1		10	84	.119
Fourth movement	10		100	308	.325
Mozart totals			1,200	2,653	.452
Beethoven (1770)					
36. Piano Sonata in C Minor, op. 13:					
First movement	11	2b, 2c	$(2 \times 10 \times .5) +$ $(2 \times 10 \times .25) + 70 = 85$	311	.273
Second movement	2		20	73	.274
Third movement	10		100	210	.476
Total for sonata					.345

37. String Quartet in F Major, op. 18, no. 1:

First movement	9	2a	(10 × .5) + 80 = 85	313	.272

38. Symphony no. 5 in C Minor:

First movement	6		60	502	.119
Second movement	2		20	247	.081
Third movement	2		20	373	.054
Fourth movement	4	2b	(10 × .5) + 30 = 35	444	.079
Total for symphony					.086
Beethoven totals			425	2,473	.172 m

Note: With minor exceptions, the titles of the works listed in the appendix are those used in vols. 1 and 2 of *The Norton Scores: An Anthology for Listening*, ed. Roger Kamien (New York: Norton, 1970). The numbers, also, are those given in the *Norton Scores*.

[a] The first instance of a $\frac{5}{4}-\frac{5}{3}$ cadence in the *Norton Scores* (hereafter *NS*) occurs in this work. The progression is one that is replicated well into the nineteenth century.

[b] Whether this progression (and others like it) was heard as "tonal" is irrelevant for present purposes. It was surely heard as cadential.

[c] The first neighbor-note $\frac{6}{4}$ progression (NN$\frac{6}{4}$) in the *NS* closes this piece. As in ex. 8, the NN$\frac{6}{4}$ is followed by a $\frac{5}{4}-\frac{5}{3}$ progression. The NN$\frac{6}{4}$ occurs in works by all the remaining composers (from Byrd to Beethoven, with the exception of Purcell) represented in the *NS*, vol. 1, and it is replicated in many nineteenth-century works.

[d] As in much Renaissance music, both cadential and neighbor-note six-four chords (see exx. 2 and 3) are followed by discords in which $\hat{1}$ is forced downward to $\hat{7}$ by the acoustic tension of $\hat{2}$, a second above or a seventh below. This suggests that, as mentioned in the text, composers did not feel that syntax alone could create unequivocal closure.

[e] As observed in the text, the first instance in the *NS* of a $\hat{3}-\hat{2}-\hat{1}$ cadence coupled with a cadential $\frac{6}{4}$ progression occurs in the first movement of this work.

[f] Because this is a ground-bass piece, the total value of all instances is divided by 4 (reduction rule 2e).

[g] The absence of cadential $\frac{6}{4}$ progressions seems surprising; but there are a number of $\frac{5}{4}-\frac{5}{3}$ and NN$\frac{6}{4}$ progressions.

[h] Notice the prevalence of cadential $\frac{6}{4}$ progressions in the solo vs. the ensemble numbers: solo = .466; ensemble = .212.

[i] This low figure, the result of reduction rule 2c, is counterintuitive; the cadential $\frac{6}{4}$ is salient.

[j] As in Handel's *Messiah*, cadential $\frac{6}{4}$ progressions articulate the Andante, not the ongoing fast movements.

[k] The unusually high percentage of cadential $\frac{6}{4}$ progressions is, I suspect, a consequence of the fact that a sample this small may not be representative.

[l] As in the Handel and Bach examples nos. 20, 23, and 26 above, the cadential $\frac{6}{4}$ progression is considerably more common in arias than in choruses.

[m] The decrease in the prevalence of the cadential $\frac{6}{4}$ progression from early (.345) to middle (.082) period Beethoven may be symptomatic of style change, or it may be a fortuitous consequence of sampling. In any case, the very low overall percentage (.172) of cadential $\frac{6}{4}$ progressions is probably a result of the fact that the Fifth Symphony accounts for more than half the music by Beethoven in the *NS*.

Appendix Table A2

Composer (Birthdate) and Work(s)	Number of Cadential $^6_4$ Progressions	Rules for Reduction (see pp. 239–40)	Total Value of Cadential $^6_4$ Progressions	Total No. of Measures	Percentage of Cadential $^6_4$ Progressions
Schubert (1797):					
1. *Heidenröslein*	2		20	16	1.250
2. *Erlkönig*	10		100	148	.677
3. Piano Quintet in A Major (*Trout*), fourth movement	10	2e	20 + (80 × .25) = 40	172	.232
Schubert totals			160	336	.476
Berlioz (1803):					
4. *Symphonie fantastique*, fifth movement	7	2a, 2b	40 + (30 × .25) = 47.5	524	.090
Mendelssohn (1809):					
5. Violin Concerto in E Minor, first movement	12	2b	110 + (10 × .5) = 115	528	.218
Chopin (1810):					
6. Mazurka in B♭ Major, op. 7, no. 1	1		10	64	.156
7. Etude in E Major, op. 10, no. 3	2		20	77	.259
8. Prelude in E Minor, op. 28, no. 4	0		0	25	.000
Chopin totals			30	166	.180
Schumann (1810):					
9. *Die beiden Grenadiere*	8	2a, 2b	30 + (50 × .25) = 42.5	82	.518
10. Piano Concerto in A Minor, op. 54, first movement	14	2a, 2b	110 + (30 × .25) = 117.5	544	.216
Schumann totals			160	626	.256

Liszt (1811):					
11. *Sonetto 104 del Petrarca*	1		10	81	.123[a]
Wagner (1813):					
12. *Die Walküre*, act 1, scene 3	24	2a, 2b	$190 + (40 \times .5) + (10 \times .25) = 212.5$	734	.290
13. *Tristan und Isolde*, Prelude	0		0 = 212.5	111	.000[b]
Wagner totals			212.5	845	.251
Verdi (1813):					
14. *La traviata*, act 1, Violetta's scene	9		90	186	.484
15. *Aïda*, act 3 (Introduction, Prayer-Chorus, Romanza-Aïda)	12	2a, 2b, 2c	$80 + (40 \times .5) = 100$	334	.299
Verdi totals			190	520	.365
Brahms (1833):					
16. *Die Mainacht*	3		30	51	.588
17. Symphony no. 3 in F Major, op. 90, third movement	6		60	163	.368
Brahms totals			90	214	.421
Bizet (1838):					
18. *Carmen*, act 4, final scene	11	2a, 2b, 2c	$80 + (30 \times .5) = 95$	212	.448
Musorgsky (1839):					
19. Field Marshall Death from *Songs and Dances of Death*	0		0	93	.000
Tchaikovsky (1840):					
20. *Romeo and Juliet*, Overture-Fantasy	0		0	521	.000
21. *The Nutcracker:*					
March, Arabian Dance	0		0	88 + 102	.000
Dance of the Reed Pipes	6	2a, 2b	$(60 \times .25) = 15$	77	.194
Tchaikovsky totals			15	267	.056

(*continued on page 260*)

Appendix Table A2 *(continued)*

Composer (Birthdate) and Work(s)	Number of Cadential $^6_4$ Progressions	Rules for Reduction	Total Value of Cadential $^6_4$ Progressions	Total No. of Measures	Percentage of Cadential $^6_4$ Progressions
Puccini (1858):					
22. *La bohème*, act 1 (Rodolfo and Mimi)	3	2b	$10 + (20 \times .5) = 20$	365	.055
Wolf (1860):					
23. *In dem Schatten meiner Locken*	6	2b, 2f	$60 \times .25 = 15$	58	.259[c]
Mahler (1860):					
24. Symphony no. 4 in G Major, fourth movement	1		10	184	.054
Debussy (1862):					
25. *Prelude to "The Afternoon of a Faun"*	1		10	110	.091
Schönberg (1874):					
26. Five Pieces for Orchestra, op. 16, *Vergangenes*	0		0	220	.000
27. Piano Concerto, op. 42, first movement	0		0	175	.000

Note: The numbers preceding the titles of the works in table A2 are those given in the second volume of the *Norton Scores*.

[a] The sample is too small to be significant.

[b] While the cadential $^6_4$ progression occurs at important points of articulation in the scene from *Die Walküre*, the Prelude to *Tristan* employs $^5_4$–$^5_3$ cadences, not the cadential $^6_4$ progression. The use of greater acoustic tension may be symptomatic of a shift in style—toward increased reliance on "natural" musical means.

[c] The high percentage here is a result of the fact that cadential $^6_4$ progressions form part of a recurring refrain.

Appendix Table A3

Renaissance (Josquin to Dowland)	.026
Baroque (Monteverdi to Bach)	.115
Classic (Scarlatti to Beethoven)	.401
Romantic (Beethoven to Debussy)	.197
Early Romantic (Beethoven to Verdi)	.223
Late Romantic (Brahms to Debussy)	.190

Note: The basis for the percentages in table A3 is explained in the main text: see rule 3f on p. 240.

A Pride of Prejudices;
or, Delight in Diversity

In the late, late Romantic ideology of our time oneness is All, and all is Oneness. A composition is considered to be more coherent and intelligible, more significant and aesthetically valuable, if every pitch and every pattern can be traced to a single germinal cell and if all relationships can be understood as instantiations of a single, underlying principle or scheme. In the Romantic view, the oneness of art is organic, and this belief is bedded with others growing in the ideological garden—for instance, nourishing notions about a composition's logic and inevitability, a bourgeois infatuation with the virtues of artistic economy, and, above all, a deeply rooted belief in the fertile force and necessity of natural relationships as opposed to the contingency and conventionality of cultural constraints.

All this yearning for the womb-like warmth of Oneness leaves me cold. I am an antediluvian empiricist who delights in discrimination, distinction, and diversity. For me, the order that entices and excites is that which is revealed when disparity and contrast, regularity and caprice are related to one another through functional differentiation. I am not a denizen of obscure, abstract depths—a diver after cosmic conceptions and unconfirmable hypotheses. I am content to snorkel along the surface, peering down just a bit to be bewitched by the pleasing patterns of luminous fish and the quiet swaying of colorful coral.

One of the ways in which the yearning for Oneness has manifested itself in contemporary theory is in an almost obsessive concern with the nature of unity in music. This concern has its roots in history—in the ideology of Romanticism, which reflected the beliefs and values of the newly reigning bourgeoisie, and in the practice of composers who sought to satisfy the needs of the middle-class audience. History is relevant because the problems that con-

Reprinted from *Music Theory Spectrum* 13, no. 2 (Fall 1991): 241–51, by permission of the Society for Music Theory.

This essay was originally presented as the keynote address at the 1988 meeting of the Society for Music Theory.

cern music theorists, and the solutions that they formulate, are consequences both of the compositional data that confront them *and* of the ideological environment that suggests and validates hypotheses. In short, music theory has a history not solely, or even primarily, because musical styles change but because culture, and especially our grab bag of beliefs and attitudes, changes. For it is ideology that establishes cultural/aesthetic goals and the values in terms of which theorists formulate hypotheses and composers choose musical relationships.

Whatever its basis is said to be, unity is neither an objective trait like frequency or intensity nor a specifiable relationship like an authentic cadence or a crescendo. Rather, it is a psychological effect—an impression of stylistic propriety, integrity, and completeness—dependent not only upon the stimuli perceived but upon cultural beliefs and attitudes ingrained in listeners as standards of cognitive/conceptional satisfaction.

Because a sense of unity is the result of a concatenation of conditions, different epochs have attributed it to different aspects of music. Indeed, what any epoch takes to be the important sources of unity might serve as a touchstone for its central aesthetic/ideological concerns. For instance, eighteenth-century music theorists considered unity to be a matter of coherent character and expression.[1] Thus, J. S. Bach might well have been appalled by the contrasts of affect present in a symphonic movement by Mozart; and, even if Rudolf Reti himself had relentlessly reasoned, demonstrating the derivation of every pattern, Bach might still have refused to acknowledge the unity of the movement. And, in our own century, Schönberg would surely have considered the stylistic/affective disparities present in some of Berio's recent works incompatible with musical unity. Yet, once cultural belief sanctions such disparity, unity ceases to be problematic.

[These observations call attention to the role of affect, gesture, and topic in musical experience. The question is not, as is sometimes supposed, how to relate character, affect, or topic to the musical pattern. For, when the claims of convention, as well as those of nature, are acknowledged, this is not a daunting difficulty.

Rather, the difficulty involves discerning and explaining the constraints that govern the *succession* of affects, gestures, or topics.[2] But, save for the most

---

1. See, e.g., Charles Batteux, quoted in essay 6, p. 243.

2. See Leonard B. Meyer, *Emotion and Meaning in Music* (Chicago: University of Chicago Press, 1956), 271–72, and also *Explaining Music: Essays and Explorations* (Berkeley: University of California Press, 1973), 246. Recently, a number of musicologists have become concerned

fundamental sequence of all (that of beginning, middle, and end), the probabilities of succession seem to be consequences of cultural, rather than universal, constraints.[3] This is evidently also the case with both "real-life" experience and verbal narratives, whether "real" or fictional.

There is, however, a crucial difference between verbal narratives and musical processes. Namely, in verbal narratives, the human motivations and goals that are represented make clear the reasons for a specific succession of affects, moods, or topics. In music, on the other hand, the basis for a specific succession of such characters is uncertain.[4]

In addition, programs tend to focus attention on the stable thematic passages that are readily characterized, whether by nature (e.g., love, anger, etc.) or by convention (e.g., festive dance, hunting music, etc.), while saying very little about the music *between* them.

Tracing a motivic transformation that connects an earlier theme to a later one will not explain the propriety of character succession. Wye J. Allanbrook, for instance, likens the way Mozart changes one theme into another to a child's game in which bit by bit one word is transformed into another—for instance, *cat* can be transformed into *dog (cat-cot-cog-dog)*.[5] But, while this explains *how* one gets from *cat* to *dog*, it does not explain *why* one didn't go, for instance, to *bun (cat-bat-ban-bun)*.

Yet the choice of word succession is not fortuitous. The game moves from *cat* to *dog* (rather than to *bun*) not because of syntactic function but as a result of class coherence, biological as well as cultural. Both words refer to animals, both animals are mammals, and both mammals are household pets,

---

with the problem of topic or affect. See, e.g., V. Kofi Agawu, *Playing with Signs: A Semiotic Interpretation of Classic Music* (Princeton, N.J.: Princeton University Press, 1991); Wye Jamison Allanbrook, *Rhythmic Gesture in Mozart: Le Nozze di Figaro and Don Giovanni* (Chicago: University of Chicago Press, 1983); and Leonard G. Ratner, *Classic Music: Expression, Form, and Style* (New York: Schirmer, 1980).

3. The denigration of convention, coupled with the failure to develop a viable theory of motivic succession, may in part explain the tendency of theorists/critics to devise narrative rationales for instrumental music. For what verbal narrative programs supply may precisely be "reasons" for such succession.

4. One problem with narrative programs is not that they are capricious but that they are too specific. As Robert Schumann observed, the same work may be consonant with quite different programs, and "different generations choose very different words and pictures to apply to music" (quoted in Leon Plantinga, *Schumann as Critic* [New Haven, Conn.: Yale University Press, 1967], 124).

5. Wye J. Allanbrook, "Two Threads through the Labyrinth: Topic and Process in the First Movements of K. 332 and K. 333," in *Convention in Eighteenth- and Nineteenth-Century Music*, ed. W. J. Allanbrook, J. M. Levy, and W. P. Mahrt (Stuyvesant, N.Y., 1992), 144.

which humans connect through behavior and language—for instance, "It's raining cats and dogs." In brief, the coupling was chosen, though probably without conscious design, because of class constraints.

The "transformation" (cat into dog) is, nevertheless, instructive because it calls attention to the fact that, whether in real life art or in art, there is no *inherent* rationale for the succession of affects or topics or emotions. For instance, in *Hamlet* (act 3, scene 1) there is a radical change in affect from the end of Hamlet's "To be or not to be" soliloquy and his "The fair Ophelia . . ." to his angry "To a nunnery go and quickly too." The affect succession is credible because we understand the motives and goals that shape the interchange between Hamlet and Ophelia.

Although musicologists/theorists have been at pains to discover the kinds of schemas, topics, and gestures that are characteristic of particular styles, there have been few meticulous studies of the nature of the relationships between successive affects, topics, and gestures and of how these are related to the kinds of transitions or juxtapositions that connect them. Finally, in what ways, if any, do the relationships among successive expressive signifiers affect the listener's sense of unity?]

In the eighteenth century, the nature of unity was not a pressing problem. This was so for two main reasons: first, because differences and contrasts in musical patterning and expression could be subsumed as parts of functional, syntactic hierarchies and, second, because such relationships were understood and explained in terms of conventions of form and genre. For instance, the relationships among the different movements of a symphony were taken for granted by both theorists and composers as being in the nature of the genre.

But the Romantic repudiation of convention, coupled with the denigration and weakening of syntactic constraints, highlighted the presence of diversity. Questions arose about the nature and basis of musical coherence and unity. What made the several parts of a composition—the movements of a symphony or the components of a collection of characteristic pieces—form an aesthetically satisfactory whole? Within movements, the problems were no less pressing. For the Romantic depreciation of convention made syntax per se seem a doubtful basis for coherence. What, other than unoriginal, uninspired convention, could account for the kinds and order of events in, say, a sonata-form movement? How could earlier themes be related to later ones if syntax seemed suspect and conventions of form were deemed arbitrary?

Of the many strategies thought to enhance musical unity, none was more important during the last 150 years than that which was based upon similarity relationships. The importance of similarity relationships—usually through derivation from, or transformation of, a single germinal motivic seed or cell—was emphasized by theorists and composers. Carl Czerny's description of Beethoven's Piano Concerto no. 3 is representative. He writes that, following the first tutti, "all other passages are drawn from the principal theme, by which means the composition obtains that characteristic unity, by which it is so highly distinguished."[6] In the same vein, Wagner wrote that "the new form of dramatic music will have the unity of the symphonic movement; and this it will attain by spreading itself over the whole drama . . . So that this unity consists in a tissue of root themes pervading all the drama. . . ."[7] And, still thinking about coherence in these terms, Anton Webern asserts: "To develop everything else from *one* principal idea! That's the strongest unity."[8]

Because specific instances of thematic development and motivic transformation have been frequently considered in historical and theoretical writing about music, my concern here will be, first, with why this view of unity prevailed and, second, with the theoretical and compositional problems that result from an account of musical organization essentially in terms of motivic and thematic similarity.

The idea of coherence and unity through *similarity* relationships prevailed because it was consonant both with the ideology of Romanticism and with the needs of the novices in the bourgeois audience.

The first, and perhaps most important, point is that the apprehension of pattern similarity is not essentially dependent upon the constraints of tonal syntax or the conventions of musical form. In this sense, the unity created by similarity is a natural one, based upon classlike identity rather than upon learned constraints. A simple example will help make this point clear. Suppose that a group of intelligent American college students was asked to arrange a number of cards of various sizes, shapes, and colors, each with a Chinese character on it. They might arrange the cards according to color or size or shape—and even perhaps in terms of the similarities between the characters. But, unless they knew Chinese, it is doubtful that the arrangements would result in intelligible, grammatical sentences. The arrangement would involve

6. Carl Czerny, *School of Practical Composition,* trans. John Bishop (London, ca. 1848), 1:164.

7. Richard Wagner, *Opera and Drama,* vol. 2 (1851), excerpted in *Wagner on Music and Drama: A Compendium of Richard Wagner's Prose Works,* ed. Albert Goldman and Evert Sprinchorn, trans. H. A. Ellis (London: Gollancz, 1970), 229.

8. Anton Webern, *The Path to the New Music,* ed. Willi Reich, trans. Leo Black (Bryn Mawr, Pa.: Presser, 1963), 35.

classification, but the order would be based on physical similarity rather than on functional differentiation. Conversely, had the cards been ordered according to the syntactic constraints of the Chinese language, the occurrence of physical, classlike coherence would have been essentially fortuitous. In a comparable way, similarities of motive (and also of timbre, texture, and the like) helped the less sophisticated members of the nineteenth century's bourgeois audience to appreciate the music they were paying for.[9]

Motivic conservation became a prevalent strategy for other reasons as well. The depreciation of conventional constraints, together with the Romantic valuing of originality and individuality, led to a burgeoning of compositional possibilities. The result was a significant increase in the number of deliberate, time-consuming choices that composers had to make. One symptom of this increase is that, since the eighteenth century, there has been a marked decrease in the output of composers: from Bach to Beethoven to Brahms to Boulez. There is no reason to attribute this decrease to a decline in the genius of composers. Rather, it occurred because the weaker the constraints of any style, the more difficult compositional decisions become. Unity through similarity was one way of coping with the proliferation of possibilities since, once a theme or motive had been adopted, its conservation served as a constraint that reduced the number of subsequent compositional choices.

To highlight the difference between the coherence that arises from the differentiation of syntactic function and that created by motivic similarity, consider the case in which a piece or movement begins and ends with the same pattern—a pattern that an experienced listener understands as a conventional closing gesture. For such a listener, the displacement of the gesture—its use as a beginning rather than as an end—generates a kind of cognitive dissonance; and, when the gesture later functions as a close, the disparity between position and function is resolved. For the syntactically unsophisticated tyro, on the other hand, the return of the pattern (for such a listener it is *not* a closing gesture) would signify closure, but it would do so for reasons having to do with innate, gestalt-like cognitive proclivities, not with learned convention.

---

9. From this point of view, the whole history of music from, say, Berlioz to Boulez can be understood as one in which nonfunctional class membership becomes increasingly important, ending in serialism, set theory, and the compositions arising from them. Thus, in the analysis of much contemporary music, the pitch class of a tone is more important than its function (see Leonard B. Meyer, *Style and Music: Theory, History, and Ideology* [Philadelphia: University of Pennsylvania Press, 1989], pt. 3).

The distinction between unity through syntactic function as opposed to unity through motivic similarity may in part explain why eighteenth-century composers constructed musical dice games while nineteenth-century ones did not. That is, the gauche motivic (melodic/rhythmic) juxtapositions that almost invariably result from the hazards of throwing dice to "choose" successive measures of music are mitigated and seem acceptable because the syntactic relationships between measures are stylistically understandable. Put differently: because coherence of *function* takes precedence over incongruity of motivic *kind,* the resulting pieces make modest musical sense.

What is ironic in the relationship between practice and ideology in the nineteenth century is that coherence by similarity of class is perhaps the least organic sort of unity. A coral reef or a sponge, which consists of collections of similar organisms, possesses only an additive unity. But an organism—whether mosquito, mouse, or man—is an integrated whole precisely because its component parts (the nervous, circulatory, digestive, and reproductive systems) perform different, complementary functions.

Motivic unity has been interpreted in two different ways: synchronically, as a relationship of similarity without regard to temporal ordering, and diachronically, as a process of successive development or change over time. The difference between synchronic and diachronic motivic relationships is the basis for Vincent d'Indy's distinction between thematic metamorphosis and organic development.[10] A comparable distinction has been made by Walter Frisch, who differentiates between *thematic transformation* (synchronic) and *developing variation* (diachronic), the latter term taken from Schönberg's writings.[11] Since these terms have become common in recent analytic writings, I will use them rather than d'Indy's designations.

In thematic transformation, the various versions of a motive, though necessarily successive in practice, are regarded as members of a temporally unordered class—a synchronic set. Of course, in actual music the versions of a motive are temporally ordered, and such ordering significantly affects aes-

10. Vincent d'Indy, *Cours de composition musicale* (1900), quoted in Daniel Fallon, "Saint-Saëns and the *Concours de composition musicale* in Bordeaux," *Journal of the American Musicological Society* 31 (1978): 321.

11. Walter Frisch, *Brahms and the Principle of Developing Variation* (Berkeley and Los Angeles: University of California Press, 1984), esp. chaps. 1–3. The fact that similarity relationships constitute a basis for classlike unity seems to underlie the concept of prolongation as a source of coherence. That is, the concept of prolongation involves the *uniformity* of class "sameness" rather than the *unity* of "return" that results from functional differentiation. Though commitment to tonality suggests that Schenker's ideas are antithetical to serialism, in this respect they seem, ironically, to be manifestations of the same mind-set.

thetic experience. Thus in Liszt's Piano Sonata it makes an enormous difference that the lyric version of the theme (mm. 163–69) follows the "malevolent" version (mm. 14–17). Nevertheless, most theorists who have been concerned with motivic unity have adopted a synchronic position; that is, they have explained how the variants of a motive or theme are related to one another—or to some abstracted imaginary pattern from which all the variants are presumably derived—by arguing for their classlike similarity.

The diachronic interpretation considers that motivic unity involves a process of change and variation. At times the nature of such a process is clear and unproblematic. For instance, one of the strategies frequently replicated in Romantic music was that of beginning a piece with a more or less inchoate pattern—one whose structuring was psychologically and stylistically less than satisfactory. The exemplary instance of this strategy is surely the opening of Beethoven's Symphony no. 9. Its nature has been described by John N. Burk: "Themes which are gradually unfolded from mysterious murmurings in the orchestra . . . all date back to the opening measures of the Ninth Symphony, where Beethoven conceived the idea of building a music of indeterminate open fifths on the dominant, and accumulating a great crescendo of suspense until the theme itself is revealed in the pregnant key of D minor, proclaimed fortissimo by the whole orchestra in unison." [12]

Change from the inchoate to the well formed cannot only be experienced, but the nature of the change can be comprehended and explained. Once the well-formed motive or theme is presented, however, the nature of subsequent developments and transformations is evidently more difficult to account for. The problem concerns the principles that govern the process of development and variation.

Many writers, for instance, have called attention to the successive variants of the neighbor-note motive that begins the first movement of Brahms's Symphony no. 2. Though the critics and analysts have described these changes (or have related each to an "ideal" source) and have classified them according to the compositional technique employed—for example, inversion, diminution, augmentation, rhythmic modification—nothing is said about the principles governing the probable (or necessary?) ordering of the variants as a diachronic development.

12. John N. Burk, *The Life and Works of Beethoven* (New York: Random House, 1943), 294. Other instances of this "germinal/prestate" strategy occur from Chopin's Etude in C Minor, op. 10, no. 12 (mm. 1–8), and Schubert's Symphony no. 8 (first movement, mm. 9–12) to Bruckner's Symphony no. 9 (first movement, mm. 1–18).

If an understanding of motivic relationships is to transcend the taxonomic, what is needed is a theory (however informal) that explains, rather than describes, the diachronic ordering of variants. The failure even to recognize that the nature of motivic succession is a crucial problem results from an obsession with motivic constancy as the presumed basis for musical unity. This obsession directs virtually exclusive attention to the synchronic similarities between motives and variants, rather than to the diachronic processes that order variants. And it is impossible to devise a theory of motivic development by attending solely to class similarities.

The problem of ordering motivic variants is compositional as well as theoretical. The technique of developing variation was not an invention of the mid-nineteenth century. It had been employed in the Baroque and Classic periods. What was new in the nineteenth and twentieth centuries was its increased importance as a compositional constraint.

As the repudiation of convention led to the attenuation of tonal syntax and form, motivic similarity was, almost by default, forced into a position of structural primacy. In the music of Wagner and his heirs, the ordering of motives depended largely upon foreground tonal syntax, sequential processes (often culminating in massive climaxes), and succession as called for by a text or a program. In the music of more Classically inclined composers such as Brahms, motivic ordering was guided by the constraints of tonal syntax and the organization of traditional forms.

With the advent first of atonality and then of serialism, motivic relationships (together with the organizing capabilities of the secondary parameters) had to bear the main burden of musical structuring. As this occurred, the need for constraints governing the ordering of motives and variants became pressing. For pure motivic variation not only lacks any "natural" order or direction but is entirely open-ended—that is, motivic variation can continue interminably. Schönberg, both the advocate and the victim of this development of Romanticism, was not only aware of the need for constraints ("It seemed at first impossible to compose pieces of complicated organization or of great length. A little later I discovered how to construct larger forms by following a text or a poem"), but he seems to have imagined the possibility of a syntax of motivic relationships.[13] This is indicated by his observations about the opening melody of "Der Abschied" from Mahler's *Das Lied von der Erde:* "All the units vary greatly in shape, size and content, as they were not motival parts

13. Arnold Schönberg, *Style and Idea,* trans. and ed. Dika Newlin (New York: Philosophical Library, 1950), 106.

of a melodic unit, but words, each of which has a purpose of its own in the sentence." [14] What Schönberg seems to be suggesting is that motival elements might be related to one another not primarily according to similarity but according to function ("purpose")—as with nouns, adjectives, verbs, and so on—in the structuring of a melody, period, or section.

But such a syntax of motivic succession was never devised, and the failure to do so explains in part why, despite the revolution in pitch organization and the "emancipation of the dissonance," the forms of Classical music not only persisted but were often used by twelve-tone composers and others in a more conservative way than in the music of the preceding generation of composers. For these forms—sonata form, rondo, theme and variations, dance forms, and so on—provided the constraints that enabled composers to choose appropriate melodic, rhythmic, and harmonic embodiments for their motives, themes, and twelve-tone rows. What I am suggesting is that contemporary composers have employed "borrowed" forms and procedures not solely (or even primarily) because they considered themselves to be heirs to the great tradition of European art music, or because of subconscious neoclassical inclinations, but because they had virtually no alternative. They could not do without some way of deciding how the motivic variants they invented should be combined with or succeed one another.

Thus there is a significant difference between Stravinsky's use of the forms and strategies of earlier music and, say, Alban Berg's in *Wozzeck*. For the appreciation of Stravinsky's neoclassical music depends on an understanding of the use of and play with learned conventions. Berg's use of the past does not. He said that he was proud that "there is no one in the audience who pays any attention to the various fugues, inventions, suites, sonata movements, variations, and passacaglias—no one who heeds anything but the social problems of this opera, which by far transcend the personal destiny of Wozzeck." [15] What I take this statement to mean is that Berg regarded the conventions and schemata of the past not primarily as communal constraints shaping the aesthetic experience of listeners but, paradoxically, as private compositional constraints that, supplementing those of atonal technique, facilitated compositional choice.

Of course, composers of all periods have probably used private constraints, sometimes casually, sometimes consistently. But the needs of twentieth-

14. Quoted in Richard Swift, "Mahler's Ninth and Cooke's Tenth," *Nineteenth-Century Music* 2 (1978): 166.
15. Quoted in *The New Grove Dictionary of Music*, s.v. "Berg, Alban," 2:531.

century composers—especially of those who eschew the conventions of the tonal tradition—for ways of limiting choice have made the nature of constraints a subject of concern. (This may partly explain why so many composers are also theorists.) And, precisely for this reason, it is important to distinguish between private, perhaps peculiar, constraints and shared, communal ones.

The distinction is important because the history of twentieth-century music can, broadly speaking, be understood as a continuing search for viable compositional constraints. The kinds of constraints used have been many and various. Some were newly devised and subsequently extended, as in the case of the twelve-tone method and serialism; some were derived from existing styles, for instance, from aspects of Baroque, Classic, folk, and non-Western musics; some made use of mathematical models, for example, the Golden Section, the Fibonacci series, or stochastic processes; and others were explicitly aleatory. Such constraints may be aesthetically irrelevant, as when my colleague George Crumb spelled out his name in Morse code in the percussion part of one of his pieces. This observation suggests that there is a continuum from the arcanely private to the platitudinously communal.

It is important to recognize that the constraints that limit and influence the choices of composers may not be those that guide the apprehension and shape the aesthetic experience of listeners. And, being a maverick, I would argue that this may also be true of some aspects of tonal music. Perhaps, for instance, the high-level key schemes in operas by Wagner or Verdi, and in symphonies by Mahler or tone poems by Strauss, should be interpreted as providing constraints that facilitated compositional choice, rather than as aspects of aesthetic experience. Indeed, there is even some empirical evidence that indicates that high-level key schemes within symphonic movements are not perceived by listeners and hence may not be aesthetically very significant.[16] What I am arguing, then, is that it is a mistake to assume that all the relationships that can be discerned in a piece of music serve aesthetic ends, creating tension and repose, enhancing closure and unity. Some relationships exist because they facilitate creation rather than comprehension.

Like the prizing of unity and economy, and of necessity and inevitability, the diligent search for high-level schemes and overarching tonal coherence is an outgrowth of the organic branches of Romanticism. And these preoccupations remind us that formalism, which has characterized and colored so

---

16. Nicholas Cook, "The Perception of Large-Scale Tonal Closure," *Music Perception* 5 (1987): 197–205.

much criticism and theory of music and the other arts in the twentieth century, is itself a remainder of Romanticism.

To support this seemingly bizarre claim, let me begin with the most Romantic master of them all, Richard Wagner. In *A Communication to My Friends,* he wrote that "Lohengrin sought a woman who would believe in him: who would not ask who he was or whence he came, but would love him as he was because he was what he appeared to her to be."[17] What Wagner here described is what is quite properly called Romantic love—a love to which lineage and tradition, social position and circumstances are irrelevant. Formalism in aesthetics is an almost perfect counterpart of such Romantic love. Like a beloved, an artwork is to be adored—even worshiped—for itself alone. The claims of social, religious, political, or biographical significance are irrelevant. And so is history.[18]

According to the aesthetics of formalism, knowledge and experience, cultural and historical context are unnecessary for the comprehension and appreciation of works of art. Each work contains its complete meaning within itself and, correlatively, the principles appropriate to its own analysis. These attitudes still pervade music theory and criticism, leading to the belief that latent in every good composition are the principles needed for its apprehension and its analysis. Related to these beliefs is the idea that the critic is the "servant of the text" since one can be a servant of the text only if the mode of criticism is, as it were, "ordered" by the text.

Behind such unmitigated formalism lies a profound faith in the primacy of nature, in the proposition that the perception, comprehension, and response to music is dependent not on learning, experience, and knowledge but solely on the gift of innate, natural sensitivity. Belief in the essentially natural, and hence universal, basis for music still pervades the psychology and the theory of music. From Helmholtz to the present, psychologists have sought to explain the power of music in terms of acoustic stimuli that, because they were natural, were presumably independent of time and place. Similar attitudes affected music theory as well. Like the analyses of similarity relationships among motives or pitch-class sets, the Schenkerian *Ursatz* is presumably a natural relationship arising out of universal principles. Such modes of analysis

17. Quoted in Carl Dahlhaus, *Richard Wagner's Music Dramas,* trans. Mary Whittall (Berkeley and Los Angeles: University of California Press, 1980), 40.

18. See Clive Bell, one of the foremost formalists, quoted in my *Music, the Arts, and Ideas: Patterns and Predictions in Twentieth-Century Culture* (Chicago: University of Chicago Press, 1994), 55.

are in principle ahistorical. They have, for the most part, been unconcerned with style differences between the musics of different cultures or with style changes within the music of Western culture.

Criticism as well as theory has been significantly affected by the positivistic tenets of Romanticism. Conceiving of the response to music as being independent of learning—of conventions characterized by time and place—is mistaken because we understand and evaluate phenomena (political actions, individual behavior, and works of art) not only in terms of what actually occurs but in terms of what might have happened. What Morris Cohen has said of history applies with equal force to our understanding of music: "We can understand the significance of what did happen only if we contrast it with what might have happened. . . . Indeed we could not grasp the full significance of what has happened, even though the facts of history were completely revealed to us, unless we had some idea of what the situation would have been otherwise." [19]

Knowing—usually tacitly—what might have happened in a piece of music depends to a considerable extent on having internalized the constraints of some specific style, that is, having learned the repertory of possibilities and probabilities that influenced the choices made by the composer. Understanding music, then, involves comprehending the relationships between actual, audible structure (relationships realized) and implied, imagined structure (relationships possible, perhaps even probable, but unrealized). Insofar as contemporary music theory slights learned stylistic relationships, it can account for only a small portion of the significance of compositions, often missing the richness and subtlety of musical relationships.

19. Morris Cohen, *The Meaning of Human History* (La Salle, Ill.: Open Court, 1947), 80–81; see also in this connection Isaiah Berlin, "The Concept of Scientific History," in *Philosophical Analysis and History,* ed. William Dray (New York: Harper & Row, 1966), 48–49.

Cohen's point is confirmed by the tendency of historians to employ counterfactual conditionals. Lars-Erik Nelson presents a convincing example of how awareness of an unrealized alternative changes our understanding of events. He writes: "This is such a stunning might-have-been that it begs amplification. Dershowitz gives it: 'Robert Bennett, Clinton's lawyer in the Jones case, never explained to him the option of defaulting. . . . If Clinton had chosen to default the case, there would have been no deposition, no Starr investigation, no perjury charge, no impeachment'" ("The Republicans' War," *New York Review of Books,* 4 February 1999, 9).

A tangential surmise: I would guess that there is a relationship between the character—yes, the *style*—of a history and the presence or absence of counterfactual conditionals. That is, counterfactuals are more frequently encountered in *explanatory* histories that seek to account for the *why* of events and must therefore be concerned with what "might have been" than in *descriptive* histories that are primarily concerned to establish and describe the *what* of the past.

[The existence of unrealized alternatives has important ramifications for the rehearing of music and the rereading of literary works as well as for the experience of the relational richness considered in essay 2. When the "plot-process" of a work of art is first encountered, attention tends to be directed to the main line of the action-pattern. The experience is like that of driving to a new destination for the first time: we give little attention to passing scenery or minor side roads but direct attention to the signs and signals that help us follow the route.[20] To take an exemplary case: as we first read a detective story, we concentrate on what seem significant clues that suggest how the solve-the-crime schema might be actualized.[21]

Similarly in music, what initially most engage our attention are the main melodic, harmonic, and schema relationships. Then, once we know how the narrative "problem" is solved, we are able to attend to nuances of structure and process—the deceptive strategies, the passing landscapes, and the intriguing side roads. This calls attention to a consequence of quality of relationship missed in the second essay in this gathering: namely, just as an uncomplicated road allows for attention to attractive landscapes and provocative trails, so grammatical simplicity makes it easier for listeners to sense the presence of, and attend to, unrealized possibilities. And, just as richness facilitates rehearing, so rehearing can enhance experiential richness.[22]

The presence of alternatives also has implications for performance. For instance, because recognizing the possibility of alternatives takes time, extremely rapid tempi preclude attending to roads not taken. For this reason, the greater the relational richness of a composition, the more moderate the speed of performance. Finally, I would suggest that what we mean when we say that a work is "deep" or "profound" is that it is rich in relational

20. Clearly this is only partly true. In a well-established style, we usually have a pretty good idea of what the structural plan of the music will be but not of how and when the expected processive and structural events will occur: e.g., in an eighteenth-century sonata-form movement, how and when we will get to the dominant, what will the character (affect, topic, etc.) of the second theme be?

21. My attempt to characterize the change in perception and experience wrought by rehearing or rereading is in some ways comparable to Edward T. Cone's account in his "Three ways of Reading a Detective Story," in *Music: A View from Delft* (Chicago: University of Chicago Press, 1989), 77–93.

22. Ramifications that I failed to see when I wrote "On Rehearing Music" (in *Music, the Arts, and Ideas*).

These observations do not, however, gainsay the view expressed in "Rehearing Music" that even the finest composition will lose its luster if a recorded performance is played too often during a limited time span.

ramifications. And it is in this sense that a seemingly simple work can be experienced as profound.]

I do not mean to deny the existence of universals or to minimize their significance for music theory. But the universals central for music theory are not those of physics or acoustics but those of human psychology—principles such as the following: proximity between stimuli tends to create connection, disjunction results in separation; orderly processes imply continuation to a point of relative stability; a return to patterns previously presented enhances closure; and, because of the requirements of memory, music tends to have considerable redundancy and is often hierarchically structured.

The reference to hierarchy suggests another way in which our Romantic heritage has misled music theory. Though the yearning for Oneness, coupled with a desire for conceptual simplicity, inclines us toward analytic monism, it is important to emphasize that hierarchies arise precisely because the constraints governing structure and process change from one hierarchic level to another. This is the case in the realm of music—as it is in the physical, biological, and social worlds. Just as the principles governing the ways in which atoms combine to form molecules are different from those governing ways molecules combine to form cells, so the constraints governing the ways in which tones combine to form motives are different from those constraining the ways that motives combine to form phrases. And comparable constraint differences distinguish other levels of a musical hierarchy. Consequently it seems unlikely that any single kind of patterning will be characteristic of all levels of the compositional hierarchy.

Since confession is the current fashion among preachers—and what else is a keynote speaker?—let me plead guilty. Like others who have extrapolated relationships discerned on lower hierarchic levels to very high ones, Grosvenor Cooper and I overextrapolated in *The Rhythmic Structure of Music*.[23] That is, we tried to use gestalt grouping ideas that work well on levels up to the phrase and period to analyze whole sections and even movements. In so doing we violated what I have since referred to as the "law of hierarchic discontinuity."[24] That is, at very high levels of structure, temporal relationships become an aspect of formal organization. New constraints shape process and structure. If these observations have merit, then one of the important tasks of music theory is to specify, for any particular musical style, the nature

23. Grosvenor W. Cooper and Leonard B. Meyer, *The Rhythmic Structure of Music* (Chicago: University of Chicago Press, 1960).
24. See *Music, the Arts, and Ideas,* 96–97, 257ff., and 306ff.

of the constraints governing the several levels of structure—and for each of the parameters of music separately.

The law of hierarchic discontinuity suggests that any theory of motivic succession would necessarily be concerned with constraints on a level higher than that of the motive itself—for instance, with a plot, a program, or a formal/ processive schema. This not only explains the need of contemporary composers for formal schemata but may be one reason why composers of the past 150 years were attracted by programs. That is, like schemata such as sonata form, programs facilitated the ordering of motivic variants.

One consequence of the discontinuity of hierarchies is that universal, high-level principles are invariably realized through lower-level, *cultural* constraints. As a result, direct, unmediated experience, à la Wordsworth's innocent infant trailing clouds of glory, is a Romantic myth. There are no innocent eyes or naive ears for any member of any culture—and to be human is to be a member of some culture. John Cage's aleatory music, for instance, tries to foist auditory innocence upon us. But his Romantic enterprise is an exercise in futility. What we know we cannot ignore: the sound of an oboe is not that of a nightingale; a cavernous auditorium is not a canyon; the rustling silence of an audience at a concert of Cage's *4′ 33″* is not that of the Maine seashore on a summer's evening. Innocence was lost not when Eve ate the apple but when she knew that it was an apple that she had eaten.

It is the nature of human beings to be nurtured by cultural constraints. And the time has come, this Walrus thinks, for music theorists and psychologists to consider seriously the claims of culture and of history. After all, our primary data—pieces of music—are a result of the choices made by composers, choices that are made in terms both of prevalent constraints and of guiding goals. Such constraints and goals are always significantly affected by culture and history.

One closing caution. I do not want to turn from one monism—one Oneness—to another: from the absolutes of Romanticism to those of cultural relativism. The claims of both nurture and nature must be allowed. The central problem then is, as it always has been, that of their interrelationships—both in general and in individual instances. And, since the individual instantiations of all constraints are invariably characterized by contingency, our theories must be formulated in such a way that they can cope with what is peculiar as well as with what is general; with what is aberrant as well as what is normal; and with what is disordered as well as with what is orderly and regular. Indeed, disorder is an inescapable fact not only of nature and life but of art. And,

since I began with delight in diversity, let me close with "Delight in Disorder," a poem by another antediluvian, Robert Herrick:

> A sweet disorder in the dress
> Kindles in clothes a wantonness;
> A lawn about the shoulders thrown
> Into a fine distraction:
> An erring lace, which here and there
> Enthralls the crimson stomacher:
> A cuff neglected and thereby
> Ribbands to flow confusedly:
> A winning wave, deserving note,
> In the tempestuous petticoat:
> A careless shoe-string, in whose tie
> I see a wild civility:
> Do more bewitch me than when art
> Is too precise in every part.

IV

Postlude

8

A Universe of Universals

Introduction

The context for this essay about universals is, paradoxically, the prevalent and pervasive preoccupation with the variability of cultural contexts. My premise is simple: one cannot comprehend and explain the variability of human cultures unless one has some sense of the constancies involved in their shaping. In what follows I have tried to be specific and concrete about the relevance of universals for the theory, history, and criticism of music.

Because we are all products of a special and limited time and space, our behavior and beliefs are invariably influenced by the cultural and personal circumstances in which we find ourselves. But, needless to say, it does not follow from this "provenance relativism" that the significance and validity of works of art, theories, and so on are confined to the time and place of their genesis. If they were, the art of the past (e.g., the plays of Sophocles) and the actions of the protagonists in history (Caesar's crossing the Rubicon) would be incomprehensible. And the same is true of concepts, whether in the sciences or in the humanities. Darwin's theory of evolution undoubtedly owes a debt to its nineteenth-century, industrial-capitalist context. The validity of the theory is not, however, affected by this provenance but depends on the empirical testing of the implications derived from the theory. This observation calls attention to questions of methodology.

Methodology

We understand the world through a collection of often tacit suppositions about the nature of things, from asteroids to zebras. Because our

Reprinted from the *Journal of Musicology* 16, no. 1 (Winter 1998): 3–25, by permission. Copyright © 1998 by The Regents of the University of California.

This essay was presented as the fifteenth annual Martin Bernstein Lecture at New York University.

My thanks to Harold S. Powers for cogent comments on, and suggestions for improving, this essay. My debt to Janet M. Levy is exceptionally wide and deep because she not only made incisive criticisms but curbed my tendency toward self-indulgent and tangential speculation.

knowledge of that world (its past, present, and future) is never more than partial, theories change, and from this variability some have inferred that truth is but a contingent social construct.[1] However, while it is plausible to argue that theories, and the hypotheses on which they are based, cannot be unequivocally confirmed, they can be, *and they have been,* decisively *dis*confirmed.[2]

In other words, when we test a hypothesis, we find out whether, given existing knowledge and experimental methods, it is presently viable or can be shown to be mistaken. And, as some hypotheses are qualified or discarded altogether while others survive the heat of testing, the probable validity of surviving ones increases.[3] The methodology I have been describing might be thought of as a kind of selectionist empiricism. That is, like natural selection, it eliminates untenable hypotheses, allowing others to endure.

This viewpoint has important implications for the flourishing field of interpretation. In this age of proliferating information—books, periodicals, and the internet—it has become virtually impossible to "keep up" in one's field. In the arts one result has been a plethora of interpretations that, when based on the personal responses of an individual critic, allow that critic to disregard the existing literature about the work being interpreted.

Anthropologist Clifford Geertz addresses what I take to be the central problem in the current vogue for interpretation: "The besetting sin of interpretive approaches to anything—literature, dreams, symptoms, culture—is that they tend to resist . . . conceptual articulation and thus to escape sys-

1. Data—the facts, the "what" of the world—can, of course, be fully verified. And it may be possible to confirm predictions derived from a particular theory. But the reasons—the "whys" of the world—can only be provisionally verified. This is because another theory may explain more relationships or the same relationships more elegantly or because data subsequently discovered may call the theory into question. John D. Sterman, e.g., argues, "Any nontautological theory (that is, any theory that refers to the world) is underdetermined and thus unverifiable" ("The Meaning of Models," *Science* 124 [15 April 1994]: 329).

2. In this connection, see John T. Edsall and John C. Eccles, quoted in essay 1, pp. 9 and 23, respectively. To take an example from music history: a number of scholars have argued that large-scale tonal relationships were a basis for coherence in Mozart's operas. But, as John Platoff and others have shown, evidence from the works of both Mozart and his contemporaries indicates that the hypothesis is, to say the least, questionable. See Platoff's "Tonal Organization in the *Opera Buffa* of Mozart's Time," in *Mozart Studies* 2, ed. Cliff Eisen (Oxford, 1997), 139–74.

3. Hypotheses exist not in splendid isolation but in relation to a framework of theory, however informally conceived. The value, if not the validity, of a hypothesis rests to a considerable extent on its relationship to—its fit with—a network of other hypotheses, at least some of which have been tested. Although it should be impartial, such testing need not be explicitly experimental. What is crucial is what Stuart Hampshire calls dispassionate "procedural process." See his "Liberalism: The New Twist" (a review of John Rawls's *Political Liberalism*), *New York Review of Books* 40, no. 14 (12 August 1993): 46.

tematic modes of assessment. . . . Imprisoned in the immediacy of its own detail, [an interpretation] is presented as self-validating, or, worse, as validated by the supposedly developed sensitivities of the person who presents it."[4] In short, though we may fully agree with an interpretation, unless the evidence and argument involved in its formulation can be comprehended, the interpretation is suspect. As in the case of hypotheses, the question is, On what grounds can an interpretation be disconfirmed?

Empiricism is indispensable precisely because it entails encounters with the phenomenal world that force us to choose among interpretations. What is crucial is whether any and all interpretations of some phenomenon—say, a work of art—are tenable.[5] If so, then interpretations are analogous to the social situation criticized by the Duke of Plaza-Toro in W. S. Gilbert's *The Gondoliers:*

> When every one is somebodee,
> Then no one's anybody!

Universals[6]

To explain why human beings in some actual cultural-historical context think, respond, and choose as they do, it is necessary to distinguish those facets of human behavior that are learned and variable from those that are in-

---

4. Clifford Geertz, *The Interpretation of Cultures* (New York, 1973), 24.

5. The exemplary collection of illuminating interpretive essays, a collection from which all of us can learn, is Frederick C. Crews, *The Pooh Perplex* (New York, 1963). Despite the many virtues of the collection—especially the hilarious sweep of hermeneutic viewpoints included—there is a glaring omission: none of the possible interpretations of *Winnie-the-Pooh* in terms of music theory have been included!

6. Universals, which are immutable constraining relationships in the physical, biological, and physiopsychological realms, fall under the rubric of what I have called *laws* (see Leonard B. Meyer, *Style and Music: Theory, History, and Ideology* [Philadelphia: University of Pennsylvania Press, 1989], 13–23). As I argue in the last part of this essay, there are also universals in the realms of human behavior (e.g., the necessity of choice and hence the need for envisaging and for a stable cultural environment). These are derivative, arising out of physiopsychological constraints.

Like all laws, the action of universals is prohibitive, stipulating what can*not* occur but leaving open a vast number of possible realizations on the levels of rules and strategies. But the action of universals can be contravened. Gravity is a universal, but both birds and airplanes fly. Such contraventions, of course, involve special constraints: e.g., wings and muscles, wings and motors.

However, the contravening constraints themselves depend on the action of universals—e.g., the physiology of living animals (in this case, birds) and the resistance of air. This suggests a further, perhaps rash, conjecture: namely, that universals can be contravened only by other universals while cultural constraints can be contravened either by universals or other cultural constraints.

nate and universal.[7] But it is a mistake—albeit a common one—to conceptualize the problem as a search for "musical" universals. *There are none.* There are only the acoustic universals of the physical world and the biopsychological universals of the human world. Acoustic stimuli affect the perception, cognition, and hence practice of music only through the constraining action of biopsychological ones.[8]

My discussion of biopsychological universals is divided into five topics: neurocognitive constraints, syntactic and statistical parameters, classification, hierarchic structures, and redundancy.

Neurocognitive Constraints

The kinds of relationships that can be perceived and processed by the human mind are limited by neurocognitive universals. And these constraints account for many features of music—non-Western as well as Western. To take an obvious case, the minimum distance in frequency between pitches in a scale depends on human auditory discrimination. As a result, intervals smaller than a half step almost always serve to inflect structural tones.[9]

More important, the *amount* of information that the human mind can process is constrained by human cognitive capacities. In general, cognitive overload, which can be a matter either of amount or of speed of stimulus input, creates confusion and anxiety. In our age of electronic resources, this hazard has become very real. Vastly to increase the *amount* of information the mind must process—for instance, playing recordings of a number of different symphonies simultaneously—is to court the vacuousness of white noise. And *speed* of both information processing and muscle response is similarly limited.[10]

---

7. From this point of view, it seems surprising that ethnomusicologists, who are especially and explicitly concerned with cultural variability, have not been more interested in what is constant in human behavior. Perhaps their preoccupation with the peculiarity of cultures led to the neglect of universals, including those of human biopsychology.

8. I am using the term *biopsychological* because the understanding and response to music includes constraints that are not generally thought of as psychological—e.g., physiological ones such as muscle tension.

9. I say *almost* because it is possible to devise microtonal scales in which, say, twelve pitches or sixteen pitches are supposed to be structural. But, to the best of my knowledge, no scales of this sort have ever become shared cultural constraints; and, unless human audition and cognition change significantly, it is doubtful that such scales will ever become so.

10. See John R. Platt, quoted in my *Music, the Arts, and Ideas: Patterns and Predictions in Twentieth-Century Culture* (Chicago: University of Chicago Press, 1967), 272.

More specifically, the number of elements in any comprehensible relationship is limited by the cognitive capabilities of the human mind—by what psychologist George Miller called "the magic number seven, plus or minus two."[11] The repertory of tones in the music of most cultures is constrained by this universal. So, too, is the number of elements that make up patterns on the various levels of a musical hierarchy—the number of motives in phrases, of phrases in themes, themes in sections, and so on.

The limitation on number is consequential. Just as, for instance, buildings increase in size not because their components (posts and beams, bricks and nails) grow larger but because the number of components increases, and just as living organisms grow not by expanding the size of units such as cells but by increasing their number, so pieces of music grow not by expanding the size of the basic elements but by increasing their number. Thus, though Bruckner's symphonic movements are much longer than Mozart's, their motives, phrases, themes, and so on are about the same length as Mozart's. And forms can be expanded through the addition of large sections, as with second developments in codas.[12]

Increase in size is, needless to say, constrained by culture as well as by nature. In the nineteenth century, the valuing of the sublime, of magnitude as a sign of power, and the taste of the audience for what I call *statistical climaxes* (see below) led to increases in the length and breadth of symphonic works. But the *ways* in which increases occurred were governed by cognitive universals.

The length of an element (pattern) on any hierarchic level also seems to be a function of the frequency of its use in a movement. In a way analogous to Zipf's law in language, it seems that the more frequent the occurrence of a pattern, the shorter it tends to be.[13] The relation of size to number seems to be a universal in realms other than human conceptualization: for instance, in the realm of organisms the greater the number, the smaller the size (more flies than humans, more humans than elephants). Size is also related to speed and register: larger equals slower and lower (tuba vs. piccolo, bear vs. bird).

11. George Miller, "The Magic Number Seven, Plus or Minus Two: Some Limits on Our Capacity for Processing Information," *Psychological Review* 63, no. 2 (1956): 81–97.

12. See, among others, Robert G. Hopkins, "When Is a Coda More Than a Coda," in *Explorations in Music, the Arts, and Ideas,* ed. R. Solie and E. Narmour (Stuyvesant, N.Y., 1988), 393–410; Robert P. Morgan, "Coda as Culmination," in *Music Theory and the Exploration of the Past,* ed. C. Hatch and D. W. Bernstein (Chicago, 1993), 357–76.

13. Length is, I suspect, also related to the presence of functionality. It seems likely that functionally governed patterns can (but need not) be longer than nonfunctional ones.

The relationship of size and frequency to form is an area of music theory and history that merits much more scrupulous and sophisticated analysis than it has yet received.[14]

Syntactic and Statistical Parameters

Because of the innate capabilities of the human mind, some parameters of sound can be segmented into perceptually discrete, proportionally related stimuli that can then serve as the basis for auditory patternings. In most musics of the world, this is the case with pitch (frequency) and duration, which are the basis for melody, rhythm, meter, and (in Western music) harmony. Because the largely learned probabilities and possibilities that govern successions in these parameters can be the basis for syntax, I have called these parameters *syntactic*.

In order for syntactic relationships to arise, the elements constituting a parameter must be related to one another in a functional way—for example, leading tone/tonic or upbeat/downbeat. Functional differentiation is a universal that is operative in all realms of being: it explains why the coherence of a starfish is greater than that of a coral reef, why a sonata-form movement is, as a rule, more tightly knit than a theme and variations movement, and why in the music of almost all cultures the repertories of pitches and durations are nonuniform.

To take the clearest example, in any syntactic tonal system there are larger and smaller intervals. The probability that this proclivity (i.e., parsing the frequency continuum into different size intervals) is a universal is supported by the recent discovery of an ancient bone flute (estimated to be at least forty-three thousand years old) in which the hole spacings are patently unequal, suggesting the possibility of diatonic pitch organization.[15]

Similarly, the existence of rhythmic groupings depends on differentiation—durational, accentual, or both. Thus, the more alike two successive stimuli are, the more likely the next will be different. It is largely because of

14. The relationship between size and structure has received considerable attention in the sciences. According to biologist Michael LaBarbera, e.g., "Size, in and of itself, affects almost every aspect of an organism's biology. Indeed, the effects of absolute size are so rich in biological insight that the field has earned a name all its own—'scaling'" (*University of Chicago Magazine* 89, nos. 1 and 2 [October–December 1996]: 19). See also G. B. West, J. H. Brown, and B. J. Enquist, "A General Model for the Origin of Allometric Scaling Laws in Biology," *Science* 276 (4 April 1997): 122–26; and Douglas E. Soltis, "Avenues for Plants" (a review of Karl J. Niklas's *The Evolutionary Biology of Plants*), *Science* 277 (18 July 1997): 327.

15. See "Early Music," *Science* 276 (11 April 1997): 205; and Bob Fink, "Neanderthal Flute," on the internet: http://www.webster.sk.ca/greenwich/fl-comp.htm.

this cognitive constraint that, as Alfred Lorenz observed, Wagner's music is characterized by bar forms (a + a' + b or 1 + 1 + 2).[16] Put the other way around, uniformity (a succession of whole tones or equal durations) precludes functionality and, hence, hierarchic structuring.[17]

Innate cognitive constraints do not, however, segment other parameters of sound into discrete, proportional relationships. For instance, there is no relationship in the realm of dynamics that corresponds to, say, a minor third or dotted rhythm. And the same is true of tempo, sonority, and timbre. Dynamics may become louder or softer, tempi may be faster or slower, sonorities thinner or thicker, and so on. But they cannot be segmented into perceptually discrete relationships.[18] Because they are experienced and conceptualized in terms of amount rather than in terms of kinds or classlike relationships (such as *major third* or *antecedent-consequent*), I have called these parameters *statistical.*

The implicative tensions of syntactic processes and the bodily tensions of statistical processes (e.g., insistent durational patterns, unusual speed, intense dynamics, extreme registers, etc.) seem to be inversely related to one another. The more forceful one is, the less compelling the other. This may be why a plaintive adagio seems more "emotional" than a persistent presto and why fulsome motor tension seems excitedly active but not very "emotional." Put crudely, marked motor activity tends to diminish cognitively generated tension (people go to the gym to "work off" their business-kindled frustrations). Similarly highly motoric music—for example, Rossini's *William Tell* overture—curbs patent emotional experience.[19]

16. The ubiquity of bar forms in Wagner's music is partly a function of the cultural/stylistic valuing of openness (characterized by frequent deceptive cadences). That is, in the absence of decisive tonal closure, bar forms provide the articulation that creates structure. Because language, too, is affected by the need for differentiation, "bar forms" are not uncommon, especially in poetry (see, e.g., essay 2, n. 36).

17. The importance of differentiation in the patterning of musical relationships (on various hierarchic levels) is discussed in my *Emotion and Meaning in Music* (Chicago: University of Chicago Press, 1956), 163–78.

18. There are distinguished theorists who argue that tempi can be comprehended as proportional (see, e.g., David Epstein, *Shaping Time* [New York, 1995]) and others who have sought to build a theory of sonority succession. Although I am frankly unsure about the perception of tempo relationships, I am more than a little skeptical about the existence of constraints governing the succession of timbres. As with the other statistical parameters, tempi and timbres are cognitively comprehended as continua; and, even though timbral differences create a sense of articulation, there seems to be no inherent cognitive disposition relating different timbres to one another in a consistent way.

19. These relationships can be related to the hypothesis that deviation from regularity is a source of affective experience. This is the case because the more forceful the regularity of motor

The distinction between syntactic and statistical parameters can illuminate relationships in the realm of theory. For instance, tonal dissonance, which is a matter of syntactic function, needs to be distinguished from acoustic discord, which is statistical—a matter of amount rather than of function. Thus the interval of a minor seventh in a dominant seventh chord implies a resolution because of our understanding of tonal syntax. But the implications of a minor seventh in a chord built of two perfect fourths are enigmatic because they are not constrained by a shared syntax. Unlike dissonance, which is functional, discord is statistical—a matter of amounts that result from factors such as the proximity of simultaneously sounding pitches and their partials, attack and dynamic level, the acoustic properties of the instruments, and so on. Thus Schönberg was right to speak of the "emancipation of dissonance," but discord remains an unliberated universal.

Awareness of the action of these cognitive universals is vital for an understanding of the history of Western music in the nineteenth and twentieth centuries. The attenuation of tonality, and hence of syntactic function, led to increased reliance on similarity relationships as the basis for form and coherence. However, because similarity cannot beget functional differentiation, form became increasingly dependent on the structuring of statistical parameters. More generally, similarity relationships give rise to class coherence (e.g., a gathering of geese, a collection of citizens, etc.) rather than the coherence created by functional differentiation.[20]

Classification

Our proclivity to comprehend the world in terms of classes—in music, classes of pitches, intervals, forms, genres, voices, instruments, performing groups, and so on—is a consequence of the finite capacity of the human mind and the resulting need for psychic economy. Put the other way around, were every sound or sound relationship perceived as unique, the amount of

---

action, the less likely deviation, and, conversely, the less emphatic motor action is, the more likely deviation (see *Emotion and Meaning in Music,* chaps. 6 and 7).

This hypothesis could be tested empirically by studying recordings by the same performer playing works with significantly different tempi and measuring degrees of durational and/or pitch deviation in relation to tempo differences. Hypothesis: fast tempi, loud dynamics, and strong accentuation result in minimal deviation; slow tempi, soft dynamics, and nonforceful motor action result in marked deviation.

20. Conversely, functional differentiation is what distinguishes return from reiteration. Put too simply: because the recapitulation in a sonata-form movement is separated from the exposition by the functional tension of a development section, the return of the first theme is understood as a "return" rather than as a "repetition."

information to be processed and stored in memory would be overwhelming. Equally important, class formation is imperative because propitious choices, which are the basis for success and survival, depend on the ability to discern alternative courses of action and to envisage their probable consequences (see pp. 294–96 below).[21] And discerning the implications of phenomena and relationships is, in turn, based on class-like probabilities, *not* on individual instances, which are always comprehended as members of some class.

Class concepts are also important because feedback from concept to choice has significantly influenced human history. In the history of music, once a replicated relationship has been conceptualized as a class, both theory and practice are forever changed. For instance, once a set of relationships was conceptualized as *sonata form,* compositional choice was a matter not only of tacitly understanding a practice but of creating in terms of *keys, themes, development sections,* and so on.[22]

The process of classification is strengthened by what psychologists call *categorical perception,* which is evidently a universal built into the nervous system, although the particular categories actually differentiated are largely learned. For instance, once the tonal relationships of Western music have been learned as categories of perception, if the third step of the major scale is gradually lowered, what we perceive is an increasingly out-of-tune major third until, at some point, a categorical shift occurs and we perceive a minor third. Were it not for categorical perception, the "blue note" would long since have lost its color.

The cognitive tendency to improve shape, discovered by gestalt psychologists, may in part be a function of the human proclivity to classify. That is, when something approximating a familiar configuration—say, a triangle, a human face, or a pitch pattern—is perceived, we tend to apprehend it within an appropriate learned cultural/experiential category and then "improve" the pattern, making it conform more closely to the class. (If this is right, then infants, who have not learned a particular class, should not "improve" shape.)

---

21. Although conceptualizing phenomena in terms of classes is indispensable, there is a danger, namely, that of reification—of treating a class, abstracted from a number of instances, as though it were an actual phenomenon.

22. Biologist Ernst Mayr has observed that there is no feedback in nature: "Variation is completely independent of the actual selection process" (*Toward a New Philosophy of Biology* [Cambridge, Mass., 1988], 98).

This calls attention to a decisive difference between biological evolution and human history: namely, the concepts, classes, and theories created by scientists, social scientists, and humanists are responsible for many of the changes—the "variations"—that constitute human history.

The universal need for conceptual classes is evident in the fact that we cling to such classes until we are forced to abandon them. We do so because classes are the basis for the relational "theories" in terms of which we envisage, choose, and act in the world. Despite currently fashionable epistemological relativism, when we change class concepts, it is because there really is a phenomenal world—a world not of our making—*out there*.[23] And, when prevalent theories and their attendant classes do not fit newly discovered data, we revise or perhaps abandon them.

Hierarchic Structures

Like classification, hierarchic structuring is an economical way of storing information in the brain. And, just as cognitive constraints give rise to two large classes of parameters, so they beget two comparable kinds of hierarchies: syntactic and statistical ones.

Syntactic hierarchies are *dis*continuous in that their functional relationships generally change from one level to another. In nature, the ways in which atoms combine to form molecules are not the same as the ways in which molecules combine to form living cells, and this holds for the relationship of cells to organs.[24] And it is because of hierarchic discontinuity that sentences rather than paragraphs, sections, or plots have been the focus of linguistic analysis. In tonal music, the probabilities of foreground chord progression are different from the probabilities of the succession of tonal areas, and the ways that pitches combine to form motives are different from the ways that motives combine to form phrases. Consequently, it seems very unlikely that different levels of a functional hierarchy, whether in nature or in culture, are governed by a single kind of process or structure.

Statistical hierarchies, on the other hand, are continuous in the sense that the constraints governing patterning *do* remain constant from one level to the next. In nature, fractal patterns exemplify hierarchic continuousness; for example, *Science Times* reporter Malcome Browne writes that "a coastline . . .

23. Those who contend that there is no "out-there" world—that all our concepts and beliefs are but social constructs—have a formidable problem, namely, that of explaining why our concepts and choices, beliefs and behaviors change. From another point of view, cultural historian Eugene Goodheart writes: "Here is a paradox: those who possess this certainty about the illusions of others usually call themselves anti-foundationalists, anti-essentialists, and anti-universalists. And they are suspicious of all claims to objectivity. So where does their certainty about the mystification of others come from?" ("Reflections on the Culture Wars," *Daedalus* 126, no. 4 [Fall 1997]: 167).

24. François Jacob writes that "the rules of the game differ at each level. New principles have to be worked out at each level" (*The Possible and the Actual* [New York, 1982], 23).

exhibits the same general appearance when viewed from afar as a portion of it does from up close."[25] In music, Isolde's "Transfiguration" is an example of a statistical hierarchy in that the smaller arch-like curves are shaped in the same ways as the larger arches that make up the overall dynamic curve.[26]

The relatively recent concern of music theorists with the detailed analysis of hierarchic structure has led to an incongruous coupling—a coupling of nineteenth-century ideology and twentieth-century science. What seems to have happened is this: the Romantic esteem for the mysteries of the "profound"—in Wordsworth's words, of "thoughts that do often lie too deep for tears"—led to the valuing of what lay beneath the surface of things. Misconstruing this belief, theorists in more than one field have been beguiled into believing that the "deepest level of structure"—for instance, the Schenkerian *Ursatz* or Jung's archetypes—is "profound" and hence more significant than the patent patterning of the phenomenal foreground.

But there is a "profound" difference between valuing a theory for its explanatory power and elegance and valuing the experience of the phenomenon that is explained. To call a work of art *profound* is to characterize the experience of that work, *not* to comprehend the general principles upon which it is based. The "thoughts that do often lie too deep for tears" result from the personal experience of "the meanest flower that blows."[27] What is profound is not the deep structure of a flower (or of a piece of music) but the experience of a particular work—its power to move us.

Clearly, depth of explanatory theory and depth of aesthetic experience got mixed up. As observed in essay 1, theories, which are propositional constructs *about* phenomena, are valued for their generality, clarity, and verifiability. The more general a theory, the deeper it is said to be.[28] But works of art are not

25. Malcome Browne, "J. S. Bach + Fractals = New Music," *New York Times,* 16 April 1991, C-5. Before I had read anything about fractals, I called such curves *statistical,* and it turns out that the analysis of fractal patterns is essentially statistical.

26. It is important to recognize that significantly different kinds of relationships may be represented by similar diagrams. This is the case with biologically generated trees vs. cognitively comprehended ones (as in music and language). For instance, tree diagrams are used to represent genetic relationships among kinds of plants and animals (from species to genus to order to kingdom). And, though the process of biological emergence may be functional, the relationships between emerged kinds (e.g., reptiles and birds) are not so—at least not in the way that motives (emerging from functional pitch relationships) combine in a functional fashion to form melodies, melodies join to form sections, and so on.

27. The quotations are from the end of Wordsworth's "Ode: Intimations of Immortality from Recollections of Early Childhood."

28. See Steven Weinberg, "Reductionism Redux," *New York Review of Books* 42, no. 15 (5 October 1995): 40–41.

propositions *about* phenomena; they *are* phenomena—phenomena that are valued for the specific experiences they provide. And, because such experiences are difficult to describe and fully explain, they are felt to be profound and often characterized as *ineffable*.[29]

Redundancy

Like classification and hierarchic structuring, the universal role of redundancy in human communication is a consequence of our finite cognitive capacity. Not only does redundancy curtail the amount of information the mind must process, but it also diminishes the effects of external interference and lapses of attention. For instance, because the English language is 50 percent redundant, if we fail to hear a word or two in a sentence, redundancy makes it possible for us to fill in what was missed.[30] Similarly, in music the existence of redundancy—of coherent stylistic constraints—facilitates perception and comprehension.

Redundancy is the complement of information. Because of the limits of our cognitive capacity, the greater the amount of information in one parameter of music, the higher the redundancy of others must be if relationships are to be intelligible.[31] From this point of view, the extensive use of a single motive in a development section does not (as is sometimes suggested) serve primarily to actualize the "full potential" of the motive. Rather motivic redundancy allows the listener to attend to the increase in harmonic information that accompanies the modulations characteristic of development sections. Similarly, the greater the speed of stimulus succession, the higher must be the rate of redundancy if the message is to be intelligible. Consequently, as in Rimsky Korsakov's "Flight of the Bumblebee," the redundancy level (per moment) of a presto needs to be higher than that of an adagio.

The way in which competent listeners understand and experience the ratio of information to redundancy is, however, significantly linked with style. For instance, in markedly goal-directed, syntactic music such as Beethoven's, patent redundancy (as in mm. 16–25 of the first movement of the Sixth

29. Note, however, that, since the uniqueness of even the most mundane experience cannot be fully captured in words, *ineffability is no guarantee of profundity!*

30. The need for redundancy in noisy environments accounts in part for the character of much elevator and supermarket music.

31. Like hierarchic discontinuity, the reciprocal relationship between information and redundancy may be a universal that constrains functional relationships in quite diverse realms. For instance, it appears that in some animal species an increase in the size of one organ or feature is inversely related to the size of another organ (see Wade Roush, "Sizing Up Dung Beetle Evolution," *Science* 277 [11 July 1997]: 184).

Symphony) creates strong expectation of change, while in contemporary, popular, New Age music, which is only weakly goal directed, redundancy gives rise to minimal tension and expectancy. The generation of these different kinds of experience is also a matter of cultural beliefs and attitudes—that is, some listeners have learned that Beethoven's music should be given devoted attention, while aficionados of New Age music find that attention can be perfunctory, even sporadic.

The relationship of information to redundancy is evident in text setting. In general, the greater the importance and amount of information in a text, the higher the redundancy level of the music will be. This might, for instance, explain why the Council of Trent ruled that the music of the Mass be such "that the words may be clearly understood by all."[32] Especially texts with a narrative message tend to be coupled with highly redundant music so that the story can be easily followed. The music of Gilbert and Sullivan patter songs—for example, Sir Joseph Porter's narrative "When I was a lad" from the first act of *Pinafore*—is highly redundant, not because of compositional incompetence, but because the important information is verbal, not musical.

Thus I question Carolyn Abbate's idea that Lakmé's music works "*against the story she narrates,* since the two musical verses, by remaining similar, by repeating, in some sense deny the progressive sequence of changing events that are recounted in Lakmé's words."[33] This view, symptomatic of a Romantic cultural stance, supposes that the "natural" function of music is to parallel and "reflect" the narrative meaning of the text. But, when a verbal message is of prime importance, music tends to be quite redundant and text reflection limited to word painting.

Conversely, when music is of prime importance, verbal information tends to be redundant. Ellen Rosand observes that in Handel's da capo arias text redundancy "liberates us to concentrate on the music. . . . [T]he da capo return is the most redundant of all: with no semantic responsibility, it offers a direct invitation to focus exclusively on the singer's embellishments of the original material."[34]

32. Quoted in Gustave Reese, *Music in the Renaissance* (New York, 1954), 449.

33. Carolyn Abbate, *Unsung Voices: Opera and Musical Narrative in the Nineteenth Century* (Princeton, N.J., 1991), 6.

One might, however, argue that the strophic organization of the music is inappropriate because it is incompatible with the other stylistic constraints or with the particular nature of the subject.

34. Ellen Rosand, "It Bears Repeating: or, Desiring the Da Capo," *Opera News* 61, no. 1 (July 1996): 20. Embellishments not only intimate "roads not taken" but direct our attention to the compelling presence of virtuosity (as manifested in ornamented varied returns). This suggests

The cognitive need for both novelty (information) and constancy (redundancy) is a universal that helps explain the concern of composers, theorists, and aestheticians with the nature of variety and unity. But the *intensity* of that concern and the ways such concern is manifested in the composition and reception of music are cultural matters.

Evolution, Choice, Culture, and Music History

Evolution and Choice

This part of my essay concerns those universals that resulted from evolution but are not themselves innate. Evolution has almost certainly influenced human behavior through the direct action of biological constraints. But what most significantly shaped humankind and gave rise to human cultures was not the existence but the *absence* of adequate innate biological constraints.[35]

It is because evolution resulted in an animal without adequate innate controls that human cultures are indispensable. This aspect of evolution is summarized by biologist François Jacob: "In lower organisms behavior is strictly determined by the genetic program. In complex metazoa the genetic program becomes less constraining, more 'open.' . . . This openness of the genetic program increases with evolution and culminates in mankind."[36]

The growth of cognitive capacity was concomitant with the development of a body design (upright posture, opposable thumb, and so on) that facilitated technologies. The result was the production of usables—from cradles to coffins—and a concomitant increase in the number of conceptual categories. This had momentous consequences because conceptual categories give rise to behavioral options and a profusion of possibilities makes choosing at once inescapable and burdensome. In philosopher Peter Singer's words: "Our ability to be a participant in a decision-making process, to reflect and to choose, is as much a fact about human nature as the effect of the limbic system on our emotions."[37]

The necessity of choice is a universal that lies at the very core of the human condition. It constitutes a basis for both ethical and aesthetic judgments. In

---

that virtuosity itself may constitute a kind of information. We are "informed," that is, not only by the musical relationships but by our appreciation of and empathy with the risk taking that makes evident the skill of an accomplished performer.

35. Since writing this passage, I discovered that Clifford Geertz made much the same point in *The Interpretation of Cultures*, 45–46.

36. Jacob, *The Possible and the Actual*, 61.

37. Peter Singer, *The Expanding Circle: Ethics and Sociobiology* (New York, 1981), 42.

ethics, as in the law, individuals are culpable only if the behavior in question can be shown to be a result of choice. Thus, for instance, finding a genetic basis for homosexuality is not simply a matter of scientific interest. It has broad social consequences because what is genetic, and hence not chosen, cannot be considered objectionable. In aesthetics, art forgeries are banished to the basement because the relationships reproduced were not created—not chosen—by the forger.[38]

Four interrelated conditions are indispensable for effective, propitious choosing: (1) the presence of constraints limiting choice, (2) the ability to envisage the consequences of alternative choices, (3) the power to realize ones' choices, and (4) the reciprocities of empathy.

Cultural Constraints

Without adequate constraints limiting the number and ordering the priority of alternative possibilities, human beings would be caught in indecision—indecision that is not only time consuming but a source of distressing psychological anxiety. Growing out of, and complementing, innate constraints, cultures provide the learned, behavioral controls without which human beings cannot function—indeed, cannot survive. The need for cultural constraints is thus a universal.

A single example clearly illustrates this point. The abandonment of common-practice tonality by some early twentieth-century composers spawned so many compositional options that new constraints were required to make choosing feasible. The invention of the twelve-tone method was, thus, a response to a universal need. The need for constraints limiting options was the necessary condition for the advent of serialism. The sufficient conditions for the constraints actually devised were largely the result of nurture— specifically, of the nineteenth-century belief that similarity generated unity. Put succinctly, if too simply: a universal (the need for constraints) produced the "problem," and culture provided a "solution."

Envisaging

In order for cultural constraints actually to facilitate choice, the world must be comprehended as stable and enduring. And, to choose intelligently, the various options available in a particular context must be comprehended

---

38. See my "Forgery and the Anthropology of Art," in *Music, the Arts, and Ideas* (Chicago: University of Chicago Press, 1994), chap. 4.

and the probable consequences of each envisaged.[39] The universal need to envisage is evident everywhere in human behavior—from soothsayers to scientists, from poll taking to fortune-telling, from economic forecasting to the search for essential, and presumably predictable, historical processes. Similarly, belief in the existence of a divinely established, unchanging order (or, subsequently, an order that changed in a regular way) was appealing because it implied the possibility of successful envisaging. Conversely, because we do not know how to act in the face of "irrational"—that is, frighteningly *un*predictable—behavior, the insane are institutionalized.

All our governments and societies, laws and customs, as well as musical styles serve to stabilize the cultural/behavioral environment.[40] And the same is true not only of theories (including even those about chaos and about universals) but of styles of behavior, whether in the arts or culture generally.[41] The need to envisage in order to choose helps explain why, as Western culture became more complex—conceptually, socially, and institutionally—the delay of gratification became an important constraint. Greater complexity meant a greater number of options and a greater amount of time for considering their consequences. It was, I think, no accident that the Protestant ethic, with its emphasis on the value of delayed gratification, arose alongside the complexities of modern industrial capitalism.[42]

Finally, and especially pertinent here, when there is a *sense* of sufficient competence and control, envisaging (bodily as well as mental) is one of the most engaging and gratifying of human pleasures—a pleasure at the heart of much aesthetic experience. This is patent in the enjoyment created by suspense in literature and by the implication-realization process in music.[43] Con-

39. The need to envisage (predict) is not confined to Homo sapiens: see W. Schutz, P. Dayan, and P. R. Montague, "A Neural Substrate of Prediction and Reward," *Science* 275 (14 March 1997): 1593–99.

40. The need for cultural/behavioral stability may be a significant source of the much-discussed question of the basis for altruism: i.e., an ambience of altruistic reciprocity—"do unto others as you would have them do unto you"—contributes to sociocultural stability.

41. It follows from this that it makes no *behavioral* difference whether theories, hypotheses, and schemas are "merely" provisional social constructs as some scholars contend. Like air, theories may be unsubstantial; but, as with air, we cannot live and act without them.

42. See R. H. Tawney, *Religion and the Rise of Capitalism* (New York, 1926).

This seems to be changing—at least in the popular culture where immediate gratification has become the norm, exemplified in the emphatic physical beat and wailing vocal style of much popular music. This change may be related to the demise of the idea of inherent progress: why delay for a tomorrow that won't be any better than today? See *Music, the Arts, and Ideas*, 146–49 and passim.

43. The difference between pleasant and unpleasant emotional experiences, commonly reified into classes of "emotions" (see n. 21 above), seems significantly a matter of the sense of—

versely, the feeling of incompetence and insecurity created by an inability to envisage is one of the most unpleasant and threatening of human experiences. Indeed, the hostility encountered by much avant-garde music can in large part be attributed to complexities and irregularities that thwart successful envisaging.

Power

To choose effectively, the power to control the outcome of one's choices is essential. The psychological importance of power and control can scarcely be exaggerated. It is a universal manifest everywhere: in animal territoriality, in the human pursuit of possession, and in the high seriousness of play, which almost always involves the enactment and testing of power. Such enactment is obvious in games like chess and football and even in noncompetitive sports like mountain climbing. In the composition and the performance of music, enactment and testing usually involve the valuing of skill or virtuosity (as a basis for power) and of risk taking (as a manifestation of both skill and power).

In lower animals power tends to be "brute"—largely a matter of physical strength. As animal intelligence increases, envisaging becomes a more and more important basis of control and power. And this shift from physical to conceptual power is a crucial consequence of evolution.

But, even in a highly developed culture such as ours, the consequences of physical power are patent. The ascriptions of masculine and feminine characteristics, for instance, are not solely a matter of sexual function and social/cultural construction. In most mammalian species, males are larger, physically stronger, and more aggressive than females, who tend to be gentler and more nurturing.[44] Thus it does not seem to be a matter of cultural caprice that themes characterized by the physical effort of disjunct intervals, forte dynamics, and unison textures are labeled *masculine*[45] while those characterized

---

beliefs about—the control exercised by the individual doing the experiencing. Without a sense of control, experiences, and the emotions they beget, tend to be unpleasant; where a sense of control exists, even potentially "unpleasant" experiences can be pleasantly exhilarating. In the arts, belief in the existence of such control seems a necessary condition for what is referred to as psychic or aesthetic *distance*.

44. It is important to emphasize that masculinity in terms of strength and aggressiveness is independent of sexual orientation. Powerful, aggressive men—athletes, prize fighters, etc.—have been homosexuals. What is thought to be effeminate behavior (or, in the case of lesbians, masculine behavior) is probably the result of cultural signaling (a kind of social semiotics) rather than anything innate.

45. Unison textures are often used to signify the power of compulsion (see Janet M. Levy, "Texture as a Sign in Classic and Early Romantic Music," *Journal of the American Musicological*

by conjunct motion, soft dynamics, and homophonic textures are said to be *feminine*.

Empathy

Human bonding begins in biology—a result of physical dependency and of the infant's ability to elicit care from others. In Stephen Jay Gould's description, "The newborn human child is about as dependent a creature as we find among placental mammalian infants. This dependency is then extraordinarily prolonged, and the child requires intense parental care for many years. . . . The adaptive premium thus placed on learning (as opposed to innate response) is unmatched among organisms."[46] With maturation and experience, bonding is transformed into empathy—that is, identification with another individual through an awareness and understanding of goals and reasons, motives and feelings. The evocation of empathy in the experience of works of art is decisively dependent on *beliefs* about the value of aesthetic experience in general, the significance of specific works, and the prestige of particular performers.[47]

Empathy enables us to imagine how other individuals will respond to our behavior and is, in this way, closely connected with the human need to envisage. And, because we presume that human nature is basically constant (though human behavior is culturally constrained), we believe that we can comprehend the behavior of those who differ from us sexually, ethnically, and culturally. It is because of this universal that we are generally able to understand and interpret human behavior arising in different cultural realms—to empathize with Achilles' wrath and Ruth's submission, with Joan of Arc's enterprise and Hamlet's indecision.

Consciousness of how others will understand and respond to our behavior is a crucial cultural constraint, one that guides the choices of composers, performers, and listeners alike. In the phrase of sociologist George Herbert Mead, we learn to "take the attitude of the other."[48] Note that the word *attitude* has two meanings. Mead's meaning is primarily socio/conceptual—a matter of interpreting the behavior of others and of imagining how others will respond to our behavior.

Society 35 [1982]: 482–531). Dynamic intensity, which is generally characteristic of unison passages, also signifies power.

46. Stephen Jay Gould, *Ontogeny and Phylogeny* (Cambridge, Mass., 1977), 400–401.

47. In this connection, see *Emotion and Meaning in Music*, 73–77.

48. See George Herbert Mead, *Mind, Self, and Society* (Chicago, 1934), 42–75.

But the word *attitude* also refers to bodily stance; and properly so since empathy often involves identifying with another in a motor-somatic way (as anyone who has been to a prize fight or a rock concert can testify). The influence of innate motor-somatic constraints is manifest not only in the physical behavior of performers and listeners but in the kinds of schemata found in the music of many cultures. The gestalt principles of *good continuation* and of *completeness* are, I suggest, a result of motor-somatic proclivities as well as cognitive ones. For instance, in a melody such as the one that begins Chopin's Waltz in C♯ Minor, the opening skip, or gap, from G♯ up to E involves a physical tension that the following fill gradually relaxes. Even the metaphors used to describe musical relationships—"up and down" motions, "high and low" pitches and intensities—probably arise out of degrees of motor-somatic effort.

These biopsychological universals also affect the relationship between interval size, duration, and affect. Large skips (especially descending ones) tend to be associated with relatively long note values because they involve time-consuming motor adjustment. Conversely, smaller intervals are generally associated with shorter note values. One result of these couplings is that interval size and tempo also tend to be related. That is, large intervals are generally associated with slow tempi and smaller intervals with fast tempi.[49] And, because physical effort in turn links tempo to intensity, our bodies incline us to couple faster with louder.

It does not, however, follow from these universal couplings that small intervals do not occur in slow tempi—as, for instance, in the Crucifixus of Bach's B-Minor Mass. Indeed, the special poignancy of that chorus is due to its interval-tempo relationships—moving very slowly with conjunct intervals—as well as to the generally descending motion of the main melodic lines and to regularity of pacing. Conversely, the expression of anger in the Queen of the Night's aria ("Der Hölle Rache") from the second act of Mozart's *The Magic Flute* is in part a result of the tension involved in the performance of large skips and extreme registers in a fast tempo. In both these cases, expression and affect are the result of deviation from a norm. As always, deviation is a matter of degree.

Our affective response to music is to a considerable extent a result of our physical identification with the motor-somatic action of the music. Indeed,

---

49. The rate (tempo) of stimulus succession is, in addition, a function of register: in general low pitches move more slowly than high ones. This is of course partly a result of the acoustic universals of the physical world—the fact that low frequencies take longer to be set in vibration.

part of the difficulty that listeners have with avant-garde music is a result of its use of motorically difficult intervals such as large descending skips and durational patterns that lack metric/rhythmic regularity. Our relationships to our fellow human beings also involve motor-somatic empathy. When another is sad and assumes a drooping stance, empathy inclines us to adopt a similar posture and to experience similar feelings. And we extend comparable empathies to the inanimate and the silent—to Michelangelo's *Pieta Rondanini* and to "weeping" willow trees. In short, not only does art imitate nature, as the ancient Greeks affirmed, but, equally important, audiences empathetically imitate the actions implicit in works of art.

The consequences of human evolution are, then, complementary: on the one hand, a vast increase in intelligence requires the presence of cultural constraints that stabilize the conceptual environment for the sake of choosing successfully; on the other hand, the extended period of infancy, which is a concomitant of increased intelligence, makes cultural learning imperative and empathetic reciprocity possible.

Explaining Music History

Given their continued concern with concepts related to organicism, it is strange that musicologists (and humanists in general) have ignored the discipline of biology, neglecting, especially, neo-Darwinian analyses of change and dissemination, which suggest fruitful ways of comprehending music history.[50] Perhaps the Darwinian model failed to appeal because it posits no inherent and necessary linear processes and hence provides no basis for envisaging.[51] Instead, evolution results from often fortuitous interactions of existing organisms with the contingencies of a variable environment.

In a comparable way, the history of music can be construed as the result of the interaction of existing compositional constraints with the contingencies of the cultural environment.[52] For example, during the eighteenth and nine-

50. Neo-Darwinian theory should not be confused with social Darwinism. Espoused by many nineteenth- and some twentieth-century thinkers, social Darwinism mistakenly construed evolution as linear and progressive, gradual, and necessary.

51. Ironically, then, the neglect of Darwinian theory might be construed as a consequence of the very evolution the theory sought to explain. That is, though evolution involves no goals, it gave rise to the human need to envisage, which in turn resulted in a world conceptualized as thoroughly goal-directed.

52. Needless to say, stylistic changes are not genetic, as most biological changes are. But neither are all biological changes. In this connection, see Virginia Morell, "Catching Lizards in the Act of Adapting," *Science* 276, no. 5313 (3 May 1997): 682–83.

teenth centuries, changes in the ideological, social environment led composers to eschew learned conventions in favor of musical relationships based on
presumably "natural" cognitive constraints—constraints more accessible to
the growing middle-class audience.[53]

Because the functioning of universals is almost invariably qualified by
historical-cultural context, it seems important to say something about the nature of historical change and about the ways in which the interaction of cultural and universal constraints have influenced the choices made by composers—the choices that constitute music history.[54] And it seems germane as
well because the process of change sketched in what follows not only is relevant to music but is itself, I believe, a universal.

In what W. H. Auden called the "realms of action"[55]—for instance, political, economic, and day-to-day behavior—the goals that affect the choices of
protagonists generally seem clear. As a result, narratives can be understood as
explanations. Consider the following account: "The slit trench that corporal
L. B. Meyer dug after landing in Normandy on 8 June 1944 was much, much
deeper than any he had dug while on maneuvers in Louisiana, USA." Because
the universal of self-preservation makes the relationship between intention
and action crystal clear, "there needs no ghost . . . come from the grave" field
of hermeneutics explicitly to theorize or explain here. As psychologist Jerome
Bruner wrote: "To understand man you must understand how his experiences
and his acts are shaped by his intentional states."[56]

More often than not, however, the "intentional states" of composers
are complex and enigmatic, and connecting them with compositional choices
requires *explicit* theorizing. The connection has usually been supplied by

53. For specific examples and discussion, see *Style and Music,* chap. 7.

54. It is generally granted that the choices made by members of a particular musical community are significantly affected by their cultural environment. Yet, despite almost ritual obei-
sance to cultural history, the ways in which the worlds outside music have affected style change
have seldom been meticulously delineated and explained.

A large segment of *Style and Music* attempts to explain how the choices of composers of the
nineteenth century were influenced by the ideology of Romanticism. And many of the matters
considered in that book are discussed in what follows. But, instead of focusing on the influence
of cultural beliefs and attitudes on the particular choices made by a compositional community,
the emphasis in the present essay is on the nature and kinds of universals that constrain the composition and comprehension of music.

55. W. H. Auden, *Forewords and Afterwords,* selected by Edward Mendelson (New York,
1974), 89.

56. Jerome Bruner, quoted in Howard Gardner, "Green Ideas Sleeping Furiously," *New York
Review of Books* 42, no. 5 (23 March 1995): 37.

culturally sanctioned models that are tacitly assumed to be universals. These models usually involve some sort of internally generated linear change; for instance, organic development (birth, youth, maturity, and death), successive stages (archaic, classic, mannerist), or dialectical processes (thesis, synthesis, antithesis).

Models involving internal linear change are still with us (despite the currency of postmodernism) because they seem to provide a secure basis for the universal human needs to envisage and choose. But linear models are, in my view, pernicious. This, for two reasons. First, because the reasons for change are posited by the model, an account of *what* happened comes to seem like an explanation of *why* it happened. Second, because, as is evident in most current analytic paradigms (including narrativity), linearity leads to the neglect of "the road[s] not taken." Just as it is in everyday experience, an awareness of "what might have been" is indispensable for the understanding and appreciation of works of art.[57]

While the appeal of the internalist, linear model is understandable, its indiscriminate application to any and all natural and cultural change is seriously misguided. This is so not only because, in T. S. Eliot's words, " 'our beginnings never know our ends!' " but, just as importantly, because hierarchies are for the most part discontinuous. Although the biological development of individual men and women generally changes in a linear way, change on the various levels of biological evolution and social and style history is not, for the most part, organic or linear.[58]

Musicologists have not infrequently been concerned with identifying beginnings—for instance, with the advent of tonality, the initial uses of pizzicato, the origin of tempered tuning, and, above all, instances of compositional novelty. Preoccupation with beginnings is problematic for several reasons. Because we cannot be certain that we know everything that happened in the past, we can never be sure that any instance was an initial one.[59] More im-

---

57. In this connection, see M. R. Cohen, quoted in essay 7, p. 274.

Awareness of alternative eventualities raises interesting and perplexing questions about interpretations of music in terms of a narrative model: Which alternatives shape implication? Those of the nonrepresentational musical "narrative" process or those of the verbal representation? In both, how are the realized and unrealized implications of the musical narrative related to, and coordinated with, the realized and unrealized implications of the verbal narrative?

58. I am arguing not against organicism per se but against the unwarranted transfer of processes discerned on the level of individual development to other levels of the same phenomenon.

59. Knowing about beginnings is historically relevant, not because of some inherent genetic power (as with racehorses), but because early instances of some relationship are necessary for delineating and hence explaining the course of replication.

portant, and consonant with the Darwinian model, I am advocating a change in our conceptual framework—in our questions and methodologies.[60] What is crucial for constructing a history of music is not the origin of kinds of relationships but the reasons—universal and cultural—for their replication, their change, and their demise and disappearance.[61]

Recognizing the existence of universals and theorizing about their nature is indispensable because we can construct a coherent aesthetic and a viable history of music only by scrupulous attention to nature as well as to nurture and by trying to understand and explain their intricate interactions. My speculations and arguments do not pretend to be definitive; they should, rather, be thought of as hypotheses. All need to be tested against the facts of human behavior. The *real* work remains to be done.

60. As observed in essay 6, Darwin's *On the Origin of Species* is not primarily concerned to explain the beginnings of species.

61. Seen thus, constructing a history of music entails, first, the careful discrimination and classification of the features characteristic of some repertory, second, an unbiased sampling of their presence in the repertory together with a scrupulous analysis of their relative frequency, and, third, the testing of hypotheses devised to account for whatever changes occur in characteristic features and in the frequency of replication. (The collection and statistical analysis of large bodies of data may involve a change in the modes of research that have been traditional in the humanities: a change from largely individual investigation to cooperative, group endeavor.)

Index

Abbate, Carolyn, 293

acoustic tension, and cadential six-four progression, 234

action, realms of: reasons for choice clear in, 301

ad hoc reasons: need for in criticism, history, medicine, and sciences, 40–45

affect, emotion, and ethos, 122–23

affect (topic, gesture), succession of: gradual transformation does not explain, 264–65; need for theory of, 265; reasons for problematic in music, 263–65

Agawu, V. Kofi, 263–64n. 2

age, creativity and: in arts and sciences, 10–11

Aldwell, Edward, 230n. 9

Allanbrook, Wye J., 263–64n. 2, 264

analysis of music, nature of (detail, length of, method), 60–61

apotheosis. *See* statistical (secondary) parameters

archetypes (schemata): analysis of example of, 195–99; Berg on, 271; and cultural continuity, 195; importance of, 157–58, 194–95; in literature, 157–58; in music, 159–61, 275; nature of, 194–95; in Romanticism, 214–15; in Bach, 225n. 50; in Berlioz's *Symphonie fantastique*, 208–14; in Haydn, 158; in Mozart and Beethoven, 199–208. *See also* Schenker, *Ursatz*

Aristotle, 29, 31, 49, 199n. 20

Arlen, Harold, "Over the Rainbow," 164–65

Arnheim, Rudolf, 32

Arnold, F. T., 136n

arts, the: choice in, 13–14; as collective activities, 18–19; as creating not discovering, 5; experience of, 6, 25; explanation and understanding, 32–33; feedback from conceptualization, 36; games com-

pared with, 6, 193; general principles in, 39–40, 192–93; great works created late in life, 10, 14; humanities and, 26–31; innovation in, 11; instruction in, 8, 29–30; not "about" the world, 6, 20–22; originality in, 15–17; presentational, not propositional, 5–7, 9, 15; profundity in, 291–92; Romantic view of, 213–15; simultaneous creation unlikely, 17–18; style and choice in, 13–14; as subjects of inquiry, 26–50; theory of, 32–37; truth and falsity not applicable to, 23–26; understanding, 6, 27–31; works not superseding one another, 9–10. *See also* creativity, in the arts; humanities

arts and sciences: analogies between, 50; apprehension of over time, 19–20; as collective activities, 18, 19; differences between, 4–20, 30–32, 36–37; learning of, 7–9

atonal music: compositional options created by, 295; need for constraints, 214n. 35, 295; pitch class displaces function in, 267n; serialism (twelve-tone music), 268n. 11, 270, 272, 295

attitude, and empathy, 298–99

Auden, W. H., 301

audience changes, and style changes, 246

authentic cadence. *See* cadence

avant garde music, 300

Bach, Johann Sebastian: cadential six-four progression in, 241, 243, 253–55; coordination processes in the *Well-Tempered Clavier (WTC)*, Prelude no. 16 in G Minor, 130n; —, Prelude no. 18 in G♯ Minor, 128–29, 130; —, Prelude no. 23 in B Major, 127–28; fugue themes in *WTC*, 127, 184, 216n. 37; influence on Mozart, 156; Mass in B Minor, 299;